Urban Life and Urban Landscape Series

A Right
to Representation

*Proportional Election Systems
for the Twenty-first Century*

KATHLEEN L. BARBER

Ohio State University Press
Columbus

Library of Congress Cataloging-in-Publication Data

Barber, Kathleen L., 1924–
    A right to representation : proportional election systems for the
twenty-first century / Kathleen L. Barber.
        p.   cm. — (Urban life and urban landscape series)
    Includes bibliographical references and index.
    ISBN 0-8142-0854-1 (cloth) — ISBN 0-8142-5058-0 (pbk.)
    1. Proportional representation.   I. Title.   II. Series.
JF1071. B37 2001
328.3'347—dc21   00-008907

Text design by Nighthawk Design.
Cover design by Gary Gore.
Type set in Fairfield by Nighthawk Design.
Printed by McNaughton & Gunn.

The paper used in this publication meets the minimum requirements of the
American National Standard for Information Sciences—Permanence of
Paper for Printed Library Materials. ANSI Z39.48-1992.

9 8 7 6 5 4 3 2 1

CONTENTS

PREFACE

IN A FRACTIOUS WORLD, the tools of democracy are critical components of self-determination. Voting comes instantly to mind as the essential instrument to hold governments accountable to us, but *how* we vote is seldom examined. Voting system reform is a critical component of peaceful resolution of violence in religiously mixed nations like Ireland and the even more fragmented societies of the former Yugoslavia. If civic life is to emerge from the rubble of death and destruction, proportional election systems are considered essential to rebuild civil society.

It is not just in strife-disrupted countries that ideas about voting systems are in the air today. In the United States, itself an ethnically and racially diverse nation, many citizens perceive that structures of public accountability are not working as they should. Misrepresentation is targeted as a fundamental flaw that needs to be fixed. Yet means to repair the electoral system are poorly understood, and earlier American experiences with alternative electoral systems that provided fuller representation were lost in selective historical accounts. In 1995, my book *Proportional Representation and Election Reform in Ohio* was published by the Ohio State University Press, highlighting accounts of proportional representation elections, their genesis, and their consequences, in five Ohio cities between 1915 and 1960. That book was an attempt to examine the circumstances under which the single transferable vote form of proportional representation (PR/STV) was advocated and adopted in American municipalities, the problems it was intended to solve, the manner of its implementation and operation, its relationship to other proposals for structural reform of American municipal government, its effectiveness, and the circumstances surrounding its abandonment. Its immediate focus, however, was on PR in Ohio.

This new book takes a much broader look at proportional election systems, placing their new relevance in the context of twentieth-century pluralism, but looking ahead at the accelerating diversity of the nation's population and culture in the twenty-first century. How will this diversity be represented in the future?

Two interrelated developments, one in doctrine and one in practice, are pointing the way. In *Shaw v. Reno,* a case decided in 1993 (and discussed briefly in my earlier book), the U.S. Supreme Court sharply limited the use of race-based districting to remedy minority vote dilution under the Voting Rights Act. The theory of this case was that the equal protection rights of white (majority) voters were violated by the establishment of irregularly drawn majority-minority congressional districts. This interpretation of the Fourteenth Amendment was rapidly applied to a succession of districting cases that severely limited what could be done to provide opportunities for minority representation within the boundaries of traditional single-member election systems. From congressional districts down to local and county councils, the federal courts invalidated race-based districting that was intended to remedy the exclusion of minority representation in winner-take-all elections.

As a result of this judicial doctrine, experiments with alternative election systems such as cumulative and limited voting began to spring up in localities around the country, providing the opportunity for minority representation in at-large elections. Moreover, a movement is afoot in Congress to repeal the statutory requirement of single-member congressional districts, to pave the way for new election systems that would enable minorities to win congressional representation through at-large or multi-member district elections in states with more than one representative. The Single Transferable Vote form of proportional representation (PR/STV), once used in almost two dozen American cities, has been put on the ballot in several communities by advocates who seek to bring it back.

The conclusion I draw from these developments is that representation in public bodies is indeed a right to be vindicated in our democratic system and that the means exist to achieve truly "fair representation" through electoral system change.

I am grateful to Charlotte Dihoff, at the time acting director of the Ohio State University Press, for first suggesting this project. I am also indebted to my collaborators on the investigations of elections in the five PR cities of Ohio for the 1995 book: Dennis M. Anderson, Ronald J. Busch, Robert J. Kolesar, and the late Leon Weaver.

Others have contributed their skills and knowledge to this new volume. Gratitude is owed to Philip A. Macklin, professor emeritus of physics at Miami University, for his critical reading of chapter 3; to Edward Still, director of the Voting Rights Project of the Lawyers' Committee for Civil Rights under Law, for reviewing chapter 5 and sharing his insights; to Daniel W. Johnson-Weinberger of Illinois Citizens for Proportional Representation for sources on the history of cumulative voting; and to Robert Richie, executive director of the Center for Voting and Democracy, for a steady flow of election data and fresh ideas. Steve Tuttle of the South Carolina Department of Archives and History was helpful in research on the South Carolina legislative election system during Reconstruction. Zane Miller, Charles Phelps Taft Professor of History at the University of Cincinnati and editor of the Urban Life and Urban Landscape Series of which this volume is a part, and Barbara Lyons, editor at-large for OSU Press, have been helpful in ways large and small. Most importantly, my friend Henry D. Shapiro has been a constant reader and critic whose hard questions and sustaining commentary have significantly shaped this book.

Finally, I wish to thank my son, John C. Barber, for sharing his computer expertise at crucial stages of this project, and my husband, D. Robert Barber, for his staunch and steady support of my commitment to the study of election systems.

INTRODUCTION _____

THIS BOOK TELLS A STORY about election systems in the United States. Election systems are rules and practices that determine how we vote and how votes are counted to determine winners. Although these rules often sound like mere technicalities, they profoundly shape the representative bodies that enable us to govern ourselves. In most democracies around the world, citizens vote by various systems of proportional representation, which allocate seats in a legislature according to the share of votes won.

In the United States, most elections are conducted by winner-take-all rules. In a single-member district, the candidate with the most votes captures all of the representation; losers' votes are simply wasted. The burden of losing falls on minorities: Republicans in a Democratic district, for example, and African Americans in majority-white districts where voting is racially polarized. Partisan gerrymanders have traditionally shaped representation to the advantage of the line-drawers. Racial gerrymanders, formerly used to prevent minorities from winning office, have more recently become the preferred means to provide representation to previously excluded groups. The Supreme Court's hostility to race-based districting, however, creates the political climate for fresh consideration of alternative electoral systems such as cumulative voting, limited voting, and the single transferable vote form of proportional representation (STV).

These alternative electoral systems have a history of their own that is little known and poorly understood. Their genesis in the context of the development of democratic governance in England and on the European Continent in the eighteenth and nineteenth centuries is the subject of chapter 1. The idea that "the people" should elect their rulers created fears of majority tyranny that representation of the educated minority could temper. In chapter 2, how and why a wing of the American Progressive movement promoted proportional representation is explored as a prelude to the introduction of proportional voting in American local elections in the twentieth century. Chapter 3 offers a pause in the narrative to explain the mechanics of the main varieties of proportional voting: party list and the single transferable vote forms of proportional representation, and the semiproportional systems called cumulative voting, limited voting, and the single nontransferable vote. The main emphasis, however, is on proportional representation by single transferable vote (PR/STV), which is sometimes called the Hare system, or in more contemporary terms preference voting or choice voting, because of the voter's ability to rank choices on the ballot.

The contemporary debate about election systems is clouded by multiple meanings of the term *proportional representation*. Both Congress and the Supreme Court have at times assumed the term to mean imposition of group quotas on the results of elections, like the Democratic Party regulations that half the delegates to national conventions must be women. But, as chapter 3 shows, proportional election systems do not mandate any particular result. What they do is to provide voters the *opportunity* to win representation (or seats) in proportion to their votes. Candidates must run, campaigns must be waged, voters must go to the polls and make relevant choices in order to be represented.

Chapter 4 resumes the narrative with actual experiences of American communities that elected their officials by PR/STV between 1915 and 1960. Ohio was the focus of a national campaign to introduce an electoral system that would diversify representation and promote social justice. Ohio's largest industrial cities—Cleveland, Cincinnati, and Toledo—adopted proportional representation, as did the smaller communities of Ashtabula and Hamilton. Linked in all five cities to other reform features, such as nonpartisanship and the city manager plan, proportional voting changed the political landscape in many ways, although the Cleveland case proved that a boss could work within and around such reform structures. Proportional representation was, however, ahead of its time, since the minority representation it produced was not always welcome. Displaced party leaders were able to incite opposition to the election system that had diversified representation, and repeal initiatives ultimately succeeded in all five cities.

With these experiences in mind, we will turn in chapter 5 to the contemporary battle over voting rights and how the American right to vote has evolved into the right to representation. Although the original Constitution left the right to vote in the hands of the states, the Fourteenth and Fifteenth Amendments and a series of statutes passed by Congress to enforce their provisions have defined its dimensions. The major thesis of this book is that the right to vote is the right to cast an effective vote, and implied in "effective" is the right to representation. This is a right that can be realized only through an election system in which the majority or plurality does not win all of the representation, but only its appropriate share, while minorities, whether demographic or political, are not forced to waste their votes, but have the opportunity to elect their share of representatives at the public table.

Evolution of the right to representation is proceeding today through conflict between contending ideas. Is the right to representation an individual or a group right? This conflict can be resolved by proportional representation, which allows for voluntary constituencies either of individuals or of groups with cohesive interests. Should representation be geographically based, or should communities of interest earn representation? This apparent conflict is also resolved by proportional representation, which enlarges the territory of an electoral district enough to allow for election of several representatives. Voters are then free to choose a neighborhood representative or one who shares their political party, ethnicity, race, or gender.

Election systems in the United States and around the world are focal points for discussion of democracy, its meaning, and its practice in a fast-changing world. Accountability and representation have moved to the forefront of political analysis as the end of the cold war and the spread of universal electronic information have unleashed aspirations for self-government from Chilton County, Alabama, to Indonesia. Election systems provide a critical but often unrecognized link between voters and the government policies that shape their lives.

In the United States at the beginning of the new millennium, enforcement of the Voting Rights Act and implementation of the Motor Voter Law are opening up new opportunities for participation in electoral choice. As voting rights expand and as the nation itself enters a period of diversification unparalleled since the enactment of the restrictive Immigration Act of 1924, enforcement of federal guarantees of these rights has brought more minority officials to power. Not only have the legitimate expectations of minority citizens been raised, but the increasing diversity of the U.S. population intensifies the need for practical ways to integrate new groups politically into the existing citizenry.

Race- and ethnicity-based districting, a strategy used in the 1990s to remedy underrepresentation, increased the presence of minorities in Congress, state legislatures, and local governments. Its use, however, is limited by Supreme Court decisions attacking the "bizarre" character of majority-minority districts. A narrow majority of the justices are not offended by the common practice of drawing districts to protect incumbents and to preserve partisan interests, but the same majority holds that lines drawn to facilitate the election of racial or ethnic minorities violate the equal protection rights of the remainder of the district's population. This judicial policy, sustained by a slim one-vote margin of the current Court, has created unexpected pressure to introduce alternative election methods that, unlike traditional American winner-take-all voting in territorial districts, could fulfill the promise of the Voting Rights Act. Experiments with various proportional voting systems have multiplied as a result of litigation and often in order to avoid litigation.

Chapter 5 shows how increasing awareness of election systems is generating popular movements around the country seeking "fair representation" in cities such as San Francisco, Seattle, Eugene, San Antonio, and Minneapolis, and at the state level in Illinois, Oregon, and Vermont. The Center for Voting and Democracy, a nonpartisan citizens' group, is building an informed network of activists committed to voting system reform. Because women, a numerical majority drastically underrepresented in political life, are naturally distributed somewhat evenly through the population, districting would not provide a potential remedy, even if women as a group were covered by the Voting Rights Act, which they are not. As knowledge of other election systems spreads, women are learning that in most democratic countries with proportional election systems women hold significantly greater shares of seats in parliament than in the few democracies that elect members in single-member districts. Women's organizations such as the League of Women Voters, the Feminist Majority, and the National Organization of Women (NOW) are undertaking or considering action to support proportional representation in the United States.

Great Britain has been the only major democratic system beyond our shores where voters have traditionally chosen their representatives by plurality voting in single-member districts. At this writing, Prime Minister Tony Blair and his Labour Party government are transforming the highly centralized British system into a federal structure in which new regional assemblies in Scotland, Wales, and Greater London are elected by proportional representation. The 1998 peace agreement between the Republic of Ireland and Northern Ireland (Ulster) established a new assembly, elected in June 1998 by PR/STV. The choice of election system was a purposeful accommodation of opposing sides by proportional representation of Protestants and Catholics as a means to end violence. Greater freedom of individual choice for candidates and parties is being realized as an integral component of the British devolution of power.

British elections of representatives to the European Parliament are, like those of the other European democracies, conducted by proportional representation, a condition of membership in the European Community. Vote shares equal seat shares in the European Parliament, a simple principle proposed almost a century ago by the PR League of the United States to guide the formation of the then future League of Nations.

Despite some progress in American electoral practices, impediments to fair representation persist. At the individual level, voters, while registering in greater numbers, are voting less. In fact, turnout has been declining since 1960. An upward blip in presidential voting in 1992, when three candidates competed seriously for public attention, was followed by a steeper drop in 1996, when less than a majority of eligible voters went to the polls to vote for president in that most visible of American elections. Turnout in the congressional elections of 1998 plunged to the lowest level—an estimated 37 percent of those eligible—since the wartime congressional election of 1942. The startling truth is that a majority of eligible American voters do not vote.

A major factor shaping the lack of motivation to vote is distrust in government. A 1998 national survey by the Pew Research Center for the People and the Press showed that "only 20 percent of Americans are satisfied with the state of the nation and only 34 percent basically trust the government" (*New York Times*, 10 March 1998, A15). The common view is that politicians are corrupt, a conviction that dates from the assassinations of the 1960s, the Vietnam War, and Watergate, and could only be sustained by the seemingly endless investigations of the Clinton administration. Popular cynicism about money in politics—the best politics money can buy—is heightened by negative and personalistic campaigns. The manipulation of images in print and on television screens drives many to despair of democracy. Apathy is seen at the bottom, greed at the top.

Beyond these psychological factors inducing the tendency not to vote lie the institutional rigidities of the two parties, winner-take-all results, and the control exercised by incumbents as they design their districts once a decade to reelect themselves. The Center for Voting and Democracy found that 83 percent of the 1998 U.S. House elections were in effect decided when the state legislatures drew the district lines almost a decade earlier, and 99 percent of the incumbents who ran were reelected. While term limit provisions around the country are bringing new faces into political office, winner-take-all voting continues to exclude minorities—partisan, racial, ethnic, or simply independent—from representation. The 2000 Census has told us how many we are and where we live; the outcome of debates about election systems will tell us whether and how we will be represented in political life.

1

Inventing Election Systems

It WAS IN THE LATE EIGHTEENTH CENTURY in the midst of revolutionary upheaval that political theorists and statesmen developed the idea of democracy as representative government based on popular elections. Rooted in the French and American Revolutions, this concept of democracy was debated on both sides of the Atlantic, not as a principle but as a problem of implementation: *who* should participate in public decisions (the suffrage question) and *how* should that participation be transformed into representation (the electoral system question). In the course of this debate, methods of voting were invented, including several intended to achieve the fair, or proportional, representation of all voters.

As participation broadened on both sides of the Atlantic, concerns grew that systems approaching majority rule could quickly tumble into majority tyranny or rule by the mob. In the face of such fears, systems of proportional representation were advocated as devices to secure the continuing presence of the educated minority in government. In the Progressive Era, the argument shifted as proponents of democratization sought to use proportional electoral systems to restore power to ordinary people from whom they believed it had been seized by corrupt party bosses and corporate monopolists. Today, proportional representation is promoted to facilitate more accurate representation of racial, ethnic, and gender groups in policy-making bodies.

Thus the history of proportional representation (PR) demonstrates both its persistence as a technical solution to the electoral problems of republican governance and its ability to bear the freight of diverse and even conflicting political ideas under differing circumstances.

[handwritten margin note:] Today they are feard because they promise to bring extreme minorities into govt.

1

Origins of PR in the Debate over Minority Rights

From the revolutionary period onward, in both the United States and France, the problem of majority tyranny in a democratic society was debated. In the American debate over the organization of government under the Articles of Confederation and then under the Constitution, *proportional representation* was used to mean representation of the states in proportion to their population instead of one state, one vote. Neither of the founding documents of the American national government, however, addressed the question of which of the persons enumerated for proportional representation in their states were to vote for the representatives or the question of how those votes should be cast. Both questions were left for the states, and ultimately the courts, to decide.

In the battle over ratification of the Constitution, James Madison justified its institutional checks and balances as democracy's strongest protection against the tyranny of the majority. Moreover, he argued that a "social check" would also serve this end through the system of representation. Representation by mere numbers was not enough. The Constitution was designed to ensure the representation of diverse existing interests, groups defined primarily in economic terms, which would check each other, preventing the dominance of any one interest. The slaveholding interest would be represented through southern delegates; commerce and shipping by men from New England and the Middle Atlantic states. But state adoption of electoral systems based on plurality voting in small districts—the English model they knew best—forced the representation of diverse interests to depend on how they were distributed geographically. Furthermore, minority interests within each district, such as small family farmers in southern districts, for example, were unlikely to be elected to represent themselves. Although Madison did not identify the problem of minority interests within districts, he recognized the danger that a "majority faction" might be elected that could carry "schemes of oppression" into effect to support its "ruling passion or interest" (A. Hamilton et al. [1788] 1945, 56–60).

Later political theorists would point to this potential outcome as an inherent flaw in a small-district plurality voting system: if a majority faction prevailed in all or most districts (with one person to be elected, the winner "takes all"), minorities would have little or no voice and the "schemes of oppression" Madison feared could indeed be executed.

The use of plurality voting in geographically based districts, borrowed from England, was rooted in the medieval practice of representing communities in decision making. The homogeneity of community life sus-

Contradiction between party-based politics and geographical representation; between cleavages that are essence of parties & homogeneity which is supposed to be the essence of community *[handwritten marginalia]*

tained territorial representation. With the growth of political parties based on cleavages in society, the familiar old electoral system persisted in both Britain and the United States, in spite of its tendency to overrepresent the majority party and systematically underrepresent small parties (Commons 1907, 25–28; Bogdanor 1991, 195).

Madison's ideas about representation became accessible in Paris when the first French translation of *The Federalist* was published in 1792 (A. Hamilton et al. [1788] 1945, vii). French theorists such as Mirabeau, Condorcet, and Saint-Just explored the significance of the American Revolution and the democratic ideas taking shape across the Atlantic in their correspondence with Benjamin Franklin, Thomas Jefferson, Thomas Paine, and John Adams, and sometimes in conversation when the Americans were in Paris (Palmer 1959, 1:270–75, 469–70). Unlike the Americans, however, these French philosopher-politicians were not content with a representative assembly that reflected merely the location of population. They wanted a representative assembly that would reflect all elements of society, not of the majority alone. A representative body, Mirabeau declared, should "present a reduced picture of the people—their opinions, aspirations and wishes. . . . [T]he value of each element is dependent for its importance to the whole and for the whole" (quoted in Sterne [1871] 1970, 50–51).

The question of how to achieve this goal was never even fully debated in France. Instead, disagreement over questions of the suffrage, direct or indirect election of representatives, and the role of the assembly itself provided the occasion for factional division.

In the turmoil that accompanied the French Revolution, protection of a system of popular sovereignty against anarchy at one extreme and tyranny at the other was a central concern. In the French National Convention of 1793, with Saint-Just as its president, mechanisms for securing broad representation of the population were discussed. Condorcet and Saint-Just both presented proposals for proportional voting systems, which were attacked and defeated by majoritarian forces led by Robespierre (Baker 1975, 325–30). The triumph of the Jacobins in the Convention, reinforced by violence in the streets, ended the debate, sent Saint-Just to the guillotine, and sent Condorcet, after a period of hiding, to prison where he died (Scott and Rothaus 1985, 232, 866–68). Robespierre himself, architect of the policy of death to dissenters and ultimately one of its victims, had called the Terror "the principle of democracy applied to the pressing needs of the country" (quoted in Palmer 1964, 2:126). But the Terror was the tyranny of the majority that the proportionalists had feared, and in France representative government was abandoned altogether in the Age of Napoleon.

During the 1830s, in the context of France's attempt at parliamentary government under a restored monarchy, the issue of the representativeness of the national assembly was again discussed. Now, however, the new "parties" were assumed to be numerous enough and representative enough to reflect the "opinions, aspirations, and wishes . . . of the people." The problem was to make certain that each *party* was represented. In 1834, Victor Considerant, a French socialist, proposed a party list system of proportional representation for election of a national assembly. His plan was based on the increasing organization of political life into acknowledged parties and on his belief that all significant parties were entitled to representation.

Proportional representation by party list (PR/PL) enabled voters to cast a single vote for their party's list of candidates for a national parliament, either in the nation as a whole or in large districts where a number of representatives could be elected to represent different parties. After votes were counted, the percentage of votes won by each party would be translated into a percentage of seats in the representative body, with the party determining which of its candidates would fill the allotted seats (Kent 1937, 133–50, 214; Cole and Campbell 1989, 43–45; Newman 1987, 386–90).

During this period Alexis de Tocqueville emerged as Europe's most vigorous proponent of PR/PL (O'Leary 1979, 3; MacKenzie 1958, 78–79; Hogan 1945, chap. 9). Tocqueville's political views were shaped by his family history: his grandparents and other relatives had been guillotined. Yet he himself was passionately committed to democracy and to the extension of political representation to the working class, a tendency he saw in any case as inevitable in modern political affairs. During his decade of service as a deputy in the French Assembly (1839–48), he attributed the political instability of his own time to the narrow base of French suffrage. Exclusion of the working class from power and responsibility inevitably created irresponsible and extremist views among its leaders, he argued. It was to avoid both a socialist revolution from the left and the tyranny of the middle class on the right that Tocqueville urged universal male suffrage and other electoral reforms (quoted in Lively 1965, 114–20; Tocqueville [1850] 1959, pt. 2, pp. 186–206). Politically marginalized by his own contradictory beliefs—his yearning for democracy against his fear of the mob—Tocqueville was unable to build support for his proposals in the Assembly.[1]

The efforts of nineteenth-century European proportionalists were to bear fruit not in France but in other European nations. PR/PL was first

used in Swiss cantonal elections in the 1860s, where its adoption was hastened by the swings between extremes experienced under plurality voting
in a society almost evenly divided by language and religion. Its first use for
national elections, in 1899, was in Belgium, where differences between
the liberal and Catholic parties, reinforced by the linguistic divergence
between Walloon- and Flemish-speakers, caused "violent and dangerous
oscillations" in the parliament. After 1899, when both major groupings
were proportionally represented, tensions were reduced (MacKenzie
1958, 75–76).

PR/PL was not widely adopted until after the turn of the century. Adoptions accelerated after the breakup of empires in 1917–21, when the issue
of choosing a voting system had to be decided in many European nations
at once. France finally adopted proportional representation by party list in
the Fourth Republic (1945–58), long after PR/PL had been implemented
in other European nations, returning to it again briefly in 1985–86 at the
instigation of Socialist president François Mitterrand. Today, PR/PL is
used in a majority of the world's democracies and indeed in all European
countries except England, Ireland, and France (O'Leary 1979, 3; Cole and
Campbell 1989, 6, 72–88, 135–41; Bogdanor 1991, 195).[2]

Party list voting, suggested by Considerant and put into practice much
later, did not, in its original form, allow for individual candidate choice.
In the eighteenth century, however, recognition of the flaws of plurality
voting had led Condorcet and his compatriot Jean-Charles de Borda, a
mathematician and astronomer, to propose procedures that would allow
voters to both choose individual candidates and express more than one
preference. If their preferred candidate could not win, who would be next
best? Borda had invented a system in which voters could rank candidates
in order of choice by assigning decreasing numbers of points to them. The
candidate with the largest total number of points would win. Condorcet,
seeking a majority winner if possible, advocated successive pairwise comparisons of candidates for an office, with the winning candidate emerging
as the one preferred to all others. This led, as Condorcet himself recognized, to the possibility of the paradox that no candidate is preferred to all
others (Reeve and Ware 1992, 148–49; Fishburn 1990, 397–99).[3]

Considerant's party list system with multimember districts avoided this
problem. With more than one candidate to be elected and parties responsible for their candidates, multiple choices could be accommodated. In
France itself, however, the single-member district was retained, and the
problem of a plurality winner was addressed by the use of a two-stage election with a second ballot (similar to a run-off election) to force majority

support for one of the leading candidates on the first ballot. The second ballot, however, was susceptible to manipulation by coalitions based on deals struck by parties in the interval between the two ballots. Often, as well, centrist candidates were eliminated in the first round, and on the second ballot voters faced a choice between extremes (Cole and Campbell 1989, 3–6, 26–27, and passim).

Although PR/PL voting manifestly cures the defects of plurality voting, it failed to take hold in the English-speaking world. Of the nineteenth-century American proponents of proportional voting systems, only Thomas Gilpin of Philadelphia, a manufacturer and a Quaker with a deep concern about the prospect of majority tyranny, advocated Considerant's party-oriented plan for minority representation. In 1844, Gilpin proposed the use of PR/PL voting for city elections to provide representation on the Philadelphia City Council of all significant interests in the community (Gilpin 1844; Hoag and Hallett 1926, 457–64). Since the revolutionary period, the working class in Philadelphia had sought representation by "mechanics" themselves (Williamson 1960, 86), but with a plurality voting system even Pennsylvania's relatively broad electorate had not elected workingmen. Gilpin believed that a party list system would give mechanics the incentive to organize their own party and put forward candidates who could win a proportional share of seats on the council. His proposal, however, did not gain the support of the council majority that was necessary to change the voting system.

Indeed, although the use of PR/PL elections spread rapidly through European parliamentary systems in the late nineteenth and early twentieth centuries, the system has never been tried in the United States. The antiparty sentiments of the framers of the Constitution shaped the American political culture, which led future American reformers to avoid an electoral system that would so enhance the power of political parties. Called "factions" by the nation's early leaders, parties were viewed as divisive elements in political life. Eminent politicians as antithetical as John Adams and John C. Calhoun shared distaste for political parties as organizations that would subvert principles for the sake of power, displacing common consent by conflict (McFaul 1975, 37; Maizlish 1983, 18–19).[4]

In spite of the critical role played by nineteenth-century parties in the development of American democracy, in conducting militant campaigns, legitimizing the opposition, and articulating the interests of a diverse nation, the parties continued to be subject to distrust. After the Civil War, as the parties' political machines became entrenched, liberal reformers capitalized on the underlying popular suspicion that parties were self-interested factions (McGerr 1986, 43–54). Debate over electoral systems would turn on how to diminish, not how to strengthen, the role of parties in American political life.

Among nineteenth-century theorists of electoral systems, however, other proportional methods to achieve both majority and minority representation were being developed. The single transferable vote form of PR, which could be used with or without the participation of political parties, was proposed as early as 1821 by Thomas Wright Hill, an English schoolmaster sometimes called "the first inventor" of PR/STV.

As in the case of PR/PL, with PR/STV more than one representative would be elected in a political unit in order to provide for representation of both the majority and the minority or minorities of voters. Instead of voting for a party that in turn would name the winning candidates (PR/PL), however, the voter would choose a list of candidates, numbering them in order of preference. Each ballot would count toward the election of one candidate only. If the voter's first choice already had enough votes to be elected, or was trailing so far behind as to be a hopeless loser, the ballot would be transferred to his second choice or, if necessary, to the third or later choice. The number of votes needed for election would be calculated by dividing the total number of votes by the number of seats to be filled.[5] The counting of ballots and transfer of preferences would continue until all seats were filled. The principle of Hill's early formulation of proportional representation by single transferable vote (PR/STV) has remained unchanged to the present, although the details have been altered in light of practical experience.

Thomas Hill's son, Sir Rowland Hill, introduced the practice of PR/STV balloting into elections in November 1821 for the governing committee of a private organization, the Society for Literary and Scientific Improvement, in order to achieve "as nearly as possible an accurate representation of the whole body." As secretary of the Colonization Commission of South Australia, Rowland Hill also introduced PR/STV in Australia, where it was used in a public election in Adelaide in 1840. It was on this occasion that Catherine Helen Spence noted that PR/STV gave workingmen a chance to elect their foreman to the city council. Later she wrote that it changed her life: she would spend the next fifty years writing and lecturing on behalf of PR, not only in her native Australia but also in Canada, Great Britain, and the United States (Spence 1910, 17; Hoag and Hallett 1926, 77, 165–70, 181).

In the 1840s, Carl George Andrae, a Danish mathematician and minister of finance, independently devised a plan for a single transferable vote as a means to integrate the German minority of Schleswig into Danish political life by giving it parliamentary representation (Bogdanor 1991, 195). A political conservative, Andrae developed comprehensive rules for counting STV ballots. His plan was used in 1856 to elect the Danish national parliament, following which Andrae became prime minister (Hoag and Hallett 1926, 172–75). What was widely viewed as a successful experience with PR/STV in Denmark encouraged its English advocates to renew their efforts (Mill [1865, 1910] 1947, 275–76).

English Electoral Reform and John Stuart Mill

The interplay of suffrage issues and electoral system reform is nowhere more evident than in the work of John Stuart Mill. He was raised by his father, James Mill, in the Utilitarian tradition, and as an adult he became a leader among Philosophic Radicals. He was continuously engaged in analysis of the benefits of liberty and the costs of democracy. His life (1806–73) spanned most of the century in which English men fought for the right to vote. As a precocious child, Mill probably knew of the working-class agitation for the vote from 1815 until 1819, when the Peterloo Massacre in Manchester ended with police killing peaceful demonstrators. At that time, less than 3 percent of the population was eligible to vote for parliamentary representatives, since eligibility was based primarily on landownership (Kingdom 1991, 162; 542).

Popular reaction against the government's violent repression of citizens seeking to participate in political life ultimately led to the Whig victory of 1830, which in turn made possible the passage in 1832 of the Representation of the People Act. This reform favored the middle class by continuing property ownership as a qualification for voting but expanding the definition of property to include income and assets, the forms of property of the rising urban industrial elite. As a result, an estimated 20 percent of English and Welsh men became eligible to vote. Continuing agitation resulted in the Representation of the People Act of 1867, which extended the vote to "all male urban householders." The addition of "male rural householders" in the Franchise Act of 1884 almost doubled the electorate to what was called universal suffrage, although under its definition less than two-thirds of the men in England and Wales qualified to vote. Women over thirty years of age won the vote in 1918, after two decades of increasingly violent agitation and imprisonment; ten years later, the Equal Franchise Act lowered the age for women to qualify to twenty-one, the same as for men (Kingdom 1991, 165–67).

During parliamentary debates about the British Reform Acts of 1832 and 1867, the American "experiment" with what was called universal suf-frage was cited by both advocates and opponents of a wider suffrage in Britain. Advocates saw the United States as an ideal society inhabited by "happy and contented" people, while opponents described poverty and corruption in American cities as evidence of the dangers of popular vot-ing (Williamson 1960, 296–98).

The struggle that generated the gradual expansion of the suffrage in England and Wales over the course of the nineteenth and early twentieth centuries was primarily about class. The assumption that the upper class was best qualified to rule was deeply rooted in feudal society. Further-more, upper-class control was legitimized by the theory of "virtual repre-sentation," which held that the lower-classes were represented by their betters who knew what was good for them, just as it was later argued that men represented "their" women (DeGrazia 1951, 241–51).

The rise of individualism and the development of the ideas of liberty and equality in the eighteenth and nineteenth centuries led to demands for direct representation that made even the most passionate advocates of these liberating ideas uncomfortable. John Stuart Mill was one of these. Like Tocqueville, he believed profoundly in democracy, which he equated with representative government. To be representative (i.e., democratic) in a system in which the people are sovereign, citizens had to exercise their sovereignty by participation. Mill rejected virtual representation out of hand. Even if rulers were wise, they could not experience the lives of ordi-nary people and hence could not know their interests, let alone represent them. People must represent themselves, he said, including both the working class and women among those who were entitled to speak for themselves (Mill [1861] 1962, chap. 3).

Mill saw democracy not only as the best form of government but as inevitable, because of demands by the excluded to participate. However, Mill was not an optimist like the Enlightenment thinkers who preceded him. He was not sure that democracy could succeed. The lessons of the French Revolution and its Terror were vivid still. Mill feared that democ-racy, like oligarchy, would degenerate into tyranny when those who ruled (in the case of democracy, the majority) failed to act in the general inter-est. Later, in his *Autobiography*, Mill would credit his study of Tocqueville's *Democracy in America* for enlightening him on both "the excellences of democracy" and "the specific dangers which beset democracy, considered as the government of the numerical majority" (Mill [1873] 1964, 142–44).[6] Drawing on both American and British experience, he recog-nized that racial, religious, or sectional minorities could be subject to

[handwritten margin note: Interesting that today group representation is the rationale for direct rep.]

oppression by a tyrannical majority. He wrote: "Suppose the majority to be whites, the minority negroes, or *vice versa:* is it likely that the majority would allow equal justice to the minority? Suppose the majority Catholics, the minority Protestants, or the reverse; will there not be the same danger? Or let the majority be English, the minority Irish, or the contrary: is there not a great probability of similar evil?" ([1861] 1962, 128).

What Mill most feared in England, however, was the tyranny of class. He considered the laboring class intelligent enough not to attack "the security of property" directly; nevertheless, such a majority might in the long run destroy initiative by unfair taxation of the rich and might lower productivity by imposing equal wages or enacting protective trade legislation ([1861] 1962, 128–29).

This fear of working-class control—as distinct from its representation—shaped Mill's opposition to the secret ballot, one of the demands of the midcentury Chartist movement of workers seeking greater political rights. Believing as he did that voting is not a personal right but a public trust, Mill wanted ballots to be cast in a public polling place (proposals in Parliament included mailed ballots that could be marked in the privacy of the home), with signatures affixed, and open to examination. An elector, he argued, like a representative, exercises power over others and therefore is under "an absolute moral obligation to consider the interest of the public, not his private advantage." Although Mill conceded the hazard of "coercion by landlords, employers and customers," he concluded that the greater danger lay in the "selfishness . . . of the voter himself," who would be tempted by secrecy to vote according to his private inclination, not the public interest ([1861] 1962, 204–7, 209).

Mill's public policy orientation is illustrated by his example of the potential power of public ballots. Supposing the suffrage were extended to all men, he suggests,

> the voters would still have a class interest, as distinguished from women. Suppose that there were a question before the legislature specially affecting women; as whether women should be allowed to graduate at Universities; whether the mild penalties inflicted on ruffians who beat their wives daily almost to death's door, should be exchanged for something more effectual; or suppose that anyone should propose in the British Parliament, what one State after another in America is enacting not by a mere law, but by a provision of their revised Constitutions—that married women should have a right to their own property. Are not a man's wife and daughters entitled to know whether he votes for or against a candidate who will support these propositions? ([1861] 1962, 212)

Still, in spite of his differences with the Chartists' agenda, Mill participated in mass meetings and, at least once in 1866, addressed a crowd of
"tens of thousands of workers" about the need for working-class suffrage
(D. F. Thompson 1976, 52). The Chartists, disappointed by the meager
results of the 1832 Reform Act, sought not only "universal" male suffrage
but also an end to property qualifications for parliamentary candidates,
salaries for members of Parliament to enable working-class people to
serve, annual elections, and constituencies of equal population, as well as
the secret ballot to protect workers from intimidation by employers (King-
don 1991, 164).

The successful opposition to this "People's Charter" was grounded in
fears for security of property such as those expressed by Thomas B.
Macaulay in a speech delivered in the House of Commons in 1842. Conceding that the Chartists' petition for universal suffrage and other reforms
had been signed by "hundreds of thousands of males of twenty-one [years
of age]," Lord Macaulay warned that, if they were entrusted with power,
"the first use which they will make of it will be to plunder every man in
the kingdom who has a good coat on his back and a good roof over his
head" (1877, 1:317). The Whig government, alarmed by what it viewed
as the Chartists' dangerous agenda, suppressed the movement, largely by
imprisoning its leaders (Kingdom 1991, 164).

Clearly, in spite of his doubts, Mill did not share the government's
extreme fear of democracy. In his view, broader political participation
would alleviate the threat of "class legislation," a term he used to mean legislation in the interest of the working class. Voting was an act that would
educate and uplift the majority, justifying the widest possible suffrage. At
a time when property ownership and male gender were the two leading
qualifications for voting in England, Mill argued that the only exclusions
from the suffrage should be based on illiteracy, failure to pay any taxes, and
receipt of parish relief. Like Condorcet in the previous century, he saw even
these limitations as temporary, placing on the government the responsibility to educate all children and to levy a modest head tax on all adults
enabling them to qualify for voting ([1861] 1962, 170–74).

To balance the high value that he placed on political participation, and
to alleviate such hazards as both he and its opponents foresaw, Mill proposed two major ways to protect the principle of competence in governing.
One proposal was that since wise persons merited extraordinary influence
in governing, they should be able to cast two votes instead of one. Weighted
voting was already practiced in England: university graduates had been
empowered since 1603 to cast votes for two members of Parliament, a

district representative and a university representative. A business owner could cast an additional vote in the district where his enterprise was located, if other than his district of residence.[7]

However, Mill rejected ownership of property as a justification for greater influence in elections. He considered "individual mental superiority" to be "the only thing which can justify reckoning one person's opinion as equivalent to more than one." To choose property as a criterion would be "supremely odious," he wrote, since "accident has so much more to do than merit with enabling men to rise in the world." He pondered the possibility of occupation as a proxy for merit, since he found employers, skilled laborers, managers, and professionals generally more able than unskilled laborers and tradesmen. Occupation, however, suffered the flaws of property as a measure of merit. Education would be the only correct standard, he concluded. Yet in the absence of a national system of education equally open to all, education as a standard too was imperfect. In the end, Mill concluded that only university graduates could clearly qualify for weighted votes, and even this existing franchise should never give any class enough weight to outvote the majority ([1861] 1962, 176–84). Given the limited access to university education at the time, a majority of double voters was not a realistic hazard.

Mill's other major proposal to prevent majority tyranny and to ensure competence in democratic governance was to change the electoral system by adopting proportional representation by single transferable vote (PR/STV). Mill had discovered PR/STV by reading English barrister Thomas Hare's 1859 pamphlet, "A Treatise on the Election of Representatives, Parliamentary and Municipal."[8] In 1861, Mill called Thomas Hare's "scheme" for proportional representation by single transferable vote, which was patterned on Thomas Hill's earlier work, "among the very greatest improvements yet made in the theory and practice of government" ([1861] 1962, 151).[9]

Mill knew of other electoral "expediencies," voting systems that would allow for some minority representation. Limited voting[10] and cumulative voting[11] were electoral reforms that had been unsuccessfully introduced in Parliament to allow for three-member constituencies in which a minority as large as a third of the electorate could return one of the three members. Although Mill felt that both of these "makeshift" plans "recognised the right principle," neither reached the "degree of perfection" of Hare's proposal ([1861] 1962, 146–47).

Mill found Hare's explanation of his purpose persuasive. PR/STV would increase both the liberty of the individual voter and the accountability of the representative. The voter would gain freedom, Hare had argued, by being liberated from a small district, and by being empowered to vote for candidates anywhere in the country. Since candidates would be nominated by petition, the voter would not be limited to the candidates presented by the major parties. These features led some to call the system "free nomination" and "free voting." The representative would become more accountable because his tie to his constituents would be direct, each voter being a member of a unanimous and voluntary constituency. In contrast, the representative in a single-member district, once elected, "represents" those who voted against him as well as those who voted for him, an unlikely if not impossible task. The direct tie between constituent and representative created by PR/STV led Hare to call his system "Personal Representation."

Like Mill, Hare advocated that each voter sign his ballot. Hare's goal was to ensure accountability by the representative. The voter would be able to trace his ballot through transfers to the candidate for whom it was counted. The voter would then know whom, in a large delegation, to hold responsible for representing him (Hare 1859, chap. 7; Mill [1861] 1962, chap. 10). Under this electoral system, Hare argued, a "natural community of interest" would gain representation untrammeled by district boundaries (Lakeman and Lambert 1959, 245; Hoag and Hallett 1926, 176). Later, Catherine Spence, who proved to be a theoretician as well as a practical campaigner, would add the idea of multimember districts for PR/STV elections, instead of voting in the whole country at-large, as Hare had assumed. This practical refinement led many advocates to call the method the Hare-Spence system (Tyson 1908b, 978).

Mill, like those electoral theorists on whose work he built, viewed plurality voting as an electoral procedure opening the way for majority tyranny. Since the candidate first-past-the-post wins, not only could a majority of voters win all, or a disproportionately large share, of the seats in a governing body, but a majority of the majority that might itself be a minority of the whole could prevail (Mill [1861] 1962, 142–43). The drawing of district boundaries, the clustering or dispersal of voters of a particular persuasion, and the actual turnout of eligible voters shaped the outcomes of plurality voting systems in ways voters seldom understood.

These were matters that, in Mill's view, were controlled by the political parties for the furtherance of their own interests. In dealing with the absence of minority representation in a single-member district plurality vote system, Mill cited as his foremost example distortions imposed by the party system. "The electors who are on a different side in party politics from the local majority, are unrepresented," he wrote. The majority itself is "misrepresented," he argued, because the majority party is capable of imposing on its followers a candidate whose opinions may differ from the party's loyal voters in all but one respect. Even candidates with no significant opinions may be nominated by the parties, since a candidate to whom no one can object may be the most electable.[12] Mill found "nothing . . . more certain than that the virtual blotting-out of the minority is no necessary or natural consequence of freedom." Minorities should not rule, but they should be present and be heard in policy deliberations in a democratic state ([1861] 1962, 144–46).

The minority whose potential powerlessness Mill found most disturbing was the intellectual elite. Under the existing system, "able men of independent thought" were unlikely to be elected by the average voter, who would be swayed by "local influence," "lavish expenditure," or party direction ([1861] 1962, 153). Even so, in imagining the "ideally best polity," Mill "support[ed] the claim of all to participate in the sovereign power," including the working class:

> Does Parliament, or almost any of the members composing it, ever for an instant look at any question with the eyes of a working man? When a subject arises in which the labourers as such have an interest, is it regarded from any point of view but that of the employers of labour? I do not say that the working men's view of these questions is in general nearer to truth than the other: but it is sometimes quite as near; and in any case it ought to be respectfully listened to, instead of being, as it is, not merely turned away from, but ignored. ([1861] 1962, 59–61)

Not only would workingmen have an appropriate voice in Parliament but "the instructed minority" could influence the entire decision-making process:

> In the actual voting, [these educated representatives would] count only for their numbers, but as a moral power they would count for much more, in virtue of their knowledge, and of the influence it would give them over the rest. An arrangement better adapted to keep popular opinion within reason and justice, and to guard it from the various deteriorating influences which assail the weak side of democracy, could scarcely by human ingenuity be devised. ([1861] 1962, 161)

Since Hare's voting system would result in the fair representation of both the independent intellectual minority and the working class, Mill would abandon his plan for weighted voting if PR/STV could be instituted ([1861] 1962, 184).

In the second and third editions of his *Considerations on Representative Government*, Mill added an analysis of the objections to PR/STV that he had heard since publication of the first edition, and he answered them as "either unreal or easily surmountable." The two principal objections were that small groups ("knots or cliques . . . or bodies united by class interests or community of religious persuasion") would gain disproportionate power and that political parties could manipulate the system by promoting "tickets," or slates of candidates (Mill [1865, 1910] 1947, 271–76).

In response to these dire warnings, Mill conceded only that organization is an advantage under any electoral system, PR/STV as well as others. Nevertheless, "able independents" would have a greater chance of election under PR/STV than under any other method, because of nomination by petition and voting in larger constituencies. A "personal merit" ticket could be effective. And "the minor groups would have precisely the amount of power which they ought to have"—no more and no less; they would be unable to control an assembly but able to be heard ([1865, 1910] 1947, 271–74).

As a member of Parliament from 1865 to 1868, Mill participated in debates on the Reform Bill of 1867, offering amendments to accomplish what he called "the two greatest improvements which remain to be made in representative government." The first of these was "Mr. Hare's plan" for election of parliamentary representatives; the other was a motion to strike out the limitation of the franchise to males. Neither of these moves succeeded, but Mill would later consider their introduction to be his most important contribution to public life ([1873] 1964, 210–11).

In 1868, a few three-member districts were established, in which voters were limited to casting two votes. This LV plan permitted some minority party representation for the elections of 1868, 1874, and 1880. The Liberal Party in Birmingham, for example, gained representation through this system (Reeve and Ware 1992, 61–62). Mill's followers, however, continued to press for the "best" means of achieving fair representation. Mill's PR/STV bill was introduced anew in 1872, when it was debated inconclusively, and again in 1884 as part of a major reform initiative. The 1884 parliamentary debate tied together the extension of the franchise (to male rural voters), the reallocation of seats from rural areas to the growing cities, and the voting system itself. Consideration was given to various devices for achieving "proportionate" representation within the existing multimember districts, including an extension of LV, CV, or PR/STV.

Despite evidence that Prime Minister Gladstone himself preferred multimember constituencies with some form of proportional representation, the Liberal government struck a deal with the Tories in which it accepted small, single-member districts in exchange for the extension of

Tories preferred single-member districts b/c it would best serve their interests the franchise. Gladstone defended his capitulation on the small-district system by claiming that minorities or "separate interests and pursuits" could secure representation in the new one-member constituencies (Bogdanor 1985, 271–77). The 1884 Representation of the People Act incorporated single-member district plurality voting for parliamentary elections, ending Britain's sixteen-year small-scale experiment with limited voting. The subsequent exclusion of minority parties within single-member districts has led to periodic reexamination of the British electoral system ever since (Lakeman 1970, app. 10; Hart 1992; Norris 1997).

Mill's advocacy and the efforts of the British Electoral Reform Society were to bear a little fruit for a time in the twentieth century. In 1917, although PR/STV for all parliamentary elections was defeated again by a narrow margin in the Commons, the 1917 Representation of the People Act established election by PR/STV for the (weighted) university seats. Between 1918 and 1945, most university seats were contested. Although Conservatives won the majority of these PR/STV elections, as they had traditionally won the university seats when they were elected by plurality, Independents were occasionally chosen (Lakeman 1970, 217–20).

The American Debate

From colonial days on, geographically based plurality voting was the universally accepted practice in the United States. The framers of the Constitution left open the question of districts, so that states could choose to elect members of Congress at-large by state, or to divide the state into districts, each of which could elect one or more members (single- or multimember districts). At the outset, just five states chose to use districts. Over time a discernible pattern developed, with the small states using at-large elections, and the more populous and diverse states using districts. Not until 1842 did Congress use its power to regulate congressional elections (Art. I, sec. 4) to require single-member districts (Reapportionment Act of 1842, chap. 47, 5 Stat. 491). Even then, four states ignored the new requirement, elected their representatives at-large, and in spite of objections were to see them seated by Congress (Issacharoff, Karlan, and Pildes 1998, 769–71).

The issue then was largely partisan. With plurality at-large elections, the majority party could elect representatives for most or all of a state's seats. The 1842 requirement was intended to protect the minority party in a state from the disproportionate results of winner-take-all elections.

In a Whig-dominant state, for example, the Democratic minority could elect one or several representatives if its voters were residentially concentrated somewhere in the state. Seldom did districting produce *proportional* party representation, but it tended to break up a majority party monopoly within a state.

In the critical and politically charged years leading up to the Civil War, however, this modest protection for congressional representation of minority interests within states was dropped. From 1852 until 1862, the states were permitted to use districts or not, as they chose (Hacker 1964, 48–50). From 1862 until 1929, Congress renewed the single-member district mandate with each decennial reapportionment act.[13] Multimember districts continued in use for state legislative elections, however, through the nineteenth century in more than three-quarters of the states (Niemi, Jackman, and Winsky 1991, 91).

The political context of the nineteenth-century electoral system debate in the United States showed striking similarities to the British framework. Assumptions about class were critical. As in England, the steady expansion of the suffrage to include men with less property or different kinds of property exacerbated elite concerns about majority tyranny. In the late eighteenth century, weighted voting had been practiced in some U.S. jurisdictions. In New York State, for example, property owners were allowed to vote in local elections in each jurisdiction in which they owned land. In 1804, the Jeffersonian-Republican majority in the state assembly abolished this practice, giving "tradesmen, mechanics, and carters" occasion to celebrate a "second Declaration of Independence" (Williamson 1960, 164).

The absence of a feudal tradition in the new United States and the patriotic passion for equality stirred by the American Revolution combined to accelerate the acceptance of democracy, but state control of qualifications for voting led to great diversity in suffrage practice. The basic notion that only property holders should vote derived from belief, as in England, that if the poor voted, they would either destroy the security of property or sell their votes to the rich, thus distorting the power of wealth (Williamson 1960, 11–12). Although the status of "freeholder" was the basic property qualification for voting in most states, the term was defined differently in different states. The amount of land owned, the value of the land, income from rents, and taxpayer status were among the criteria for granting suffrage to men of property. Property qualifications, however, were steadily undermined in practice. In several states, depreciation of paper money after the Revolution broadened the franchise by making specified monetary requirements, such as "being worth 50 pounds," easy to achieve. Men without property and youths less than twenty-one years of age who had fought in the Revolution were admitted to the franchise by some grateful state legislatures (Williamson 1960, 83, 113, 121).

In addition, party competition contributed to broadening the franchise. Jeffersonian Republicans (later Democrats) strove to expand their support through efforts in state legislatures and constitutional conventions to achieve universal male suffrage. Although Federalists (and later Whigs) opposed extension of the suffrage, they were known to manufacture votes by giving temporary deeds for small lots to potential supporters who would return the deeds after the election (Williamson 1960, 168–69).

In 1802, Ohio's first constitution was hailed as symbolic of democracy on the new frontier because the only property restriction was payment of a tax (Ohio Const. 1802, Art. 4, sec. 1). While this tax appeared to be a tax on real property, the difficulties of surveying land and granting titles on the frontier made literal application of the requirement impractical. Otherwise eligible men were permitted to meet the qualification by "work[ing] out a tax on the public highway" (K. H. Porter [1918] 1969, 36–37). In 1851, Ohio's new constitution dropped the taxpaying requirement for voting altogether.

Racial restrictions on voting were not uncommon outside of New England. Five states admitted to the Union between 1796 and 1821 confined voting to white males (Williamson 1960, 219). For example, Ohio's 1802 constitution limited the suffrage to "white male inhabitants" (Art. 4, sec. 1).[14]

The period of Jacksonian democracy was actually restrictive for black voters in America, as race came to replace class as a qualification to vote in states that had not discriminated earlier. Agitation against slavery in the North and slave rebellions in the South led to racist fears of a democracy that would include blacks as participants in political life. Southern states that had once permitted free blacks to vote disfranchised them between 1835 (North Carolina) and 1851 (Virginia). White supremacy, binding poor whites to the interests of slave owners, was promulgated to prevent the development of unified interests among propertyless whites and blacks (Williamson 1960, 232–40). In the North as well, states such as New York, Pennsylvania, and New Jersey, which had permitted black freeholders to vote, withdrew the privilege by confining the suffrage to white adult males. By 1858, free blacks still voted only in a few New England states (Williamson 1960, 278–79; Litwack 1961, 75).

Ohio's new constitution of 1851 retained the racial qualification ("every white male citizen," Ohio Const. 1851, Art. 5, sec. 1). Whigs had advocated a literacy test instead of either property or racial qualifications, but Democrats controlled the 1851 convention and prevented debate on the issue (Williamson 1960, 267). Strenuous efforts by advocates of "negro" suffrage to get their petitions accepted for consideration were futile. "Even petitions advocating the expulsion of all free negroes from the state had a better reception," reported an early twentieth-century historian (K. H. Porter [1918] 1969, 108). In 1867, three years before the Fifteenth Amendment to the U.S. Constitution was adopted to prohibit the states from denying the vote on account of race, Ohio voters rejected a proposed state constitutional amendment that would have enfranchised blacks and disfranchised all who bore arms in support of insurrection or rebellion against the United States (Patterson 1912, 170).

Women had voted only in New Jersey, where "free adults" had been enfranchised in the original state constitution. By 1810, when women had actually voted for a few years, which perhaps no one anticipated, the right to vote was restricted to men (Litwack 1961, 180–81). Later, Elizabeth Cady Stanton would attribute this setback to male corruption: incidents were reported of men voting early in the day and returning to the polls a second time in women's dress to vote again (Stanton, Anthony, and Gage [1881] 1969, 1:453). With the initiation of the women's rights movement in 1848, inclusion in the suffrage became an issue that would grow in importance for the rest of the century (Stetson 1991, 45). American woman suffrage activists were familiar with Mill's work. Stanton, the leading intellectual of the suffrage movement, shared Mill's philosophy of individualism and natural rights. In 1868, she wrote that the ballot alone was not what women needed, but "a revolution in society, politics, and religion" (quoted in Banner 1980, 88).

Interested Americans corresponded with Mill about electoral systems, and his writings were widely read in the United States.[15] Disciples of his theories of liberty and representation included Philadelphian J. Francis Fisher, who published *The Degradation of Our Representative System and Its Reform* in 1863, in which he advocated the use of PR/STV. Like Mill, Fisher believed that the electoral system could affect policy outcomes. He argued that the Civil War could have been averted if minority political views had been represented in both Northern and Southern delegations to Congress. Antislavery Southerners and pro-states' rights Northerners, incapable of winning election in winner-take-all elections, could have been elected in PR/STV contests, in Fisher's view, and, once in Congress, would have introduced moderate perspectives that might in turn have led to more serious consideration of alternatives to war (Fisher 1863).

Simon Sterne, another Philadelphian, went to England in 1865, met with Hare, Mill, and other British advocates of PR, and returned with their encouragement to lead a PR movement in the United States (Sterne [1871] 1970; Hoag and Hallett 1926, 183). Like Mill, Sterne was eager to secure the representation of the educated minority in order to protect democracy from the demos. He did find it "odd," however, that Mill, and Hare as well, should advocate women's suffrage at a time when women were to him so obviously ignorant and manipulable (Sterne [1871] 1970, 176–78; Mill, 1972–88, 19:370).

Although captivated by Mill's electoral system analysis, Sterne rejected his feminist theories on the ground that "to one . . . Mrs. Stanton, there are half a million of women whose political education is nil; and though the ballot-box has an educational influence, that much-be-praised and overrated education machine is as yet very far from having fully impregnated [sic] every suffragan with sound politico-economical ideas" ([1871] 1970, 178). In Sterne's view, Mill's vision of PR as a mechanism to allow representation of the educated minority should not include the educated female minority.

Ironically, the fear of too much democracy was shared by suffragists themselves. Concerned about the illiteracy of both freedwomen and immigrant women, many suffrage leaders supported an "educated franchise" (Flexner 1975, 225, 309). Furthermore, many nineteenth-century feminists deemed immigrant women to be controlled by their husbands, who were mere pawns of the machine bosses, powerful politicians who instructed male legislators to vote down any public policy steps toward women's equality.

While suffrage would remain at the top of the feminist agenda until 1920 (when the vote was at last won), the grounds for women's claim to the vote shifted significantly in the late nineteenth century. Since 1848, arguments for political rights had rested on the theory, articulated as well by Mill, that women were persons equal to men, entitled to the franchise on that ground alone. As the decades slipped by and women won few battles for self-representation, they began to assert entitlement based on their higher moral capacity. By the 1890s, woman suffrage leaders were contending that if only women had the vote, they could clean up corruption in the cities; improve education, sanitation, and health; and help to alleviate the harsh burdens that industrial life had imposed on society, particularly on women and children (Stetson 1991, 48). These claims activated new enemies—the liquor interests, antiregulatory forces in business, and above all, the bosses—but they also placed the women's movement in the mainstream of developing Progressive thought.

BETWEEN THE CIVIL WAR and the end of the nineteenth century, the fear of majority tyranny or an "excess of democracy" was reignited in both the North and the South by several major social and political forces. Demographic and political trends led such minorities as white men in the South, Protestant elites in the urban North, Republicans in Democratic-dominant states, and Democrats in Republican-dominant ones to try experiments with electoral systems that would preserve their influence or control in the governance of cities, states, political parties, and even Congress. The limited vote (LV) and the cumulative vote (CV) were most often considered, but PR/STV was also debated.

In the South, racial issues continued to dominate the debate. In 1867, by military rule, Congress enfranchised the newly freed male slaves and disfranchised former Confederate leaders. Black majorities existed in the new electorates of five states. State constitutional conventions were convened, and new state constitutions were proposed and adopted, confirming the black male franchise under state authority. Although the new black voters did not win control of any state government, many black office-holders were elected, and in South Carolina blacks won a majority of the lower house of the state assembly (Holt 1977, 96).

White reaction was intense and violent across the South. Northern friends of Negro suffrage, many of them from states that had disfranchised blacks before the Civil War, were alarmed by reports from Southern states of white retaliation that ranged from intimidation of black voters to murder. The Radical Republicans in Congress determined that only a federal constitutional amendment to prohibit state denial of the vote on account of race could resolve both the issue of hypocrisy in the North (outside of New England) and the threat of betrayal of the promise of black freedom in the South.

While the struggle over Negro suffrage in the South was raging, some members of Congress searched for peaceful ways to reach an accommodation that would support gradual change. Alternative electoral systems were proposed as means of protecting black voters against exclusion from representation in the new South. The focus of this debate over electoral systems was a bill introduced in the Senate in 1867 by Democrat Charles R. Buckalew of Pennsylvania, to require the use of cumulative voting (CV) for members of Congress from the reconstructed states of the former Confederacy. Identifying "plurality rule" as the "evil which exists," Senator Buckalew argued that CV ("the free vote") would alleviate growing racial antagonisms in the South by allowing Negro representation from that region in Congress. Buckalew's proposal was defeated by opponents who contended that such a major change in congressional election procedures should not be sectional in nature (*Cong. Globe* 1867, 40th Cong., 1st sess., pp. 533, 573–79).

In 1869, Buckalew chaired a Select Committee on Representative Reform that issued a report advocating the use of CV for election of representatives in Congress, presidential electors, state legislatures, town councils, and other elected bodies (U.S. Senate 1869, Report no. 271). The committee report promoted minority representation through CV elections most importantly as "just." Other "great reasons" for this reform were said to be its potential to check corruption, to prevent the gerrymander, to improve the "character and ability of the House," and to guarantee peace. "The free vote," the report asserted, "will now allay the antagonism of race." Senator Buckalew reintroduced his bill to elect members of the House by the cumulative vote, expanding its reach to all states electing more than one representative, only to have it defeated again (*Cong. Globe* 1869, 40th Cong., 3d sess., 1769ff. and App., 268–78; Buckalew 1872, 82–86).[16]

In the South, the debate about alternative electoral systems focused instead on protection of the white minority. Not surprisingly, the locus of action was South Carolina, where blacks were 60 percent of the population and where more black leaders were elected to public office than in any other state (Holt 1977, 96). The ratification in 1870 of the Fifteenth Amendment, a federal guarantee of black voting rights, precipitated large protest meetings, billed as Taxpayers Conventions, in 1871 and again in 1874. The assembled bodies objected to high taxes, the increase in the state's public debt, underrepresentation of white voters, and general mismanagement of state government. Among the reforms proposed "to protect the rights of minorities" was cumulative voting to elect the legislature and boards of county commissioners. The purpose was to enable white property holders to gain what they considered adequate representation in the making and execution of laws (*New York Times*, 14 May 1871, p. 1; Dutcher 1872, 43–45, 61–62; Commons 1907, 248–49; Zuczek 1996, 137).[17] The governor and legislature were urged to implement the recommended reforms, and although the governor expressed his support, there is no evidence of legislative action by the assembly, where the majority was both black and Republican (Holt 1977, 97).[18]

Many years later, W. E. B. DuBois would write that the South Carolina legislature replied to the charges but did not take action on the recommendations of the Taxpayers Conventions, since they were "composed of the former ruling class which wanted to regain power" (DuBois 1935,

414). White control was achieved instead by the rapid disfranchisement of black voters following the withdrawal of Northern military power. After 1877, the white minority used literacy tests, the poll tax, intimidation, and violence to prevent blacks from voting[19] and, safely in control again, continued to use plurality elections. *whites were not interested in fairness but the protection of their interests.*

POLITICAL LEADERS IN THE NORTHERN STATES were becoming preoccupied with their own problems of democracy. The massive immigration of European workers, often illiterate and inexperienced in the ways of democracy, made universal male suffrage controversial in the North as well. Between 1870 and 1900, more than 11 million immigrants poured into the United States, most of them building their new lives in the cities of the Northeast and the Middle West (Boyer 1978, 123). Moreover, political party organizations became adept at recruiting these new residents into their ranks, developing their loyalties by serving their basic needs, and collecting their reward at the polls on election day.

New York City was often used as an egregious example of political corruption. Edwin L. Godkin, editor of the *Nation* and one of Mill's American intellectual heirs, worried about the abuse of universal suffrage by "the boss" in governing a large city such as New York. He saw control of the city shifting into the hands of poor, illiterate immigrants, "the dangerous classes," who voted as told by the demagogue who helped them. The "respectable classes," on the other hand, he complained, split their votes between parties and thereby allowed crime and ignorance to prevail in municipal affairs (Godkin 1894, 879–81).

Reformers who deplored the ability of party organizations to gain and hold power through the ballot box promoted electoral system experiments that might maintain at least some representation for independents and for antimachine partisans. Semiproportional electoral systems such as limited and cumulative voting were used in a variety of settings.

Limited voting, which had been used for some local elections in Pennsylvania, was adopted for the election of delegates to the New York Constitutional Convention of 1867.[20] The success of the LV strategy in producing what was believed to be fair representation of New York's Democratic minority in a Republican-majority convention led to further consideration of electoral system change. In the course of the convention, Republican Horace Greeley proposed the use of cumulative voting (CV) for election of New York's U.S. senators and representatives in order to end the "tyranny" of election results in which plurality or majority winners could take all of the representation. This proposal was defeated, but partisans were aware that electoral system experiments might serve their own purposes (DeGrazia 1951, 187–89).

In 1872, the Republican majority in the New York legislature attempted to impose the cumulative vote on New York City, then firmly in the hands of the Tammany (Democratic) machine, which routinely elected all council members by the winner-take-all plurality system. The measure was vetoed by the Democratic governor of New York, but the following year the legislature tried again to introduce some partisan proportionality into New York City elections, this time successfully with a limited vote plan. For council elections the city was divided into nine districts with three members each; no voter could cast more than two votes. This plan, which remained in effect for almost a decade, enabled the Republican minority in the city's electorate to elect at least one member in several of the new districts (Commons 1907, 251, 261). Still, this reform did not last, and the city returned to one-party rule.

The cumulative vote was to meet with more lasting success. In the wake of the Civil War, Illinois was torn by sectional politics. The conflict had left allegiances in the state deeply divided between the North and the South. Plurality voting allowed Republicans to monopolize representation in the northern districts of the state, whereas in southern Illinois only Democrats could win district elections. A plan for the cumulative vote for the lower house of the legislature was proposed to the Illinois Constitutional Convention of 1869–70 by its Committee on Electoral and Representative Reform as a solution to the problem of sectional cleavage. Committee chair Joseph Medill, editor of the *Chicago Tribune,* urged the convention to adopt a legislative election plan which provided that in each district voters would elect one senator by plurality vote, and three representatives by cumulative vote. Voters' options for the lower house included casting three votes for one candidate, one and a half votes for each of two candidates, or one vote for each of three candidates. By limiting nominations and concentrating votes, the minority party in each district could secure representation. Medill told the convention:

> This great measure of reform will carry our pure democratic equality and equal rights for all men in the legislative halls; secure the equal representation of every citizen, the minority with the majority, man for man; allay partisan strife, reform legislative corruption, purify the electoral system, inspire good and quiet citizens to attend the polls, enable virtuous citizens to elect pure and able representatives. (*Debates and Proceedings of the Constitutional Convention of the State of Illinois* 1870, 2:1727)

The CV plan was accepted by the convention, but because of concern that the new electoral system might lead to defeat of the whole proposed constitution, it was submitted as a separate amendment. Both the amendment and the constitution passed, but the CV plan won by a narrower margin (Ill. Const. 1870, Art. 4, sec. 7; G. S. Blair 1960, 10).[21]

From the first implementation of CV elections in 1872, partisan representation improved markedly in the Illinois lower house. Between 1872 and 1898, the division of seats approximated the division of the two-party vote statewide. Third parties were usually unable to win seats in spite of significant support statewide, because they were unlikely to win over one-fourth of the vote in a district. With some modifications, such as extension of CV to primary elections in 1910, the system was retained for over a century, its persistence making it an exception to the usual pattern of fleeting electoral reform (G. S. Blair 1960; Argersinger 1989, 83–86; DeGrazia 1951, 187–89).[22]

It was also in 1870 that Illinois became the first state to provide for CV elections for directors of corporations. The measure was modeled on the provision for CV legislative elections, but was less controversial and therefore was inserted into the proposed constitution itself (Ill. Const. 1870, Art. 11, sec. 3). In the headlong post–Civil War expansion of the American economy, corporate corruption, particularly in the railroad companies, led to the dissipation of the investments of many small stockholders. Medill, who chaired the convention's Committee on Corporations (as well as the Committee on Elections and Representation) argued on the floor of the convention that cumulative voting for directors would "afford every stockholder more power of self-protection than he now possesses. Its object is not to cripple or injure the rights of the majority in any respect. Their power to control the offices of the company remains intact; but this is to protect the minority from being plundered and robbed out of house and home, their stock confiscated and lost for the want of some representative to look after their interest" (*Debates and Proceedings* 1870, 2:1666).

Other states quickly followed Illinois's example either to require or to permit CV elections for corporate directors, often by state constitution, or, as in Ohio in 1898, by statute (Williams 1951, 20–25, 34).

BY THE END OF THE NINETEENTH CENTURY, although in a few state and local legislative bodies the use of cumulative and limited voting continued as a means of achieving minority representation, agitation for opening up the system of representation to minority parties or interests failed. In 1894, for example, Boston adopted a limited voting system to elect its aldermen (each elector could vote for seven of the twelve aldermen), but plurality voting was restored in 1898 (Hoag and Hallett 1926, 42–43). With the notable exception of the Illinois House of Representatives, existing electoral systems contained an insuperable barrier to lasting change. The two dominant parties, which benefited from the exaggeration of their strength implicit in small-district plurality voting, controlled Congress and most state legislative chambers, the very bodies that held the power to change—or preserve—the winner-take-all electoral system (Argersinger 1989, 65). Electoral reformers clearly understood this power structure and began to unite in support of nonpartisanship as a critical step on the road to achieving their other goals.

[handwritten margin note: Party the main obstacle]

Electoral System Reform Efforts in Ohio

Ohio was hardly immune to the agitation arising over electoral systems and representation in the late nineteenth century. Congressional debates about minority representation were fueled by electoral results distorted by winner-take-all voting. Ohio offered a particularly flagrant example because of the close division of popular sentiment and intense competition between the two major parties. In the last quarter of the nineteenth century, the percentage of votes won for a party's congressional candidates in Ohio had little relationship to the share of seats won by the party. The switch of a small margin of votes from one party to the other would swing a significant number of districts into the other party's camp. From election to election, party control of the Ohio delegation swung from Republican to Democratic and back again. These swings in turn drove repeated redistricting as each majority party of the moment in the Ohio legislature sought to retain its temporary advantage.

Ohio's assembly districts were based on county lines (from 1852 until 1966) and were therefore immune to manipulation by districting authorities, but congressional district lines were (and still are) drawn by state legislative enactment. The party that controlled the legislature drew the lines. When party control changed in mid-decade, the new legislature upon convening would quickly draw new congressional districts. Between 1876 and 1886, a new districting plan was enacted in Ohio for each of six successive elections (Argersinger 1989, 71).

Even some members of Congress whose seats were secure worried that the legitimacy of the political system as a whole was being undermined by what they called "practical disfranchisement." In 1870, when Congress was debating an apportionment bill that would add fifty-eight members to the lower house to represent the rapidly increasing population of the United States, Rep. Samuel S. Marshall (not surprisingly of Illinois) introduced an amendment to provide for the new members to be elected by cumulative voting. He explained that the purpose of his amendment was to ensure fair partisan representation among this significant augmentation of the membership of the House (Dutcher 1872, 56–60). This was the occasion for James A. Garfield, Republican congressman from Ohio and later president, speaking on the floor in support of Marshall's amendment, to criticize the existing winner-take-all electoral system because "a large portion of the voting people [are] permanently disfranchised. . . . There are about ten thousand Democratic voters in my district, and they have been voting there for the last forty years, without any more hope of having a Representative on this floor than of having one in the Commons of Great Britain." However, the amendment was defeated (*Cong. Globe*, 41st Cong., 2d sess., 23 June 1870, pp. 4737–38).

In 1874, under the rubric of another popular term for the same problem, "virtual disfranchisement," representation became a leading issue in debates over Ohio constitutional revision, and the Illinois experiment with cumulative voting attracted intense interest. In a proposed new constitution, CV was introduced for state legislative elections in the multimember urban counties in Ohio, then Cuyahoga (Cleveland) and Hamilton (Cincinnati) Counties. The declared purpose of CV was to enable minority party voters in those counties to gain some representation in the assembly (Proposed Art. 14, sec. 12, 1874; in Patterson 1912, 176).

Because Ohio's elective judiciary was also perceived as captive of the majority party, the bench was targeted for reform as well. A separate constitutional amendment, called the "Minority Representation Amendment," was submitted to Ohio's voters, providing for limited voting (LV) for state judges in the counties in which more than one judge was elected at a time (Proposition 1, 1874). Voters would be permitted to vote for only as many judicial candidates as constituted a majority of judges in their county, not for all seats on the bench. For example, if three judges were to be elected countywide, voters could vote for two judicial candidates; if five judges, three votes. Both of these provisions attempted to break the monopoly that the majority party could achieve with countywide multimember plurality voting, and both the proposed constitution and the separate amendment were defeated by the voters in 1874 (Patterson 1912, 176, 223).

A different path proposed in Ohio to secure minority party representation was the division of multimember counties into single-member districts

for the election of state legislators. Three times in the nineteenth century—in 1857, 1889, and 1893—constitutional amendments were initiated to "subdistrict" the populous urban counties in Ohio for state legislative elections. Although plurality voting in single-member districts would
still produce winner-take-all results within those districts, subdividing the
large multimember counties would have facilitated some minority party
representation from urban areas in the General Assembly. However, like
the cumulative and limited voting amendments, all three proposals were
defeated at the polls. The prevailing argument against single-member districts was the horror of the gerrymander, which had been practiced so
effectively by the dominant party in the legislature from 1802 until 1852,
when Ohio's new constitution established counties as the basic unit of legislative representation (Patterson 1912, 166–67, 259, 274). Not until
1966, following passage of the Voting Rights Act of 1965, would single-
member districts be established for the Ohio House of Representatives.

Since power in competitive party states depended on the geographical
distribution of partisan voters, the small-district plurality voting system
enhanced the stakes in districting and apportionment decisions. The gerrymander has historically been a key tool in the hands of the party that
controlled the state legislatures for shaping in turn the party composition
of Congress and thus its policy output. Ohio congressional districts were
frequently used as examples of partisan misrepresentation by means of the
electoral system. It should not be surprising that it was Rep. Tom Johnson of Ohio (later mayor of Cleveland) who introduced into Congress in
1892 the first bill to elect its members by proportional representation
(Commons 1907, 114–15).

Conclusion

By the end of the century, the major parties had secured a firm lock on
access to power in the United States. While the parties were intensely
competitive nationally and in states like Ohio, and participation of those
eligible remained high, the political system seemed undemocratic and the
economic system unjust to growing numbers of citizens. The drive for
more democracy would coalesce outside the party organizations, and the
parties would become leading targets of attack in the name of democracy
instead of its instruments.

Electoral system reform came to the fore because representation was
at the fulcrum of controversy. Who would be allowed to vote was still a

key issue to the excluded—primarily to women and African Americans. There was, however, a growing awareness that how votes were translated into power, the reality of representation, profoundly affected the ability of voters to influence public decisions.

In structuring the American government, the framers of the Constitution had relied on institutional checks and balances—the separation of powers and the federal system—to prevent the tyranny of the majority so feared in that revolutionary period of western political development. The need for Madison's "social check" on the potential tyranny of the majority was believed to arise out of the inequalities deeply embedded in human nature and therefore built into the politics of the system. As the citizenry became more diverse, however, through both the end of slavery and new waves of immigration, nineteenth-century Americans confronted different problems.

Unable to break into the multifaceted structure of political practices and institutions, a significant number of antiparty reformers gradually narrowed their focus to local elections and to alternative electoral systems. Both limited and cumulative voting had been tried in a variety of settings. As these turn-of-the-century Progressives took up the challenge of expanding grassroots democracy while attempting to preserve competence in governance, they were drawn to PR/STV by its technical elegance, its reliably proportional results, and its unqualified endorsement by John Stuart Mill.

The Progressive Crusade
for Proportional Representation

BETWEEN 1890 AND 1920, American political life was charged with optimism about the potential for improving the human condition and with anger about social, economic, and political inequities, particularly in the rapidly expanding cities. At the same time, insecurity spread among native working-class and upper-middle-class professionals about their ability to maintain their way of life in the face of industrialization and the massive new immigration of Europeans to the United States.

A transition was taking place in American life from the individualism of the framers, the settlers and pioneers of the eighteenth and nineteenth centuries, to more collective modes of political awareness. Ideas of representation were constantly changing under the pressure of mutating forces in the social and economic realms.[1] By the end of the nineteenth century, the consolidation of economic power in corporate structures appeared to be displacing governmental decision making. As the population grew and became more diverse through immigration, internal migration, and the pressures of industrial life, social control loomed as a problem. In a democratic system, how was order to be maintained? Some reformers projected mass democracy as a goal, but others supported specific policies that when adopted made participation more difficult. In the North and West, registration laws, nonpartisan ballot requirements, and other measures were passed to control potentially volatile political movements. In the South, outright disfranchisement of the black population was effected by both legal and illegal means. Between 1896 and 1926, turnout dropped steadily and the American electorate appeared to shrink in size. Regular voting among lower-income voters especially seemed to decline in both North and

South. With the apparent loss of function in the public sphere, apathy came to characterize a large portion of the citizenry, while the anonymity and complexity of industrial life appeared to marginalize politics.

The development of modern pluralism in the early twentieth century is rooted in these concerns. Social scientists analyzed the "social disharmony" that resulted from the conflicting interests of economic and ethnic groups. Sociologist Arthur F. Bentley wrote of the coalescing of groups in the struggle for power and described politics as process, the flow of activities that interest groups engaged in to shape policy outcomes (1908). Ideas of representation evolved from the right of the individual to elect a personal representative, so compelling to Hare, Mill, and Buckalew, to group identity and collective claims on the body politic, as delineated by political scientists Charles E. Merriam and Harold F. Gosnell and by historian Charles A. Beard. The debate about electoral systems was a critical element of this development because of growing awareness that the electoral system shaped how voters' choices were translated into policy outputs. Which social and economic groups would prevail?

The Organized Campaign for PR

In 1893, in conjunction with the Chicago World's Columbian Exposition, a Proportional Representation Congress was called. This was but one of a series of meetings held that summer in Chicago to showcase nineteenth-century American scientific advancement. The International Congress of Anthropology and the World's Congress of Historians and Historical Students were among the learned societies that gathered to explore "the science of man." Out of papers presented and discussions held grew concepts of nationality and ethnicity that combined culture and place as a ground for first individual and then group identity. These ideas formed the basis for a twentieth-century understanding of social reality as pluralist in form (Shapiro 1983). Developing notions of pluralism supported the group-based representation that PR systems could provide. In addition, the contemporary desire for a scientific approach to the improvement of the human condition was fulfilled by the mathematical precision of PR/STV.

Although Progressivism had not yet coalesced as a movement, it was at the PR Congress of 1893 that the Proportional Representation League (PRL) of the United States was founded.[2] The league was modeled on the British Proportional Representation Society, which had been organized in 1884 to conduct an educational campaign on behalf of PR/STV elections for Parliament. British reformers believed that John Stuart Mill's bill for PR/STV elections had failed to pass because of inadequate understanding of the problem of minority representation in a plurality election system.

American advocates adopted the educational approach of the British proportionalists. Lectures and discussions occupied the Congress, and mock elections were held to illustrate practical applications of various proportional systems. Speakers included Catherine Helen Spence of Australia, John R. Commons, W. D. McCracken, William H. Gove, a Massachusetts legislator who had devised a form of transferable vote known as the "Schedule System," and Alfred Cridge, a friend of Senator Charles R. Buckalew of Pennsylvania (Hoag and Hallett 1926, 55, 186). Out of this PR Congress grew the organization that would provide leadership of the electoral reform movement in the United States for almost four decades. With William Dudley Foulke of Indiana as president and Stoughton Cooley of California as secretary, the league attempted to reach consensus on the one best form of PR.

Unity in support of a single system of voting, however, was difficult to achieve. The term *proportional representation* was used loosely in the United States as well as in Britain to apply to limited voting (LV), cumulative voting (CV), the party list system, and PR/STV. The league agreed to back a bill introduced a year earlier in the U.S. House of Representatives by Ohio Democrat Tom Johnson, later mayor of Cleveland. Johnson's bill provided for election of members of the U.S. House, in states with more than one representative, by the "free list system," a modified PR/STV. Electoral experiments with other proportional proposals were also encouraged (Commons 1907, 114–15; Hoag and Hallett 1926, 187).

Consensus on a general purpose was more readily achieved:

[T]o promote reform of legislative assemblies, by abandoning the present system of electing single representatives on a majority or plurality vote in limited territorial districts, and by substituting the following provisions:
(1) That all representatives be elected "at-large," on a general ticket either without district divisions or in districts as large as practicable.
(2) That the election be in such form that the several parties or political groups shall secure representation in proportion to the respective number of votes cast by each. (Tyson 1908a,38)

Following the British precedent, these American proportionalists decided that they needed staff and a publication. The *Proportional Representation Review* (PRR), edited by Cooley, was launched in 1893 to inform the public about their view of the system of representation as a critical link between voting and policy, and about the variety of voting systems to achieve what they saw as better representation. The technical and abstract nature of voting systems limited the journal's appeal; after three years of publication, funds ran out and the quarterly ceased to appear. However, champions of electoral reform persisted, and meetings of the league followed in Buffalo (1899) and Detroit (1901). At these meetings Robert Tyson of Toronto conducted sample PR/STV elections for participants, building a growing consensus in favor of this "perfect" strategy for representation. One of many Canadians involved in the activities of the PRL, Tyson edited and published the *PRR* from 1901 until 1913 as a department of various other publications, and he served as secretary of the league until 1909. He was succeeded as secretary for two years by William Hoag of Boston, a former member of the Massachusetts legislature, and then by Hoag's brother Clarence, a professor at the University of Pennsylvania. ("It was pretty academic then," remarked Richard S. Childs, a fellow activist and chronicler of the movement.) Academics were indeed among the most active participants, but a growing interest in political reform generally enabled Clarence Hoag to reposition *PRR* as an independent publication from 1913 until 1932 (Hoag and Hallett 1926, 187–88; Childs 1952, 242).

Foulke drew together a governing council for the PRL that included such eminent Americans as historian Charles A. Beard; Jane Addams, founder of Hull House; scientist Charles P. Steinmetz; Charles Frederick Adams, great-grandson of an American president; Margaret Dreier Robins of the Women's Trade Union League; Richard S. Childs, founder and secretary of the National Short Ballot Organization; Charles W. Eliot, president emeritus of Harvard University; Professor Felix Adler of Columbia University; and Professor Jeremiah W. Jenks of New York University.

In the early years, the PRL aimed its efforts at reform of state and national elections. Its stated intent was to enlarge participation in political life for "those considerable classes of voters, like farmers, mechanics and laboring men" who were underrepresented in Congress and the state legislatures (*PRR* 1894, 1:105). Foulke advocated the use of the party list system for congressional and state legislative elections, a position supported by the League (Foulke 1915, 76; *Equity* 1914, 16:193–97). Presidential elections were also identified as unrepresentative of a large portion of American voters because the states had adopted winner-take-all rules that eliminated votes for the minority candidate or candidates in the electoral college. A proportional division of the electoral vote for president within states would permit minority choices for president to be aggregated to the national level, providing a more representative count. In a close vote, such a division might even change the outcome (proposed amendment, art. 18; *Equity* 1914, 16:43–47; 1917, 19:42–44).[3]

Economist and statistician N. I. Stone, who was a member of the U.S. Tariff Commission and who held several other government posts in the area of economic policy, provides an illustration of the kind of wide-ranging electoral debate that occurred in the early years of the twentieth century. In an article in *Century*, he differed from the PRL on presidential elections, advocating the direct popular vote for president, with a second or runoff election between the two top candidates if no candidate received a majority of the vote (Stone 1915, 131). The problem of misrepresentation in Congress seemed to Stone more critical. Supporting the PRL position, he urged the state-by-state adoption of proportional representation elections for congressional delegations, to be chosen "within the broad boundaries of the State, or large natural divisions of the State," in order to allow both majority and minority parties their fair share of seats in Congress. Although he would start with New York ("Let the Empire State blaze the way for a reform which will be certain to sweep the country"), he argued that PR's greatest impact would be felt in the South where it could break up the "solid South." Political and economic issues would replace sectionalism in a "more wholesome division of the electorate." Stone showed how control of Congress had swung back and forth between Republicans and Democrats from 1888 to 1912, owing to marginal changes between parties in the total vote (outside of the South), creating instability on such issues as tariff policy, his special area of expertise. PR, he argued, would in contrast allow opposing views to be represented fairly from all states, provide the opportunity for aggregation of policy preferences across the country, and therefore create more continuity in policy development (Stone 1915, 136–37, 141–43).

Well before the League of Nations was established, the PRL encouraged debate about how nation-states would be represented in an international assembly. When the League of Nations emerged as a concrete proposal, the PRL advocated a guarantee, first of all among member states, that "fair and true representation of all elements" would occur in their own parliaments, and then that these representative national assemblies would choose delegates to the international body by proportional election. By this means, internal minorities could combine with minorities of similar views and needs from other nations in worldwide deliberations. The purpose of PR elections was to create capacity in the new international body for representatives to "think internationally" about the issues confronting them (*Equity* 1919, 21:74).

In 1908, the drive for adoption of PR to elect large units of government led to a single and limited success at the state level. Proportionalists in Oregon initiated a ballot measure permitting (but not requiring) PR/STV elections in the state's multimember legislative districts where elections were conducted by plurality at-large. A groundswell of support for the initiative was fueled by the distorted outcome of the 1906 contest for the sixty-seat Oregon House of Representatives: fifty-nine Republicans and one Democrat were elected. Voters, however, had divided their choices among candidates of four parties as follows: 57 percent Republican, 32 percent Democratic, 7 percent Socialist, and 5 percent Prohibitionist (Tyson 1908b). With a Republican majority in all but one district, the 44 percent non-Republican minorities had won less than 2 percent of the representation. The campaign for PR in Oregon targeted the "defective electoral machinery" (namely, plurality voting) that could so misrepresent the voting public. However, in subsequent years the permissive authority granted by the initiative was not used; four efforts to enact the reform, one in the Oregon legislature and three by initiatives, failed to pass (Hoag and Hallett 1926, 188–89).

Since no adoptions of PR elections occurred in the deeply majoritarian American system for almost two decades after the founding of the league, efforts began to shift to local elections. The PRL did not abandon its long-range goals for state, national, and international election reform, but in 1912 C. G. Hoag persuaded the organization to target city council elections as a more realistic immediate goal. Hoag believed that small-scale demonstrations of PR's merits were necessary if broader acceptance were to be achieved (Hoag and Hallett 1926, 188). Chester C. Maxey, a political science professor at Western Reserve University in Cleveland (now Case Western Reserve University) and PRL activist, identified a secondary but tactical purpose in shifting the PR campaign to the municipal level. The city manager plan, he argued, was a more popular structural reform; to link the PR electoral system to this new mode of administration would facilitate its acceptance in the United States (Maxey 1924; Hermens [1941] 1972, 360).

Dayton, Ohio, where business leaders were promoting a new charter to "clean up" their city, was a promising venue for the experiment. In 1913, a charter commission had been elected that was committed to consideration of the city manager plan. Progressives were joined by the local Socialist Party in petitioning the commission to propose PR/STV city council elections as a critical institutional partner to complement professional administration. Only PR elections, they argued, would ensure the fully representative council needed to make policy that the city manager would be obliged to carry out. This rationale was not persuasive in Dayton, but it was widely discussed in reform circles. Dayton subsequently became the first large city in the country to adopt the city manager plan, but the policy-making body that was adopted was a commission, elected by plurality at-large (Warner 1964, 450-51). J. L. Conger, a friend of PR, lamented a few years later: "To those of us who try to see in the city manager the ideal form of city administration none can fail to see that the fundamental weakness in the Dayton scheme as at present constituted is the nonrepresentative character of the commission, which must stand between the city manager and public opinion" (1920, 59).

This linkage between PR elections and the city manager plan strengthened the partnership of the PRL and the National Municipal League (NML). Founded in 1894 by Progressives to advance a broad "good government" agenda at the state and local levels, the NML's principal concern was the governance of cities. State control of municipal affairs, however, forced it to address both state and local issues. Inefficiency and corruption were seen as the overwhelming ills of American cities; the party bosses were the villains. The NML's agenda to attack these afflictions from its founding to 1914 featured nonpartisan elections and the short ballot. By 1914, with William Dudley Foulke as president of both organizations, it is not surprising that the NML endorsed both the election of city councils by PR/STV and the city manager plan, stressing the linkage between them. The NML promoted the PRL's theory that enhancing efficiency in municipal government by assigning the executive function to a trained expert called for a more representative council to make municipal policy. In its deliberations all important elements of the city should be heard.[4]

By 1921, the NML's commitment to PR/STV extended to the state level. The *Model State Constitution* published by the NML in that year recommended a single-house legislature, to be elected by PR/STV from districts electing from three to seven members (Hoag and Hallett 1926, 123).[5] The unicameral principle, it was argued, derived from the kind of representation produced under PR/STV. "When one legislative body is made really representative, why try to check it with another?" asked Hallett (1940, 167). By 1930, the NML sought to encourage these structural reforms at the county level and endorsed adoption of a state law that would explicitly permit counties to adopt a county manager plan with a county council to be elected at-large by PR/STV (Cassella 1990, 322). For the next two decades, the NML circulated its model county charter, finally published in 1956, incorporating these features.[6]

During the years in which the NML was developing its broader reform agenda, the PRL pursued its own campaign for electoral system reform. For two decades, from 1913 to 1932, its staff traveled the country to testify, exhort, write PR charter provisions, provide expert advice on the conduct of PR elections, and defend existing PR systems under attack in repeal referenda. The addition of a field secretary in 1917, Walter J. Millard, and an assistant secretary in 1919, George H. Hallett Jr., to the PRL staff expanded the capacity of the organization. Hallett became the executive secretary in 1926 (Hoag and Hallett 1926, 194). By this time, other renowned reformers had joined its council, including historian Arthur N. Holcombe of Harvard and economist Paul H. Douglas of the University of Chicago, journalist Walter Lippmann, suffragists Carrie Chapman Catt, founding chair of the National League of Women Voters, and Belle Sherwin, the first president of the Ohio League of Women Voters and second president of the National League; and Senators George W. Norris of Nebraska, Robert L. Owen of Oklahoma, and George Wharton Pepper of Pennsylvania.

Cooperation in electoral reform between the PRL and the NML led Ferdinand Hermens, an opponent of PR who taught at Notre Dame University, to complain that "the great authority of the official reform movement in this country has been behind PR" ([1941] 1972, 360).

The Progressive Coalition and Its Agenda

The place of proportional representation in the reform movement can be understood only in the context of the coalition of individuals and groups calling themselves "Progressives." These reformers generated a flow of reform activities to solve the problem of social justice they identified as critical to the health of the nation. At federal, state, and local levels, they actively sought to secure protective labor legislation, antimonopoly laws, and tax reform to mitigate the impact of unregulated capitalism on workers and small businesses. They also sought to change the very institutions of government through which such meliorative laws were to be passed and by which they were to be administered, from women's suffrage and direct primaries to the direct election of U.S. senators. Although there were strong agrarian elements in what came to be called the Progressive movement, it was in the cities that the most egregious wrongs were seen, and it was among urban reformers that issues of representation seemed most pressing.

Diversity of views characterized these urban reformers. Some were concerned primarily with political participation. Attempting to stem the tide of apathy, they worked for direct democracy in the form of initiative, referendum, and recall, women's suffrage for school board and municipal elections, and nonpartisan elections to remove control of city government from political machines. Others, eager to attack economic inequality, worked for public ownership of utilities, tax equity, minimum wage/maximum hour legislation for municipal workers, and local measures to protect women and children in the workplace. Economy in public affairs ranked high in importance for some, as they viewed with alarm the rising cost of government at all levels. Still others placed a high priority on structural changes in municipal government, including electoral systems. This complex agenda was held together, if only in an amorphous way, by an underlying yearning for morality in public life and by confidence that political change could make a difference.

The first barrier the reformers found to promoting change in the fast-growing cities was the traditional and widespread state control of municipal affairs. State control was entrenched in state constitutions and reinforced in forty-six states by the common law principle known as Dillon's Rule, which required a narrow construction of municipal power as opposed to state power. Cities could do only what states permitted them to do, either expressly or by necessary implication of expressly granted powers (*Clinton v. the Cedar Rapids R. R. Co.* [1868]). In the period of rapid urbanization following the Civil War and accelerating at the turn of the century, rural legislators tended to keep control of the state assemblies, either by failing to reapportion or by deliberate malapportionment. Reformers contended that rural-dominated state legislatures oppressed the cities by blocking their efforts to change their form of government or even to legislate locally on critical health and safety issues. "Home Rule" therefore became a Progressive rallying cry and a precursor of further reform (Cassella 1975, 442).[7]

In the heated competitive politics of the late nineteenth century, urban party organizations consolidated their power, providing services not otherwise available to dependent immigrant populations in exchange for their votes. The expanding black populations of these cities were also more welcomed by "the bosses" than by urban elites; black community leaders became precinct captains and occasionally elected officials as well as voters. Services provided by the urban machines were financed by the growing corporate sector, which was willing to pay the required graft to obtain the utility franchises and tax favors that facilitated their consolidation of private economic power, and by kickbacks from gamblers and vice-ring operators whose illegal activities were in turn protected (Warner 1964, chap. 1; DuBois [1899] 1967, 383–84). The large, ward-based councils of major cities provided the building blocks of the bosses' power to govern through patronage practices (Z. Miller 1968).

Opposition to this structure of power united diverse forces of reform. Key structural proposals to undermine or destroy that power were the city manager plan and small councils to be elected at-large by proportional representation (PR/STV). Citywide office, many reformers believed, would draw "better men" as council candidates, instead of the parochial ward politicians then holding sway in the large, single-member-district councils of the machine-dominated city. PR/STV elections would be conducted at-large, creating representative councils that could legitimately debate and determine policy. The city manager, responsible to this representative council, would bring expertise to bear on the problems of the city, with impartial administration replacing favoritism and graft. The application of scientific techniques to government operations would increase economy and efficiency in the public sphere (Haber 1964; Svara 1990).

Yet PR/STV was the one element of this institutional agenda that was omitted from the reform charters of most cities. The adoption of citywide plurality elections for either small, at-large councils or commissions resulted in homogeneous representation that lent credence to the notion that the reforms were elitist in purpose and character. These governmental arrangements were similar to the corporate form, in which the city manager was said to be in effect the president of the corporation, the city council its board of directors, the voters its shareholders. The separation of politics from administration was seen by many Progressives as the key to scientific management, which would in turn insulate government from "both class prejudice and the ballot box" (Haber 1964, 103).

However, while some reformers were concerned exclusively with management and social control, others stressed "economic justice, human opportunities, and rehabilitated democracy" (Wiebe 1967, 176; see also Link 1959; Huthmacher 1962; Filene 1970; Buenker 1973). Among this latter group were the proportionalists, such as historian Charles A. Beard of Columbia University and labor economist John R. Commons, a professor at the University of Wisconsin. In 1907, Commons flatly rejected the analogy between the city and a business corporation. The business corporation's sole purpose was to increase dividends, he said. By contrast, "the city is a compulsory corporation into which men are born."

In a political corporation different classes of citizens have often different interests. Therefore all interests and classes should be represented in its administration. In what direction its sovereign powers shall be employed is a political question, involving justice and expediency as well as business. Shall taxes be levied to protect health, to extend free schools, to cleanse the slums, to buy water-works or street-car lines?— these are a few of the political questions which cities must consider. (Commons 1907, 200-201)

Commons, like Beard, became a leader of the proportional represen- tation movement. With all interests represented on the local legislative body, he argued, differences would be negotiated and social cooperation would prevail in the making of policy, which it was the executive's job to carry out. As noted earlier, the legislative supremacy implicit in the city manager plan magnified the importance of a representative council (Hoag and Hallett 1926, 193, 230).

Commons's vision of group representation illustrates a changing clus- ter of ideas supporting the use of PR/STV. He contrasted the "worry" of Mill's day—protecting representation of the educated minority—with new concerns: "PR is no longer needed to defend the rich against the poor. Its problem now is to defend the masses against the monopolists." Commons identified campaign contributions from corporate elites to unelected party leaders as the mechanism for monopoly control of the political process (Commons 1907, 352).

He noted that the urban political machines won working-class votes, but then ignored their needs for schools, decent housing, parks, and play- grounds. He called for "social invention," promoted by the science of soci- ology, to advance human progress. But "science alone is inadequate," Commons argued. Only by having all interests represented in a city's council could human feelings and needs be taken into account in the mak- ing of municipal policy. Social invention could then "proceed, not by the coercive arm of the state, but by mutual concession" (Commons 1907, 224–30).

Commons was careful to distinguish this kind of representation from the rigid rule by special interests that he saw as the vice of machine con- trol. Free nomination, by which he meant nomination by petition, and free voting, or choosing individual representatives unfettered by small-unit boundaries, acknowledged the fluidity of people's real interests (Com- mons 1907, 361–62).

As the appeal of PR was expounded in journals and newspapers, broader representational goals for PR were expressed, expanding from class to "political, racial, religious, ethnic, and vocational groups and classes" the need for self-representation (Hatton 1915; R. A. Burnham

1992, 205–6). Proposals for representation of functional groups and for occupational rather than territorial groupings were widely discussed (Beard and Lewis 1932). Economist Paul H. Douglas countered proposals for occupational representation by arguing that proportional representation would allow voters, "rendered powerless [by territorial representation] to make their real preferences and interests effective" by choosing the basis on which they wished to be represented, whether through occupation or other interests (1923, 140). If diversity itself was a problem, proportional representation was its solution.

Prevailing accounts of Progressive-inspired electoral reform present a polarity between the bosses' practical dependence on plurality single-member district (ward) elections, on the one hand, and the reformers' advocacy of plurality at-large elections, on the other. The record, however, shows that PR advocates among the reformers rejected both of these polar alternatives. In fact, they saw PR as drawing together representational qualities from each type of system. PR elections would be held citywide, freeing voters from geographical limitations on choice. If large, multi-member districts were preferred, candidates could run in districts other than their place of residence and appeal to voters in districts of their choosing. At the same time, because constituencies within this larger framework would be voluntary, voters could select their personal representative by whatever characteristics were important to them. In this way, the mechanics of PR were seen by these Progressives to meld the advantages of citywide election promoted by defenders of the plurality at-large system and the personal relationships more likely to develop in the plurality single-member district (ward) system.

Clarence Hoag, secretary of the PRL, found it a "strange belief" among many Progressives that lines of division among voters would vanish if elections were held by plurality at-large voting. Of course, all should work for the "good of the city," he wrote, but "*what is* for the good of the city" could not be imposed by one group. "All shades of opinion" should be represented in council, he argued, to "foster mutual understanding and cooperation" (Hoag 1913, 80–81).

The accuracy with which the PR/STV system could translate votes from the electorate into seats in a legislative body was a key attraction, not only to Commons and Augustus R. Hatton but also to those Progressives who placed a higher value on scientific method. The quantitative details of the count, the complexity of which would become the focus of later attacks on PR systems, were clear enough to its advocates. Proportional representation thus provided a significant conceptual linkage between the ideas of the technical and professional elites of the Progressive movement and those of their more participatory and populist allies. In the first instance, PR/STV elections were believed to provide a scientifically demonstrable, nonpartisan method of selecting the best council; at the same time social and cultural pluralism could be accommodated in governmental decision making, because minorities (identified by whatever characteristics were important to them) would be represented in proportion to their actual strength in the voting population.

The Progressive Party itself, organized in 1912 to capture national power from the old parties, did not officially support proportional representation elections, although proportionalists were well represented among the organizers. Jane Addams, for example, social feminist and early member of the PRL's advisory council, played a leading role in the organization of the party and seconded the nomination of Theodore Roosevelt at the party's national convention (Flexner 1975, 266, 271). The party's platform included a section entitled "The Rule of the People," endorsing women's suffrage, the short ballot, and the initiative, referendum, and recall, but election system reform was not an explicit priority.

The coalition promoting electoral reform was broader than the organized Progressive Party, and its attack on the ills of industrial capitalism drew allies on particular issues from the ranks of old Populists and new Socialists. The high tide of Socialist electoral success in the United States was reached in 1912, by which time over a thousand Socialists had been elected to public office in the United States. Most held local office, but in 1910 Socialist Victor Berger was elected to Congress from a Wisconsin district, and in 1912 Eugene V. Debs won 6 percent of the vote for president on the Socialist ticket (Draper 1957, 41–42). The Socialist Party endorsed both direct legislation (the initiative, referendum, and recall) and "proportional representation nationally as well as locally" (K. H. Porter 1924, 336, 367).

In 1913, Carl D. Thompson, head of the information bureau of the national Socialist Party in Chicago, published an article in the *National Municipal Review* explaining the party's position on charter reform. Guided by the "vital and necessary principles" of good city government, "democracy and efficiency," he wrote, certain basic elements were needed: home rule, direct legislation, proportional representation elections, and the city manager plan. The professional administrator was endorsed as a means of effectively carrying out the "steadily increasing extension of the functions of municipal government" advocated by Socialists (C. D. Thompson 1913, 426). Two important caveats, however, limited these forthright endorsements of the Progressive municipal reform agenda. The recall, an important feature of direct legislation, would have to "operate against the whole group and not against a single councilman," in order to protect the minorities elected by PR from arbitrary recall by the majority. Furthermore, the PR ballot should identify the candidates' parties in order to enable voters to relate their choices to the policies they wanted adopted (C. D. Thompson 1913, 419, 421–23).

This attack on nonpartisanship led C. G. Hoag and Robert Tyson to concede that "it may be necessary where the Socialists are strong for those who would prefer the Hare system to accept instead . . . a party-list system." Ultimately, however, Hoag and Tyson hoped that "the Socialists would come to realize that the Hare system without party names is not only fair to all parties, but also fair to all factions of any one party" (*Equity* 1913, 15:231–32).

Although many Socialists and later Communists rejected the reformist Progressive agenda as backward and irrelevant, such "fusion" attempts at cooperation were frequent. During World War I, when Socialist members of city councils and school boards, as in Cleveland, were expelled from public office for their opposition to the war, pro-war Socialists established a separate organization, the Social Democratic League of America. In 1917, drawing together activists from the ranks of Progressives, prohibitionists, and woman suffragists, the group anticipated developing a new political party. Its platform featured proportional representation for state and federal legislative elections, along with women's suffrage, prohibition, direct legislation, the short ballot, public ownership of railroads and public utilities, old age pensions, and the abolition of child labor. Charles A. Beard and Frederic Howe were among the PR advocates on the platform-writing committee. To be called the National Party, this coalition did not survive beyond its organizational stage (*Equity* 1917, 19:206; Shannon 1955, 103).

More tenacious was the post–World War I Conference for Progressive Political Action (CPPA), pulled together by leaders of the railroad brotherhoods and including the Socialist Party (Communists were vigorously excluded), the Farmer-Labor Party, the Non-Partisan League, and church groups such as the Methodist Federation of Social Service, the Church League for Industrial Democracy, and the National Catholic Welfare Council. The Socialist Party was committed to forming a third party like the British Labour Party, but labor leaders resisted this. Conferences, aimed at building an electoral coalition if not a party, were held in Chicago (February 1922), Cleveland (December 1922), and St. Louis (February 1924). A CPPA convention, held in Cleveland on 4 July 1924, nominated Robert M. La Follette as an independent candidate for president. The

CPPA served as an alliance of his supporters, who could not form a party but called themselves "Progressives" throughout the campaign. Their platform demanded such electoral reform as the direct nomination and election of the president and national direct legislation, but not proportional representation. Municipal PR campaigns, however, such as the successful one in Cincinnati that year, were conducted out of local CPPA offices. The Socialist Party accepted La Follette as its presidential candidate and did not publish a separate platform (K. H. Porter 1924, 516–22). La Follette's loss in the November election brought to an end, at least for the time being, the "socialist experiment in cooperating with nonsocialist progressives" (Shannon 1955, 181).

The Appeal of PR to the Conventionally Excluded: Women and African Americans

After 1920, with their suffrage battle won, many of the more political women among the suffragists joined the effort to adopt the PR/STV electoral system. Like the broad coalition of Progressives of which they were a part, they had diverse goals. Some had pursued political rights, especially the right to vote, while others battled for social and economic goals, such as child labor laws, mothers' pensions, and social justice. In the late stages of the battle for suffrage, women had used traditional stereotypes to justify the vote, such as women's special role in protecting their homes and children. In part, this revealed the conservative character of the women themselves; but it was also a strategic move, designed to reassure conservative men that women's suffrage posed no threat to the social order (Cooley 1913). In this spirit Jane Addams explained women's support of the city manager plan and PR/STV: "City housekeeping has failed partly because women, the traditional housekeepers, have not been consulted as to its multiform activities" (Addams 1960, 115).

PR/STV was promising to reform-oriented women because of their independence of parties. Nomination by petition, the nonpartisan ballot, and the single transferable vote were all features that would facilitate the election of independents. Because of the influential role that political machines had played in delaying women's suffrage, feminists decried the influence of parties in political life and supported reforms to undermine the bosses' power. They also believed that with PR/STV, women could form "voluntary constituencies" in multimember districts or at-large to elect women to municipal office.

Moreover, electoral reform was seen as instrumental in that the "better" councils elected by PR could implement substantive reforms in the fields of housing, public health and welfare, cleaner air, and city planning. The National League of Women Voters and local leagues across the country were in the forefront of municipal reform battles, along with club women who in many cities had been organized since the late nineteenth century to improve their communities (Lemons 1973, chap. 4; Chafe 1972, 12–18).

Women in the settlement house movement also entered the fray on behalf of PR. From the 1890s on, settlement house activities had attracted well-educated women who, like many of their male counterparts in the Progressive movement, understood the economic roots of the evil conditions of life in cities and saw the immigrant as "the victim of bad conditions" (Higham [1955] 1988, 117). Their central commitment was to live in the settlement houses among the immigrants, not apart from the people they wanted to help. These women seemed to appreciate the diverse ethnic cultures they came to know in crowded urban neighborhoods. Rejecting the prevailing "melting pot" theory of Americanization, they promoted the validity of cultural "contributions," which the immigrants brought from their previous lives, as enrichments of American culture (Addams, in Warner 1971, 23–25; Higham [1955] 1988, 120–22; Grabowski 1986, 32–33). These ideas of cultural pluralism were congruent with the political pluralism that proportional representation would foster.

Jane Addams and Lillian Wald, founder of the Henry Street Settlement in New York City, tried to bridge the cultural and political gap between suffrage advocates and working women, especially immigrant workers living in the slums, where the urban machines were most strongly rooted. In 1903, these social workers joined women trade union organizers to create the National Women's Trade Union League (NWTUL) "to help industrial women help themselves through the trade union movement." Its primary efforts were directed toward organizing women into trade unions; once organized, these new unions were "turned over" to the American Federation of Labor. To protect unorganized women, the NWTUL worked for passage of protective labor legislation to improve conditions of work, to establish maximum hours and minimum wages for women, and to prohibit child labor (Lemons 1973, 142). Yet this work was constantly rendered ineffectual by women's political powerlessness. Thus suffrage became an important tactical goal for these women who at an earlier stage had seen the vote and "equal rights" as a middle-class frill. Endorsing women's suffrage in 1907, NWTUL leaders concluded not only that working women should vote but also, explicitly, that working women should represent themselves. It was only a small step from this belief to the endorsement of PR. Through direct political representation, these women could improve their conditions of life and become integrated into the community (Dreier 1950; Flexner 1975, chap. 18; Dye 1980, 122–24).

Little such collaborative activity was attempted to bring African American women into the struggle for municipal reform. Most African Americans were at the bottom of the economic heap and had more pressing concerns. In both the North and the South, however, there were Colored Women's Clubs, organized in the late nineteenth century to improve life conditions of their race and "of *all* humanity," whose members shared many of the reformers' values. In 1896, two national federations of local and state clubs with an estimated 300,000 members joined to form the National Association of Colored Women (NACW) with Mary Church Terrell as president. Women's suffrage was one of its goals, and its suffrage department conducted "training classes" on the Constitution to prepare its members for civic responsibilities (Lerner 1992, 440-46). These women might have been recruited for the causes of municipal reform, but their social and organizational segregation was pervasive. White suffragists rejected alliances with these "colored" women's groups for what they called the greater goal of winning the support of southern senators for a federal suffrage amendment. The constitutional requirement of a two-thirds vote to propose an amendment, impossible without southern backing, shaped their strategy and submerged virtually every other consideration (Flexner 1975, 190). In spite of this exclusionary policy of the suffragists, important black leaders endorsed women's suffrage—not only Mary Church Terrell but also W. E. B. DuBois and Ida Wells-Barnett—with a view to the long-range importance of expansion of the suffrage for African Americans as well (Flexner 1975, 318, 374n. 22). Still, few interracial collaborations were established in the trenches of municipal reform. Not least important in explaining the racial cleavage afflicting electoral reform efforts was the role of the urban boss in meeting the daily needs of black constituents. DuBois had noted this before the turn of the century:

> The growth of a higher political morality among Negroes is to-day hindered by their paradoxical position. Suppose the Municipal League or the Woman's Schoolboard movement, or some other reform is brought before the better class of Negroes today; they will nearly all agree that city politics are notoriously corrupt, that honest women should replace ward heelers on school boards, and the like. But can they vote for such movements? Most of them will say No; for to do so will throw many wor-

thy Negroes out of employment: these very reformers who want votes for specific reforms, will not themselves work beside Negroes, or admit them to positions in their stores or offices, or lend them friendly aid in trouble. Moreover Negroes are proud of their councilmen and policemen. What if some of these positions of honor and respectability have been gained by shady "politics"—shall they be nicer in these matters than the mass of the whites? Shall they surrender these tangible evidences of the rise of their race to forward the good-hearted but hardly imperative demands of a crowd of women? Especially, too, of women who did not apparently know there were any Negroes on earth until they wanted their votes? Such logic may be faulty, but it is convincing to the mass of Negro voters. And cause after cause may gain their respectful attention and even applause, but when election-day comes, the "machine" gets their votes. ([1899] 1967, 383–84)

The reform movement's very reason for being was to destroy the power of those political organizations that effectively served the most downtrodden of the black communities of Progressive Era cities. Instead of addressing their needs themselves, civic association reformers, both women and men, criticized African American voters for their "blind" partisan loyalty.

Ohio as Trailblazer

Ohio's ruling party organizations were largely Republican. Dayton's Joseph E. Lowes, Cleveland's Robert S. McKisson and Maurice Maschke, Cincinnati's George B. Cox, and Toledo's Walter F. Brown were prototypical bosses, all Republicans who operated in these now legendary ways. The local Democratic Party organization in these cities was often a subservient satellite of the dominant Republican Party, accepting a modest share of patronage in exchange for quiescence on reform (Warner 1964, 5–6). This failure of the "opposition" to oppose created the opportunity eagerly seized by a shifting Progressive coalition to promote multiple reform agendas. Reacting against such party organizations, forces loosely called "Progressive"—often united only by their opposition to the existing paradigm of power—sought reform.

Ohio Progressives saw themselves as national leaders in reform endeavors. Independent Republicans such as Mayor Brand Whitlock of Toledo, city council members Frederic Howe of Cleveland and Washington Gladden of Columbus—who also led the Social Gospel movement of American Protestantism—campaigned across the country for home rule for cities, as did such Democrats as Tom L. Johnson and Newton D. Baker. Johnson, elected mayor of Cleveland in 1901 after his two terms in Congress, served to wide popular acclaim until 1909. He was known nationally as the "prototype of the best of the Progressive Era" (Griffith 1974, 146). To the muckrakers such as Lincoln Steffens, he exemplified the best of Progressivism in his commitment to expansion of city services, public ownership of utility companies, and equitable taxation (Steffens [1906] 1968). Johnson organized fellow Democrats and lobbied at the state level, not only for home rule but also for beneficial labor legislation and redistribution of the burden of taxation (Warner 1964, p. 55 and chap. 4). Historians who view the "good government" reformers as patricians treat Johnson as an exception, not a prototype, however (Buenker 1973, 26–27). To those who believed their property interests were threatened by his regulatory measures, he was considered a "traitor to his class" (Swanstrom 1985, 47). Baker, his aristocratic ally, would write Ohio's home rule amendment, as well as Cleveland's first charter, and under the latter would become the city's mayor in 1912 (Howe [1925] 1988; Warner 1964, 488–89).

Ohio's Progressive leadership was primarily urban and emerged from the large cities where Republican machines had kept a tight grip on the perquisites of power and policy. Although these reformers were largely native-born Protestants, in other ways they were a diverse lot. A study of the lives and careers of ninety-one Ohio Progressive leaders included a small number who were foreign-born and several Catholics and Jews. Fewer than half were college educated; about a third were lawyers; eleven were businessmen; eight were labor leaders. Others were journalists, ministers, and educators. Two-thirds were Democrats; the rest were independent Republicans and Theodore Roosevelt Progressives.[8] Many, like Tom Johnson, believed in the economic theories of single-taxer Henry George; some claimed religious inspiration for their political activities, citing the Sermon on the Mount as the source of their social and political activism (Warner 1964, 22–24, 46n. 2).

The Republican-dominated Ohio legislature had blocked structural changes in government that might undermine the rule of the Republican bosses in Cincinnati, Cleveland, Toledo, and Dayton. The 1900 census, which showed the state's population approaching an urban majority, frightened the legislature and then the state's voters into adopting a constitutional amendment in 1903 to guarantee rural control of the lower house. Called the Hanna amendment, in honor of its sponsor, U.S. Senator Marcus A. Hanna, this provision allotted at least one representative to each of the state's eighty-eight counties, no matter how small its pop-

ulation. Previously, apportionment of both houses had been based primarily on population, with the county as an integral unit of representation.
Before the Hanna amendment, in rural areas, whole counties could be
combined to form districts; in urban areas, counties became multimember
districts with members added to accommodate population growth after
each decennial census.[9] While the Hanna amendment's impact was relatively limited at first, it contained the seed of resistance to the changes
sought by the Progressives. As in other states, this deliberate, turn-of-the-
century malapportionment preserved a structural barrier to reform initiatives at the state level (Ohio Const. 1851, art. 11; Barber 1981, 257;
Buenker 1973, 14).

The Ohio Republican Party, led by an uncomfortable but powerful partnership between Ohio's two U.S. senators, Hanna and Joseph Foraker,
developed an unusually strong rural-urban alliance. The urban delegations in the Ohio legislature were elected by plurality in the counties at-
large. Candidates were virtually nominated by the bosses and elected
routinely by Republican majorities. Once in Columbus, they seemed to fit
comfortably into the Republican Party's rural-urban power structure. The
struggle over tax policy illustrates the state-local linkages that dominated
policy outcomes. When reform mayors such as Johnson of Cleveland and
Whitlock of Toledo attempted to enact equitable taxation of utilities
locally, the legislature reorganized the tax review boards of cities and
shifted them to state control (Warner 1964, 100, 104n. 39).

In reaction to this and other regressive measures, the state's Progressives pursued a reform agenda characterized by the slogan "antibossism."
Virtually written by Mayor Tom Johnson of Cleveland and adopted in 1905
by the Ohio Democratic Party as its platform, this urban revolt called for
home rule for cities, the initiative, referendum, and recall; popular election of senators; women's suffrage; railroad rate regulation; municipal
ownership of utilities or taxation of utilities at full value; protective labor
legislation; and tax equity. Seeking "economic, not personal reform,"
Ohio's reform leaders tried to avoid the issue of prohibition, which they
saw as a diversion from the "real" issue—"the struggle of the people
against Privilege."[10] Their waffling on the issue of prohibition opened
Ohio reformers to the charge of selling out to the bosses, but they kept
prohibition off the state Democratic platform and added to their arguments for home rule the option for cities to remain wet when their surrounding counties went dry (Warner 1964, 70, 185–91).[11]

The election results of 1905 demonstrated the popular appeal of the
Progressives' claim to be battling against privilege. Ohio was a state in
which being Republican was, according to independent Republican Brand

Whitlock of Toledo, "elemental . . . a synonym for patriotism, another name for the nation. . . . One became a Republican just as the Eskimo dons fur clothes" (1914, 27). Yet in this year of Progressive revolt, a Democratic governor was swept into office; Cleveland, Columbus, Dayton, and Cincinnati elected Democratic mayors; and Toledo elected Whitlock as mayor on an antimachine platform (Warner 1964, 160-65). Assisted by revelations of graft and fraud in the offices of the Republican state treasurer and auditor, the reform momentum continued to build for the rest of the decade. Six legislators were convicted and four were imprisoned for soliciting bribes in exchange for their votes against labor legislation and for a bill sought by the insurance industry. Although these six official miscreants were both Democratic and Republican, urban and rural, they nevertheless shared a common antipathy to the reform agenda (Warner 1964, 276–77).

Major reform victories followed. In 1910, a Democratic governor was elected as well as a Democratic majority of both houses of the legislature and sixteen of Ohio's twenty-one members of Congress (Warner 1964, 258–60). The newly Democratic legislature called for the election in 1911 of a constitutional convention to meet in 1912 for the purpose of removing state constitutional barriers that stood in the way of the Progressive agenda. The question of calling a constitutional convention would have been on the ballot automatically in 1912 (the Ohio Const., art. 16, called for the question to be put before the voters every twenty years), but momentum toward reform led the legislature to advance the date. Groups agitating for their particular reform are given credit for successfully promoting constitutional revision: the Ohio State Board of Commerce, seeking classification of property for tax purposes; liquor interests, seeking the licensing of saloons; and the Direct Legislation League, advocating the initiative and referendum (Warner 1964, 295).

Delegates to the constitutional convention, equal to the number of representatives in the lower house of the assembly, were to be nominated by petition and elected by county on a nonpartisan ballot (102 O.L. 298 1911, in Ohio 1912, *Proceedings,* 21–22). Progressives—independents as well as reform Democrats and Republicans—proceeded to win a 75 percent majority of delegate seats at that convention.[12] Although they were unable to reach consensus on repeal of the Hanna amendment, the delegates proposed forty-two amendments to the Ohio Constitution that furthered their goals. Among the thirty-four amendments subsequently adopted by the voters were those providing for home rule for cities, the statewide initiative and referendum, which enabled the voters to circumvent the legislature by taking proposed laws and constitutional amendments to the voters for approval or rejection, nonpartisan election of state judges, the direct primary for nomination of state elected officials, and permissive authority for minimum wage and maximum hour legislation (Warner 1964, chap. 12).[13]

Under the home rule amendment, the municipal corporations of Ohio were at last permitted, if their voters so chose, to write their own governing charters and to exercise all powers of local self-government, including municipal ownership of public utilities (Ohio Const. 1851, art. 18, secs. 1, 3, 7, 1912). In 1913, Cleveland became the first Ohio city to adopt its own charter. Three other cities—Columbus, East Cleveland, and Lakewood—soon followed with charters that, among other reforms rejected at the state level, permitted women to vote in municipal elections.

In Cleveland and Columbus (and later Toledo), as part of the antiboss strategy of the reformers, the new home rule charters provided for mayor and council members to be nominated by petition, replacing the party primaries which had enabled party leaders to control access to public office. Party labels were banned from the election ballots, creating another barrier to party control. A third step in this strategy was the introduction of the Bucklin, or (then-called) preferential, ballot. The ballot's purpose was to expand the choices voters could make for their mayors and city councils, yet retain the popularly elected mayor and the familiar ward system for council elections, presumably facilitating the ballot's adoption.[14] The Bucklin ballot permitted voters to indicate their first, second, and "other" choices of candidates for election. A candidate with a majority of the first-choice votes would be declared the winner. If the leading candidate won only a plurality, second choices would be added to the candidates' totals. Again, a majority winner would end the count. If there were still only a plurality candidate in the lead, "other" choices would be added to the totals, and a majority or plurality winner would be declared the victor (*Equity* 1916, 18:50; Kneier 1957, 367).

The potential for local action under home rule charters exhilarated the activists. In Ohio, and in many other states at this time, the urban reformers now had the opening they had been seeking.[15] Home rule made possible a broad array of structural reforms in the cities, and its adoption signaled the growth of a civic culture that fostered change.

PR/STV Is Put into Practice

PR/STV elections came to rank high on the agenda of Ohio's municipal reformers, sharing such local priorities as the city manager plan, the local initiative, referendum, and recall, the eight-hour day for city workers, and municipal ownership of utilities. The earlier electoral reform, the Bucklin preferential ballot, had proven flawed and lost favor. In practice, the Republican and Democratic Parties constantly attacked the preferential ballot, even as they learned to use it to their own advantage. By instructing their regular voters to cast first-choice votes only, the parties denied second- and other-choice votes to independent candidates. Independent voters tended to use more options, marking two or more choices and thus helping to elect the parties' candidates over their own first choices (*Cleveland Plain Dealer,* 18 November 1915; Maxey 1922a, 85). Moreover, experience showed that the ballot allowed the defeat of the candidate with the most first-choice votes by the addition to the final count of second and other preferences of some of the same voters, tallied at equal value. Although this seldom happened, a few dramatic instances, such as the 1915 mayoral defeats of Peter Witt in Cleveland and George Murphey in Toledo, dismayed voters and drove demands for further reform (Kneier [1934] 1957, 365–70; Warner 1964, 449; Mingle 1974, 11).

As in the earlier battle for home rule in Ohio, independent Democrats and Republicans affiliated with the state's Progressive Party were leaders in the campaign for electoral reform. Whitlock and Gladden continued to travel and exhort on behalf of the Progressive agenda. They were joined in the fray by Democratic attorneys Florence Allen and Susan Rebhan of Cleveland and by populist minister Herbert Bigelow and Democratic attorney Edward Alexander of Cincinnati, who held out successfully for PR/STV elections in exchange for supporting a small at-large council for their city. Antimachine Republican leaders, such as attorney Murray Seasongood, later mayor of Cincinnati, Agnes Hilton, suffrage leader and organizer of the Cincinnati League of Women Voters, and Marietta Tawney, president of the Woman's City Club of Cincinnati, campaigned both locally and in national forums for the adoption of PR/STV.

Election reform was advanced as part of a "cosmopolitan revolution," in which social welfare and city planning would be advanced by new political practices. Z. Miller and Tucker note that the at-large feature of PR elections "sought to encourage city council to focus on the welfare of the city as a whole, PR acknowledged the legitimacy of cultural group pluralism, and nonpartisanship made it easier for minority representatives to secure a place on the ballot" (1998, 15–16).

Women's organizations in Ohio were particularly active and gained national prominence for their persistence in organizing members and other voters and campaigning for electoral reform (Abbott 1949, 107–19;

Lemons 1973, 125). The women's city clubs of Cleveland and Cincinnati were known nationally for their skill in organizing workers to canvass for votes on behalf of new charters embodying the city manager plan and PR/STV (Beard [1915] 1972, 320; Kornbluh 1986, 27). With these local activists leading the charge, it is not surprising that the national PRL would pour its resources into winning over voters in Ohio.

Ashtabula was just one of many Ohio cities that Clarence Hoag visited in the wake of the adoption of home rule, but there he met a sympathetic local labor leader, William E. Boynton, a railroad engineer and former city council president who invited him to return for further conversations with other leaders and eventually for a well-attended hearing before the city charter commission. The seed planted by Hoag would grow by 1914 into the adoption of a new charter with the city manager plan and by 1915 into the first American adoption of PR/STV (Hoag and Hallett 1926, 193).

Adoptions followed in Boulder (1917), Kalamazoo (1918), and Sacramento and West Hartford (1921). Because these were relatively small cities, there was jubilation in the movement in 1921 when Cleveland adopted PR/STV elections with its new charter. Not only was Cleveland the largest city yet to try this electoral system, it was ethnically and religiously the most diverse—"polyglot," in contemporary terms. With favorable press emanating from Cleveland and intense intercity campaigning by reformers in Ohio, Cincinnati (1925), Hamilton (1926), and Toledo (1935) also adopted PR/STV charters, as did nearby Wheeling, West Virginia (1935).

In 1936, over the strenuous opposition of the Tammany organization, which had a virtual monopoly on council, the nation's largest city adopted PR/STV. A state legislative investigation in 1931–32 of corruption in New York City, headed by Judge Samuel Seabury, led to the appointment in 1934 of a charter commission which in turn recommended a new charter for the city. PR elections for the city council, viewed as the most controversial element of the commission's plan for improving city government, were proposed as a separate ballot issue lest the debate over PR drag the charter down to defeat. These proposals reached the ballot in the presidential election of 1936, along with Franklin D. Roosevelt, running for his second term as president. In the campaign, the city's Democratic organization warmly supported Roosevelt and stridently opposed both PR/STV and the new charter. However, voters approved both reforms and overwhelmingly reelected Roosevelt. The new charter and the separate provision for PR/STV council elections carried all boroughs except Staten Island. The reform spirit, with its interest in changing political arrangements, seemed to persist at the local level and to blend into the national revival of the spirit of Progressivism in the New Deal (Hallett 1940, 147; Zeller and Bone 1948).

Eleven more cities joined the PR/STV roster between 1938 and 1948, seven of these in Massachusetts, where the system was (and continues to be) called "Plan E" under state law. These cities were Yonkers and Long Beach, New York; Coos Bay, Oregon; Hopkins, Minnesota; and Cambridge, Lowell, Worcester, Medford, Quincy, Revere, and Saugus, Massachusetts (Childs 1952, 250).

The successes for electoral reform that could be tallied in the 1920s and 1930s on the Progressive agenda, however, were limited by existing structures of political power. Proportional voting proposals reached the ballot in other large cities, but reform efforts were often obstructed by powerful party organizations, operating in the legislature or in the courts, where the judges were elected or appointed through partisan channels. As a center of PR activism on the West Coast, Los Angeles had been the first major city to vote on a PR charter amendment. On 24 March 1913, the amendment lost by a narrow margin (*Equity* 1913, 15:137). The issue of fair representation was a lively one for at least a decade in Los Angeles, but during renewed debate there over adoption of PR in 1922 the state supreme court upheld lower court rulings that PR (as adopted in Sacramento) violated the state constitution (*PRR* 1931, 3d ser., p. 30; *People ex rel. Devine v. Elkus* 1922), ending at least for the time the agitation for election reform in California.

Twice during the 1930s, the Pennsylvania legislature refused to grant Philadelphia a PR/city manager charter, sought by its citizens and even recommended in the second instance by a charter commission appointed by the governor. In Massachusetts, where the legislature passed an act in 1937 to permit PR/STV elections for both city and local school board officials, legislators from Boston forced the exclusion of their city from coverage as the price of passage (*NMR*, October 1938, 513; Hallett 1940, 165).

Like the National Municipal League, the PRL kept its collective eye on future opportunities for PR/STV at the state and national levels. Committed advocates within the PRL and the NML continued to campaign for election by PR/STV of county councils, state legislatures, the U.S. House of Representatives, and a proportional division of the vote count for presidential electors (Hallett 1940, 166–76).

During the period of American adoptions, PR/STV was spreading elsewhere in the English-speaking world as well. The system was adopted not only for the university representatives to the British House of Commons but also for some municipal (council) or provincial (legislative) elections in Canada, Australia, New Zealand, South Africa, India, and Malta (Hoag and Hallett 1926, 223–34, 253–54; Hallett 1940, 158–60; O'Leary 1979, 5).

Ireland, however, became the seat of the most thorough and long-lasting use of PR/STV. The PR Society of Ireland, founded in 1911, was well organized and militant, urging PR/STV elections in the south to facilitate the representation of Unionists, a Protestant minority, and in the north to promote eventual unity through representation of Ulster's Catholic minority. The Government of Ireland Act of 1920 incorporated these provisions. The subsequent 1923 Irish Free State Constitution for the southern twenty-six counties retained the PR/STV system, which has been used for election of the Dail ever since. Municipal, school board, county, and special district elections have also been conducted by PR/STV throughout the Irish Free State (now the Republic of Ireland). In the six northern counties, however, the British and Protestant majority, while supporting PR/STV in the south where their analogues constituted a minority, reverted to plurality elections after only four years of PR/STV. The resulting exclusion of the Catholic minority from power in Ulster through winner-take-all plurality elections is believed to have contributed to the increasingly violent polarization of that society (O'Leary 1979, chap. 3).

The Precarious Existence of PR Elections

In the United States, the PRL experienced declining financial support during the Great Depression. Lack of funds forced the PRL to merge into the NML in 1932, and its continuing efforts were conducted by volunteers.[16] Still, the innovation continued to spread. By 1964, about 160 PR/STV elections had been held in the United States, including thirty-seven school board elections in Massachusetts.

Additional adoptions in some cities, however, took place even while other communities, where PR had been in use for a decade or more, were reverting to more traditional arrangements. In 1929, Ashtabula, the first city to adopt PR/STV, became the first to repeal it.

The attack on PR voting was not always launched by popular vote. State legislatures and state courts were also battlefields, where political party leaders who felt threatened could act without the risk or expense of a referendum. Childs would write: "Other reforms have a way of staying put— cities hardly ever go back on nonpartisan elections or council-manager charters or the merit system in the civil service or shortened ballots. But

PR greatly irritates the politicians and they come back at it unceasingly"
(1952, 244). The Republican-controlled Connecticut legislature was hostile to PR because of the 1921 results of the first and, as it turned out, only
PR election conducted in West Hartford, a strongly Republican suburb.
The Republican organization lost its majority on the city council to independent Republicans. At that time Bridgeport and other Connecticut cities
were considering adoption of PR as well. In 1923, the legislature acted
quickly to outlaw "preferential or so-called 'proportional' ballot[s] . . . in
any election, any charter provision or municipal ordinance of any town, city
or borough" in the state (Hoag and Hallett 1926, 208). Later the Massachusetts legislature attempted a similar move. In 1947 alone, five Massachusetts cities adopted PR/STV in addition to the earlier adoptions in
Cambridge and Lowell, and several other cities in the state were considering joining what seemed to be a trend. The established political parties grew
alarmed and instituted legislative action to outlaw PR. Officials in the seven
Massachusetts PR cities and many of their constituents apparently rose up
in protest, forcing the legislature into a partial retreat. In 1950, any *further*
adoptions of PR in the state were prohibited by law (Childs 1952, 249).

The state courts became an arena for challenges to PR. In Kalamazoo,
where PR was adopted in 1918, Michigan party leaders who had been displaced in PR elections joined business leaders who had been adversely
affected by tax reforms enacted by the first PR council to challenge the
PR system in state court. In 1920, the Michigan Supreme Court overturned the electoral system, finding it a violation of the state constitution's
guarantee that voters had a right to vote "at any election." Each candidate's race in an at-large election was interpreted to be a separate election. Therefore, in a multicandidate election, a PR/STV ballot that was
ultimately counted for one candidate only was held to prevent the exercise of full voting rights (*Wattles ex rel. Johnson v. Upjohn*, 1920).

This interpretation was repeated two years later in the California
courts. The PR/STV section of the Sacramento charter, adopted in 1920,
was invalidated on the same grounds, based on a provision in the California Constitution, similar to Michigan's, that guaranteed the right to
vote "at all elections" (*People ex rel. Devine v. Elkus,* 1922). In both states,
the judges had ties to their respective Republican Party organizations.

In 1923, however, in cases brought to challenge Cleveland's adoption of
PR/STV, the Ohio Supreme Court upheld its validity under both the state
and federal constitutions (*Reutener v. City of Cleveland et al.,* 1923; *Hile v.
City of Cleveland,* 1923). Judge Florence Allen, author of the opinions in
the Ohio cases, was an independent Democrat who, before election to the
court, had been a vigorous proponent of proportional representation and

other Progressive reforms (Tuve 1984, 92–93). In the first Ohio case, the plaintiff claimed that his state right to vote "at all elections" was violated by a system that allowed a ballot in a multimember district to count for only one council member. Rejecting this claim, Judge Allen wrote: "The Hare System of Proportional Representation does not violate the Ohio constitution, for the elector is not prevented from voting at any election. He is entitled to vote at every municipal election, even though his vote may be effective in the election of fewer than the full number of candidates, and he has exactly the same voting power and right as every other elector" (*Reutener v. Cleveland* 1923, at 137).

Federal constitutional issues were settled in *Hile v. Cleveland* (1923). George D. Hile, a taxpayer, attempted to equate plurality voting with the republican form of government guaranteed in Article 4 of the U.S. Constitution. PR/STV, he argued, was not a "republican" mode of election. He also claimed that his equal protection of the laws under the Fourteenth Amendment was violated by his subjection to a form of voting not imposed on citizens of other communities in Ohio. Both arguments were rejected. Judge Allen wrote for the court that the "republican form" was a political, not a judicial, question. If, however, republican form were to be defined as by Lincoln, "of the people, for the people, and by the people," Cleveland's charter could not be attacked on this ground, since it "establishes a form of government by express vote of the people, in which the people are by vote to control the government for their own purposes" (*Hile*, at 151). Furthermore, the charter provision could not violate the federal equal protection of the laws, since it applied equally to every citizen of Cleveland. The Fourteenth Amendment did not require every municipality of the state to have the same electoral provisions (*Hile*, at 152–53). In 1924, the U.S. Supreme Court declined to review the Cleveland case (*Hile*, writ of error dismissed, 266 U.S. 582).

In New York City, a state constitutional challenge to PR/STV was brought on grounds similar to those of the first Ohio case. As in Ohio, no violation of the state right to vote was found (*Johnson v. City of New York* 1937). In 1941, the Plan E form of local government in Massachusetts withstood a constitutional challenge under the state constitution, which the court said did not require plurality voting. Furthermore, the use of PR/STV was not unreasonable, C. J. Field of the Massachusetts Supreme Court wrote, since its purpose was to permit minority representation. The plan was also held immune to attack under the federal Constitution, following Ohio Judge Allen's reasoning in *Hile* and *Reutener* (*Moore v. Election Comm'rs of Cambridge* 1941).

The municipal referendum, however, itself a Progressive reform tool to

expand popular participation in government, became a formidable wea-
pon in the hands of PR's opponents. Political party leaders easily grasped
the mechanics of petition drives and devised ballot issues to restore the
political structures through which they were accustomed to operating.
Forty-nine repeal issues were placed on the ballots of American PR/STV
cities between 1920 and 1961, with some cities, such as those in Ohio,
experiencing repeated referenda. Most repeal initiatives were unsuccessful until the late 1940s, but with the gathering tensions of the cold war,
exacerbated in the case of PR by the election of two Communists to the
New York City Council, the repeal strategy gained strength. Repeal issues
were ultimately successful in twenty-one cities, leaving Cambridge, Massachusetts, the only American city continuing its adherence to PR/STV
elections (Childs 1965, 67; City of Cambridge 1998).

No single factor adequately explains the popular support won by party
leaders in the wave of repeals by referendum. Contemporary accounts by
PR's opponents ascribed their successes to the complexity of the PR/STV
count and its time-consuming character; advocates of PR blamed the
domination of machine politicians who had lost power in reformed cities
and sought to recover it. In Cincinnati, for example, where the PR system
grew deep roots over three decades of local use, the Republican Party
repeatedly launched repeal initiatives with the hope that its demise would
"kill the Charter Party, the group that engineered the adoption of PR in
the 1920s" (Z. Miller and Tucker 1998, 46).

Since the electoral system had been voted in as a corollary of the city
manager plan, it was occasionally voted out in the same way. The former
city manager of Cleveland, William R. Hopkins, explaining the repeal of
Cleveland's PR/STV elections to a New York City audience, said, "[A]s to
PR . . . the manager plan was the dog and PR was only the tail" (Hopkins
1935, 29). Hopkins's wry evaluation might have been the advice that led
New York City to become the only municipality in the United States to
adopt PR/STV without the city manager plan. Yet New York City's PR elections would be overturned by referendum in 1947, and many other cities
separated the two reforms—administrative and electoral—retaining their
city managers when they discarded PR/STV.

The cold war provided fertile political ground for opponents of PR to
try to stigmatize the system as "un-American." Few minor party candidates
were elected to American city councils in PR/STV elections, but the election of two Communist Party members to the New York City Council
between 1941 and 1945 figured prominently in repeal campaigns that followed. Raising the "red menace" had been an unsuccessful strategy in
repeal campaigns before and during World War II, but in 1947 New York

City's voters were vulnerable to Tammany Hall's resolution calling PR "the first beachhead of Communist infiltration in this country," and asserting that "no effort will be spared to throw out this Stalin Frankenstein known as PR on Election Day" (resolution of the Executive Committee of the Democratic Organization of the City of New York, 1947, quoted in *New York Times,* 8 October 1947, p. 21; Zeller and Bone 1948; Kolesar 1996).

Beyond the search for explanations of repeal in the context of particular cities and their social and economic development, an underlying cause of repeal seldom recognized in the literature is the fact that PR/STV did what it was supposed to do, that is, facilitate the representation of minorities of various sorts. The repeal of PR/STV in New York City demonstrated that voters generally were not as open to diversity as PR's sponsors had been. The political diversity attained on city councils by PR was seldom radical but more often was the partisan minority in single-party-dominant cities. In addition, independent professionals often replaced small businessmen, such as tavern owners and undertakers who were ward leaders in their party organizations, thus realizing John Stuart Mill's fondest hopes as well as the expectations of many reform leaders. For the first time, ethnic, religious, and racial minorities and, in many cases, women were elected to council seats. These results may not have been well understood; in many cases they were not welcome in the 1930s, 1940s, and 1950s. The election of African Americans in Toledo and Cincinnati led to the charge in repeal campaigns that PR allowed "racial bloc voting," a code phrase that was never applied to white voters electing white candidates. In the absence of a coherent theory of a right to representation, these charges were not effectively countered by PR's proponents.

The abandonment of PR/STV in twenty-one of the twenty-two cities where it was used in the United States has been attributed to a changing political climate less friendly to experimentation and reform. However, the innovation of PR/STV was still spreading during the period of repeals. The last two successful repeal votes did not occur until 1960 (Hamilton, Ohio, and Worcester, Massachusetts). Voters in Cambridge, Massachusetts, defeated five repeal referenda, the latest in 1965, and the city continued to practice PR at the end of the century, sixty years after its adoption. In 1970, PR/STV was adopted to elect thirty-two community school boards in New York City, established in a major initiative to decentralize a school system believed to be in crisis (Weaver and Baum 1992).[17] These are instances of the Progressive influence still at work at state and local levels among the forces of organized labor, urban Democrats and independents, independent Republicans, social workers, and champions of public power. Advocates of PR/STV persisted in all of these groups.

Conclusion

During the so-called Progressive Era, political life in the United States was characterized by low voting turnout, patronage-based political parties in the cities, and a throng of interest groups formed by shifting coalitions in the electorate. The intense partisan loyalties that had driven the politics of the late nineteenth century dissolved into fluid, issue-oriented commitments by activists seeking ways to ameliorate the conditions of industrial life. Self-styled reformers were diverse; some tried to shrink government and decrease its costs to promote efficiency, while others struggled to expand democracy by improving representation and extending public services to people who needed them. These distinct strands of the reform movement appeared to join forces mainly in opposing their common enemies, the party bosses, and in trying to undermine partisan ways of doing business.

One of the electoral tools advanced for the purpose of improving representation was proportional representation. At first, election reformers advocated the use of party list systems, CV, LV, or PR/STV for international, federal, and state legislative elections. They adapted to failure in their grander schemes by focusing on local elections as small-scale experiments to prove the merits of their case. Since the parties were viewed as sources of corruption in the cities, reform forces did not consider the party list system for local elections. They chose instead the single transferable vote, which worked well on nonpartisan ballots, as the best mechanism for restoring control of urban policy to "ordinary people." By "ordinary people" they often meant people like themselves, but they believed that the working class needed its own representatives as well. If the workers on whom the burdens of industrial growth fell most heavily could represent themselves in the governing of cities, they might alleviate the harsh conditions of their lives. Social justice could be advanced while the advantages of electoral reform would be clear for all to see.

This endeavor succeeded in twenty-two cities, at least for a time. Five of these cities were in Ohio, where the Progressive coalition included labor leaders and women who worked resolutely for electoral reform. The state proved to be a particular locus of adoptions of PR/STV in both large and small cities. By 1960, however, voters in all the Ohio PR cities, and all but one elsewhere in America, had repealed their PR election systems.

Explanations abound. Conflicting views among reformers sometimes hobbled efforts to defeat repeal referenda. Occasionally when measures to repeal PR were on the ballot in these cities, supporters of PR would confuse the voters by their differing views on the size of council or over the question of multimember districts versus at-large election. Strong barriers existed to retention of innovative electoral systems: The major parties were hostile to changes that could threaten their perquisites and their virtual monopoly on power. Some voters' faith in their traditional winner-take-all elections made them reluctant to question their fairness, while others feared the loss of social control through election of representatives from unwanted groups. Finally, the rhetoric of reform often raised expectations beyond the ability of mere institutions to deliver results.

But did representation improve? Did these new electoral systems work? It is often said that all politics are local, and the struggle over representation may be better understood in the context of particular communities. Before turning to a comparative look at the experiences of voters, candidates, and public officials in the five PR cities of Ohio, a more detailed explanation of electoral systems and how they work seems appropriate. The reader may choose to skip the next chapter or return later to its pages for more insight into the operation of the seemingly obscure set of practices that determine how people's votes are translated into representation.

3

How and Why Proportional Election Systems Work

Proportional representation is a simple principle, derived from democratic theory, that in a representative body the share of seats won should correspond to the share of votes won. The electoral system is thus the link between the preferences of the voters and the making of policy. As Ernest Naville wrote in 1865, "In a democratic government, the right of decision belongs to the majority, but the right of representation belongs to all."

The term *proportional representation* is often used loosely to encompass all electoral systems that break up the winner-take-all effect of plurality voting. Strictly speaking, however, proportional representation applies to a much more limited universe of electoral rules. There are two major variants of such electoral systems: party list (PR/PL) and the single transferable vote (PR/STV). Both can be used, and are currently in effect, in various partisan systems; in nonpartisan systems only the STV form of PR is appropriate (Gallagher 1992). Today, the terms *preference voting* and *choice voting* are sometimes used to refer to PR/STV.

Over time, the definition of minorities that the PR theorists worried about has shifted in emphasis from the propertied or educated elite and minority political parties to the farmer and the blue-collar worker and, more recently, to groups identified by religious, ethnic, racial, or gender traits. The core of PR thinking has remained constant, however. In a democratic system, individuals and groups with differing views and identities are entitled to their share of representation in the policy-making process. Minorities are not entitled to rule, but they should be heard, and they should have influence in proportion to their numbers.

The misrepresentation inherent in plurality systems is analyzed here in order to clarify why change in electoral systems has been sought and what differences can be anticipated if a different method of casting ballots and counting votes is adopted. Alternative electoral systems in use today are then explored, including cumulative and limited voting, which are semi-proportional systems. The principal emphasis, however, is on the STV form of proportional representation (PR/STV).

Plurality Voting

Plurality voting describes a decision rule. The candidate with the most votes wins, whether a majority or a plurality produced the winner.[1] This common British and American practice has led European observers to call such elections "horse races" because the first horse past the post wins, no matter by an inch or a mile (Rae 1967, 26). In city elections, plurality voting may be used for candidates running either at-large for seats on a small council (plurality at-large) or in small wards (plurality single-member district), in which the winner-take-all feature applies in each of many locales. Minor variants include systems in which single members are elected at-large to numbered seats, or to seats with residence requirements, resulting in geographic distribution of representation but selection by the entire electorate. Still, the plurality wins.[2]

A popular plurality-based alternative at the local level has been the "mixed system," in which some seats are elected by plurality at-large and some by plurality in single-member districts or wards. In these mixed systems, both at-large and district winners are victorious because they have received the most votes (a plurality) in their respective jurisdictions. In Ohio, Ashtabula, Cincinnati, and Hamilton all used such mixed systems before they adopted PR/STV, each city choosing a different combination of district and at-large seats. The mixture was considered a partial reform of the plurality systems described above, preserving the localism of neighborhood representation while balancing this localism with the whole-city perspective of the at-large members. Victory for all seats, however, was still determined by plurality.

The most obvious political effect of these winner-take-all electoral rules is the exaggeration of majority or plurality representation and the shrinkage or elimination of minority representation. Winning an election in which representation is not distributed in proportion to voter preferences means winning a bonus for one's party, race, ethnic group, or whatever identity is politically relevant.[3] This consequence is sometimes called the "balloon effect" to describe the distortion of representation by the puff of the electoral system, not by actual votes. The inevitable effect of plurality voting shapes the resulting representation, no matter the magnitude of the district, whether a multimember (at-large) or single-member district.

Plurality At-Large Voting Systems

In a plurality at-large election, the voter places an X beside the names of (up to) as many preferred candidates as there are seats to be filled. Thus following the repeal of PR/STV in Hamilton and Ashtabula, where seven members of council were to be elected, the scheme was called "7X" and in Cincinnati and Toledo, where nine members of council were to be elected, "9X" served as an abbreviated designation. The seven or nine candidates with the most votes are elected. No candidate is required to win a majority of the vote (that is, 50 percent plus one). However, a plurality or majority of the voters casting bloc votes for all candidates of plurality or majority identity (say, by party, race, gender, religion, or ideology) can win all of the seats. Thus, 51 percent of the voters with characteristic C may elect up to 100 percent of representatives who also are C's. When both Cincinnati and Toledo repealed PR/STV in favor of a plurality at-large system, their first post-PR elections produced all-white councils, although one or two black members had been elected with some regularity under PR/STV.

Minorities can win one or a few seats in a plurality at-large election in one of two ways, but both ways require majority-group cooperation. First, the plurality or majority may voluntarily choose one or several minority candidates when they vote for all seats, in which case those elected to represent the minority are still candidates preferred by the majority. This is a political strategy not uncommonly used by knowledgeable majorities when plurality at-large systems are under attack for their exclusionary effects, as white voters did in Houston, Texas, in the 1970s (Davidson and Korbel 1981, 1004).

Second, if both majority and minority voters voluntarily limit the number of candidates they select to a number that roughly corresponds to the group's proportion of the electorate as a whole, both groups may elect candidates. For example, if the majority votes for five, six, or seven instead of nine in a 9X election, and the minority votes for two, three, or four, representation can be shared. But to succeed, this method requires sophisticated strategic voting by a substantial share of the electorate.[4]

Minorities can increase their chances of representation (without majority group cooperation) by withholding votes for candidates favored by the majority, since adding to such candidates' vote totals increases the likelihood of defeat of any minority-preferred candidate. If a voter has one intense preference, it is most powerfully expressed by voting for that single candidate, thereby not assisting any other candidate toward a winning total. This strategy, called "bullet voting" or "plunking," is seldom overtly organized, but it is not uncommon among voters who implicitly or explicitly understand how plurality at-large systems work.

A bullet vote is a choice of intensity over numbers, a method of rationalizing the arbitrary effect of plurality at-large voting. Since a plurality at-large election is a free-for-all, in which each candidate competes with all others, all voters may actually help defeat their most preferred candidate or candidates if they vote for all seats. The burden is most severe for small minorities who must give up voting for even a second choice if they hope to get their leading choice elected.

Plurality Single-Member District Voting Systems

Plurality voting in single-member districts (or wards) is the other common form of plurality voting. If minorities are residentially segregated, as Catholic immigrants tended to be in the Progressive Era and as urban blacks in the North became after World War I, they can achieve representation in a plurality single-member district system. With wards as basic political units of party organization and districts determined by ward lines, the parties have historically valued this electoral system as a structure that maximizes their control of city councils. If the wards are small enough, and lines are drawn to create wards with majorities or pluralities of minority voters, representation of minorities ensues. For example, Cleveland adopted a thirty-three-district (ward) council when PR/STV was repealed. Three black council members had been elected by proportional representation before its repeal. Because of the combination in Cleveland of housing segregation and majority-minority wards, black representation on council continued through the 1930s (and to the present) despite the change in electoral system.

The characteristics of a plurality election by single-member district are clear. The election is still by plurality vote. With one seat at stake, the candidate with the most votes is elected ("first past the post" or "winner-takes-all"). If there are only two candidates, the district majority can elect its candidate, thus winning 100 percent of the representation. If there are three or more candidates, a plurality winner, the candidate of the largest minority, is possible. If 45 percent of the voters (a plurality) support the winner, then 55 percent of the voters, having divided their votes between two other candidates, go unrepresented. In this way, a majority in a council or in a legislative body may be "manufactured" by the electoral system (Rae 1967, 74–77).

Prior to the adoption of PR/STV in New York City, the Tammany organization traditionally controlled the board of aldermen, elected by plurality from single-member districts. Machine-organized majorities ranging from half to two-thirds of the voters would elect all or almost all of its members. The last pre-PR board of aldermen was composed of sixty-two organization Democrats out of sixty-five members elected in single-member districts (Hallett 1940, 149), a dramatic example of the balloon effect.

When single-member districts are used, representation in the city or the state as a whole depends on the way the population is geographically distributed and on how the district or ward lines are drawn. Partisan loyalists, racial groups, or ethnic groups may be clustered or dispersed. Traditional techniques of gerrymandering have often determined the composition of a council or a state legislative house, either by bunching (often called "packing") partisan, ethnic, or racial groups into a district so that votes contributing to unnecessarily large majorities are wasted; or by spreading minority populations thinly across several districts so that they do not constitute a majority in any district ("cracking"). More recently, the affirmative gerrymander has been used to advance representation of minorities historically subjected to discrimination in districting.

The goal of minority representation is more easily accomplished for groups that suffer from housing segregation, such as African Americans, than for minorities such as Hispanics and Asians, whose housing choices are less constricted by discrimination. The size and therefore the number of single-member districts in a given political system will affect the number and variety of minorities represented in a council or a legislative body. New York City, which in the 1990s no longer had an ethnic or racial majority, recently expanded its council from thirty-five to fifty-one members to allow for greater diversity of representation. The task of creating distinct minority districts fell to computer experts, who could draw convoluted shapes within the city to produce the desired demographic results (*New York Times*, 13 September 1991, A1).

In this way, single-member districts provide structural support for residential segregation. Moreover, in a heterogeneous community with several minorities, political authorities decide by drawing the district lines which minority is entitled to representation in a district. In a larger multimember district system, voting by PR, the voters would decide how to allocate representation between majority and minority, or among minorities.

The Special Cases of Majority Formulae

So far in this chapter we have been treating plurality and majority wins together. A cohesive majority can use a plurality electoral system effectively, but it should be clear that the decision rule is victory by plurality (the most votes); a majority (50 percent of the total plus one) is not necessary. There are, however, two single-winner district systems that permit or require a majority victory at some stage of the process. One is the second ballot system, used in France and in some American primary elections, where the second election is called a runoff. The other system is the "instant runoff" (IRV), more traditionally known as the alternative vote (AV), or the majority preferential vote (MPV), used for election of the Irish president and in single-member district elections for members of the Australian lower house.

As practiced in France, the second ballot system provides that if any candidate in the single-member district receives a majority of the votes on the first ballot, he or she is elected. Because there is no primary election, few candidates receive a majority vote. Therefore, a second election is held, usually a week later, at which a plurality winner is elected. This system is used to elect the French president (with the nation as a single district) as well as to elect the parliament. Deals struck in the interval between ballots may include withdrawal of individual candidates in exchange for some post-election benefit. In French parliamentary elections, candidates must win support of at least 12.5 percent of the registered voters in the first round to enter the runoff. The interval between ballots is used by small parties to trade districts by withdrawing candidates on a reciprocal plan to maximize opportunities for electoral success on the second ballot (Cole and Campbell 1989, 60–63, 67–70, 93–94, 158–60, 167–72; Rae 1967, 23–25, 107–10). Significant misrepresentation may result, as in 1993 French parliamentary elections. In the first round, only 14 percent of the seats were filled (by majority vote), leaving 497 of the 577 members to be elected in the second round. The outcome of the second round a week later saw a conservative coalition, the Union for France, win 84 percent of the seats in the National Assembly with 39.5 percent of the vote in the single-member district winner-take-all runoff (*New York Times,* 29 March 1993, A3).

The second ballot system is handicapped not only by the opportunity for manipulation by candidates and parties in the interval between the election and the runoff but also by the expense to taxpayers and the inconvenience to voters of two-stage elections. Moreover, the runoff typically draws fewer voters, even different voters to the polls, introducing arbitrary factors to the outcomes of the second ballot.

The instant runoff avoids these drawbacks by creating the opportunity for voters to rank their choices on the ballot. The election of the president of the Irish Republic is conducted by this method. In October 1997, Mary McAleese was elected to the position from a field of five candidates who were ranked by the voters on the IRV ballot. When the three lowest-ranked candidates were eliminated and their ballots transferred to second or subsequent choices, McAleese won with 58.7 percent of the vote, a strong majority, while the runner-up took 41.3 percent of the vote (*New York Times*, 1 November 1997, A6).

In Australia the instant runoff is used to elect members of the federal lower house of parliament, requiring a majority winner for election and expanding the voter's choices in a single-member district by providing for ranked voting. The voter marks the ballot by placing numbers beside each candidate's name in order of his or her choice.[5] As in the Irish presidential race, if any candidate wins a majority of first-choice votes, he or she is elected. If not, the lowest ranked candidate is eliminated and his or her second preference votes are added to the first choices of the other candidates. This process continues until majority winners are produced in all districts (Parliament of the Commonwealth of Australia, House of Representatives 1994, Factsheet no. 8, 2).

In the United States, this instant runoff voting could be used instead of plurality voting for the election of one candidate nationwide (the president), statewide (governors and U.S. senators), and for members of the House of Representatives, who run in single-member districts, giving voters expanded choices and strengthening the claim to power of officials who win with majority support (Richie 1997). For legislative elections, however, both the two-ballot system and the instant runoff suffer from the flaws of voting by plurality in single-member districts. Minorities are excluded from representation when a single candidate is elected, and outcomes do not depend on the total votes parties receive. Instead, outcomes are biased by the geographical distribution of party supporters and by the configuration of district lines (Bogdanor 1984, 44).

Semiproportional Voting Systems

Cumulative voting (CV), limited voting (LV) and the single *non*transferable vote (SNTV) are alternative electoral systems that enable a jurisdiction to maintain at-large voting in a multimember district, city, or county, but that at the same time provide the opportunity for minority representation. The term *semiproportional* is applied because the decision rules do not guarantee a close relationship between the share of votes won by a group and the share of seats allocated to that group in the governing body. Votes may be wasted both by overelecting some candidates and, owing to vote-splitting among similar candidates, defeating others.

Cumulative Voting

Cumulative voting (CV) gives voters (up to) the same number of votes as seats to be filled in a multimember district but permits voters to concentrate their support on one or more candidates instead of voting to fill all seats. The most persistent exercise of this option was the 110–year-old practice in Illinois (1870–1980) for electing the lower house of its legislature. The house was composed of three-member districts. Each voter could cast three votes in one of the following ways: one vote for each of three candidates; two votes for one candidate and one vote for another; one and a half for each of two; or three votes aggregated or "cumulated" for the same candidate. By this system in Illinois, one Republican was generally elected to serve in a Democratic-dominant legislative district, and one Democrat in a Republican-dominant district. A minority (either Democratic or Republican, depending on the district's composition) making up one-third of the voters was capable of capturing one of the three seats. The decision rule was still by plurality; the candidates with the most votes won, but the intensity or depth of voter preference was to some degree accommodated (G. S. Blair 1960; Everson and Parker 1983).

A problem inherent in cumulative voting surfaced in Illinois in districts where so many of the second party's candidates ran that their support was dispersed too widely, and none could win. To deal with this issue, in 1910 when CV was extended to the primaries, party committees were given the power in each three-member district to establish a maximum number of party nominees who could be selected in the primaries to run in the general election. Over time this party control of nominations evolved into a stable system in which Democratic and Republican committees approved the nomination of only as many candidates as could be reasonably expected to win. By the 1950s, the primary would become the major arena of voter choice, depriving voters of contested general elections in more than half the districts. While this provided considerable stability in the legislature, with members serving longer periods of time than in the legislatures of comparable midwestern states, long tenure became a contentious issue in the successful repeal campaign of 1980 (G. S. Blair 1960, 129; Everson and Parker 1983). CV increased in popularity in the United States in the late twentieth century as a remedy for minority vote dilution in Voting Rights Act cases, a development discussed in chapter 5.

The most common use of CV in the United States today is in private elections for corporate directors. Between its initial adoption in Illinois in 1870 (see chap. 1) and mid-twentieth-century practice, twenty-two states required CV elections for corporate directors, and another seventeen states adopted constitutional provisions or statutes permitting such elections. In the 1980s, some states changed their statutes from mandatory to permissive corporate CV elections, and by 1992 only six states retained CV as a requirement for these private elections. However, efforts to secure minority shareholder representation on corporate boards increased again in the 1990s. The American Society of Corporate Secretaries reported that provision for cumulative voting to elect directors was among the most common proxy proposals, although few stockholder proposals were adopted. The difficulty for minority shareholders seeking representation on corporate boards in the permissive states is inherent in their minority status (Williams 1951, v; Gordon 1994, 145; M. Blair 1995, 74).[6]

Limited Voting

In the case of limited voting (LV), the voter is restricted to voting in an at-large election for fewer candidates than the number of seats available. For example, the voter may be allowed to cast votes for up to five candidates for a seven-seat council. The minority party or minority groups will quickly learn to maximize their strength by voting for only two or three candidates. This method is used in nonpartisan elections in some Connecticut cities and towns and in Pennsylvania county elections. A variation of this system, which can be used in partisan elections, provides for limited nominations (LN), restricting the number of candidates each party may nominate but allowing voters to vote for all seats. A combination of LN and LV limits both the number of candidates nominated by each party and the number of votes each voter may cast. At-large members of the Philadelphia City Council have been elected by this combination of limited nomination and limited voting (Weaver 1984). The more limited the vote is, the smaller the minority that can gain proportionate representation. If the limit is one vote, LV becomes the single nontransferable vote.

The Single Nontransferable Vote

The single nontransferable vote (SNTV) is the most limited version of limited voting: each voter casts a ballot for only one representative in a multiseat at-large election. SNTV is little known in the United States, but is being considered again as a possible remedy for minority vote dilution. This system has been used in some form since 1900 in elections for Japan's lower house. From 1947 to 1993, when a mixed-member proportional system was adopted, Japanese voters cast one vote for their representative in a three-, four-, or five-member district (not, as in a plurality election, three, four, or five votes). In a four-member district, a candidate winning about 20 percent of the vote could capture a seat (Lijphart 1994, 40–42). The larger the number of seats, the greater the proportionality that could be achieved. This electoral system can be recognized as somewhat similar to PR/STV, but without the transfer feature (to be discussed below), which minimizes wasted votes. With SNTV, votes for winners in excess of those needed for election as well as votes for hopeless losers are still wasted (Cox 1997, chap. 13; Reeve and Ware 1992, 147–48; Newland 1982, 34–35).

Limited voting systems (including SNTV), like other semiproportional systems, are handicapped in another important respect. The opportunity to achieve minority representation is likely to attract more minority candidates to a contest, inevitably inviting dispersal of minority votes over too many candidates. As a result, minority candidates may defeat each other. Indeed, majority representation may be limited if too few majority candidates run. To produce reliable results from limited or cumulative election systems, parties or groups seeking representation must attempt to exercise control over the number of candidates that enter a given race, and individual voters must understand how to vote strategically. Minorities that may or may not be residentially segregated but that learn to limit nominations and vote cohesively can gain representation in at-large LV or CV voting systems. But if all groups or parties correctly estimate their electoral strength, the total number of candidates will equal the number of seats available, and the voters are stripped of choices (Zimmerman 1978, 655–56). Current use of LV to remedy discrimination in Voting Rights Act litigation will be discussed in chapter 5.

Proportional Voting Systems

Proportional Representation/Party List

The party list system is the most common application of PR, found in presidential as well as parliamentary systems around the world in national, state, or provincial elections for legislative assemblies. By aggregating voters' interests, preferences, and ideologies into meaningful collective action, the political party system provides a base for democratic representation in governance. On the PR/PL ballot, candidates are listed by party or, in a few places, such as Israel, only the parties are listed.

Voters choose their preferred party or party list of candidates. The percentage of total votes won by each party is then translated into the share of seats earned, determining the representation of that party in the legislature. The parties decide which candidates will be on their lists (therefore no primary is necessary), and if the entire list is not elected (a likely event, since the winner does *not* take all), the parties decide which of the listed candidates will actually serve to make up the party's voter-determined share of seats. A popular variation of the party list ballot is to allow the voters to rank their choices of candidates within a party list, as in Norway, or even to choose a few candidates from different lists, as in Switzerland, but the emphasis is on fair translation of voters' party preferences into power in the parliament (Rae 1967, 39–45). A party that wins 55 percent of the votes will have about 55 percent of the seats; a party that wins 10 percent of the votes will have about 10 percent of the seats, and so on.

Most PR/PL systems today have a threshold percentage that a party must win in order to get any seats at all, 5 percent being a common minimum requirement (Bogdanor 1984, 10). This threshold corrects what was viewed as a defect in the system of the Weimar Republic of Germany, under which extreme fragmentation made difficult the coalescence of a majority in the parliament. Israel is an example of a contemporary party list system that has a very low minimum required percentage of votes to achieve representation. In the 1988 Israeli election, when the threshold was 1 percent, a 5 percent threshold would have excluded from the Knesset thirteen parties that won between 1.2 percent and 4.7 percent of the total vote. Only the two major parties, Labor and Likud, received more than 5 percent of the vote. In 1992, the threshold was raised to 1.5 percent, a minimal increase but one that reduced the number of parties winning representation from 15 to 10. Facing a higher threshold (3.5 percent has been considered), the very small parties could either accept exclusion as the price of purity or build a coalition among themselves to surmount the threshold as a few parties did in 1992. Their third option would be to join with one of the two major parties to share in power. Raising the threshold is a leading change sought by Israeli reformers (Cox 1997, 62, 240; Bogdanor 1993, 68, 73).

Different formulae for allocation of seats and different district magnitudes (ranging from 2 in Iceland to 150 in the Netherlands, a district of the whole) add variety to the practice of PR/PL but do not change the basic principle (Rae 1967, 18–36). Constituencies are territorial, but they tend to be whole political communities such as cities, counties, or provinces. When the population grows or declines, the principle of equality of representation is maintained by raising or lowering the number of members from a district instead of redrawing district lines or further subdividing a political community (Steed 1985).

In Germany, a hybrid variety of PR/PL called a "mixed-member proportional" system (MMP) is practiced, as it was formerly in West Germany. Half of the Bundestag's seats are filled by plurality voting in single-member districts, and the other half by PR/PL, with the overall composition of the body determined by the party shares won on the party list ballot (Cox 1997, 63, 197–98; Rae 1967, 11–13). In November 1993, by popular referendum New Zealand became the first English-speaking democracy to adopt this system for its parliamentary elections. Variants of this mixed-member system have also been adopted recently in Japan, Russia, Italy, Hungary, Bulgaria, and Mexico (Nagel 1994, 525).

Because proportional representation was originally promoted in the United States as an antiparty measure, and because PR has been adopted only at the local level where most governments use nonpartisan ballots, PR/PL has not yet been practiced in the United States.

Proportional Representation/Single Transferable Vote

In the proportional representation/single transferable vote (PR/STV) paradigm, it is not the parties alone but all interested persons, including independents, that deserve representation.[7] Because the election is conducted at-large in a city or state, or in a multimember district, the share of seats elected corresponds to the share of votes won by independents, by a political party, or by a group with common interests. The single transferable ballot makes this possible by giving the voter the opportunity to rank-order his or her preferences. The ballot ultimately counts for one candidate, as it does in a single-member district system, or under SNTV, but it is used where it is needed to best reflect the voter's choices. If the voter's first choice is a very popular candidate who needs no further votes to be elected, or if the first choice was cast for a hopeless loser, the ballot is not wasted. Instead, it is transferred to the voter's second, third, or subsequent choice and added to that candidate's total. Thus, the greatest possible number of voters is represented by a candidate for whom they voted.

In this way, the PR/STV ballot integrates the advantages of an at-large

d a single-member district system without their attendant costs.
is not constricted by district boundaries in choosing a repre-
~~~~~~ but may join with other like-minded voters throughout the city,
state, or multimember district, creating a voluntary constituency for their
council member or legislator. If geographical representation is important
to the voters, they are free to give neighborhood candidates preference in
marking their ballots. If party, race, ethnicity, gender, or ideology is important, voters can join with others of similar interests to elect a candidate.

For the voter, the task is simple. Given a ballot with a list of candidates
either running at-large in a city (as at one time in Ashtabula, Cincinnati,
Hamilton, and Toledo, and at present in Cambridge, Massachusetts), in
large multimember districts (as formerly in Cleveland and New York City,
and still in Ireland), or in states (as in Australia for the upper house of the
federal parliament), the voter marks the ballot with numerals, giving his
or her first preference a "1," the second a "2," and as many successive preferences as desired up to the total number of candidates. As a practical
matter most voters will not rank candidates whom they do not prefer at
all, except in Australia where voting is compulsory and all candidates must
be ranked.

As with PR/PL, the voter is relieved of the duty of voting twice, first in
a primary and then in the general election, since candidates are nominated for the PR/STV ballot by petition and the electorate's rank-ordering
of choices serves to both narrow the field and pick the winners.

Although PR/STV has frequently been criticized as too complex for the
average voter to understand, it is only the count, for which the voter is not
responsible, that is complicated. Advocates of PR/STV often point out that
voting becomes, like telling time, driving a car, or buying insurance, something that ordinary people do all the time without any need to understand
the underlying technology. They need only have confidence in the coun-
ters, a condition relevant to all types of elections. Here, however, an
overview of the count will help to explain how proportionality is achieved.[8]

First count. The first step is to sort all ballots by first choices, eliminating invalid ballots (for example, those marked with X's instead of
numerals).[9] First-choice votes are counted and the total number of valid
ballots is determined. This makes it possible to establish the minimum
required number of votes that candidates must earn in order to be elected.
This number becomes the threshold for election. In order to minimize
wasted votes, the threshold is set at the smallest number that can elect no
more members than there are seats. If, for example, there are nine seats

to be filled, a majority of voters (5 x 10% = 50%) will elect a majority of seats (5 of 9). One-tenth of the total vote plus just one more vote will prevent ten candidates from being elected. No votes are wasted in an unnecessarily large majority, as they would be if the threshold were set at (what might seem to be the obvious) one-ninth of the total vote.

At the time that PR/STV was adopted in cities in the United States, the threshold was calculated by a formula developed by British barrister H. R. Droop (then called the "Droop Quota"), essentially the method used today. The total number of valid votes cast is divided by one more than the number of seats to be filled, and one digit is added to the quotient. If $V =$ the total number of valid ballots and $N =$ the number of seats to be filled, the threshold (T) is found as follows: $T = V/(N + 1) + 1$.

If 1,000 valid ballots are cast to fill nine seats, the threshold is $(1000/10) + 1 = 101$. This is the smallest proportion of the total vote that can elect each of nine candidates (Lakeman and Lambert 1959, 105, 251–52).[10] At the end of the first count, all candidates receiving the established threshold or more of votes are declared elected. Any excess votes—that is, more than the number necessary to be elected—are declared "surplus."

Second count. The surplus ballots are redistributed to the second preferences marked on these ballots. The method for this transfer varied in the American cities using PR/STV. In Cincinnati, all ballots were numbered consecutively on the first count so that the appropriate proportion could be drawn from all wards and precincts. If candidate A's total first-choice votes exceeded the threshold by 25 percent, then every fourth ballot of A's total vote was withdrawn and allocated to the second choice on that ballot. If the second choice was already elected, the ballot was allocated to the third or, if necessary, subsequent choice.

In Toledo, however, the surplus ballots were those counted last, so that the sequence of counting determined which ballots were redistributed to second or later choices. In the first count, when Candidate A reached the threshold, he was declared elected, "his" ballots were set aside, and all subsequent ballots on which he was given first preference were allocated to second or later preferences (Zimmerman 1972, 75). This practice gave rise to the criticism that the PR count was a lottery.

A third system, used originally in Boulder, Colorado, and statistically refined today, distributes the surplus by a simple mathematical formula, as follows: the elected candidate's surplus (s) is divided by the total vote for the elected candidate (v); the quotient is then multiplied by the number of second preferences (sp) for each unelected candidate, and these fractional votes (fv) are then allocated to the designated unelected candidates. The formula is then: (s/v) x (sp)= fv (Rae 1967, 37).

For example, if the threshold is 15,000 and candidate A receives 20,000 votes (v), the surplus is 5,000 (s). On A's 20,000 first-choice ballots, second choices are divided among five candidates, say 4,000 each (sp) for candidates B, C, D, E, and F, or 20 percent each. Then 20 percent of 5,000 (or 1,000) surplus fractions of votes (fv) are transferred to each of these five candidates. Thus a fractional vote or vote value is actually transferred, representing the proportional share of second or subsequent choices for unelected candidates among the total first-choice votes of an elected candidate. This method is accepted today as the fairest and most accurate distribution of the surplus and is easily accomplished by a computer-programmed count. After the transfer of all surplus votes from the first count, any candidates reaching the threshold are declared elected.

Third count. At this stage, the lowest-placed candidate on the list is declared eliminated, and his or her ballots are transferred to other unelected candidates in order of second, third, or subsequent viable choices. Any candidates reaching the threshold will then be declared elected; the next lowest candidate will be eliminated, and so on, until the required number of seats has been filled. Unlike the transfer of the surplus, these votes transfer at full current value, since they are the universe of votes for eliminated candidates.[11]

Although some ballots may be exhausted before they are allocated to a winning candidate, the number is far smaller than those wasted in a single-member district plurality election in which only one choice is counted.[12] As noted earlier, in a three-or-more-candidate race decided by plurality in single-member districts, a majority of ballots may be wasted. In a PR/STV election, a ballot is wasted only if the voter opted not to make enough choices to keep the ballot in play, or if each of the voter's choices represented too small a minority to make up one ratio of representation (for example, one-tenth of the total vote plus one for a nine-member council). Typically, 80–90 percent of the ballots are effectively counted to elect a member of council, as opposed to 45–55 percent in a plurality election.

Final count. On the final count, it is possible for candidates to be elected without reaching the threshold. If the next-to-last remaining candidate has been eliminated, her ballots transferred, and one or more seats remains unfilled, the surviving candidate(s) will be declared elected. In Cleveland council elections—which took place in four large multimember districts, two of which elected seven members, one elected six members, and one elected five members—it was not uncommon for several members in each district to be elected without reaching the threshold. With a small number of seats and therefore a relatively large required number of votes, it is not unusual for leaders on the first count to be the winners on the final count (Lakeman and Lambert 1959, 109; Hermens [1941] 1972, 413).

If most of the council members who were finally elected after the transfer process were also among the leaders on the first count (90 percent was the average in these Ohio cities), does it really make much difference whether an at-large election is held by plurality or by PR/STV? The answer is a resounding yes. Not only would (and did) 10 percent minority representation itself make a difference, but a different array of candidates is likely to enter a PR race because of the different opportunity structure. When a citywide minority of 10 percent to 15 percent of the electorate has a chance of electing a candidate, as in a seven- or nine-member PR/STV election, there is a distinct incentive for a minority candidate to run. This incentive is absent in a winner-take-all situation, such as 7X or 9X voting, since such a candidate would probably lose out in the plurality contest at either the primary or the election stage. Furthermore, the transfers significantly increase the proportion of voters actually represented on the policy-making body. In contrast to plurality systems, few ballots are wasted.

In the American communities that adopted PR, there were ardent followers of the count. The count was conducted publicly, with succeeding totals marked up on large chalkboards. Frequently it would take a week to complete the transfers and reach the final results. Some observers have portrayed this process as a civic celebration, as it has been experienced in Cambridge, Massachusetts, where many voters mourn the rapidity and invisibility of its new computer count. Others complained of the delay in learning the outcome.

Computer tally. Computer technology has now made expeditious—indeed, virtually instant—counts a reality. The first official computerized count of a PR election in the United States occurred in November 1997 in Cambridge, Massachusetts. Both city council and school committee ballots were tabulated by electronic sorting, counting, and transfer of votes in what was reported to be a few seconds.[13]

Impact of the number of seats. The number of seats on a city council, in a state, or in a multimember district will affect the diversity of representation in a PR/STV system. With a nine-member council, for example,

of 10 percent of the voters has a chance of electing a rep-
of its choice. A seven-member council would provide the
opportunity of representation to a minority of 12.5 percent. The Australian Senate allocates twelve senators to each of the nation's six states
(plus two each from the two territories), for six-year terms, staggered so
that in each state six senators are elected every three years. In a six-seat
election, conducted at-large in each state by PR/STV, just under 17 percent of the voters can win a seat (Parliament of the Commonwealth of
Australia 1994, Senate Brief no. 1, 2–3).

In contrast to LV and CV, a minority-preferred candidate in a PR/STV
election is unable to defeat another minority-preferred candidate because
rank-order voting prevents lower preferences from being counted until
higher-ranked preferences are elected or eliminated. Cleveland's twenty-
five-member council, elected in four multimember districts, was sized to
permit representation of more minorities in that highly diverse community than was possible in the seven- or nine-member councils of the other
Ohio PR cities. Its multimember districts in which voters elected five, six,
or seven representatives were intended to provide some geographical distribution of representation as well as to ease the transition from wards to
at-large voting.

Ireland's experience over more than seventy-five years of PR/STV elections illustrates the impact of district size in a party-based system. From 1923
to 1977, Dail districts varied in size from three to nine members, depending
on district population. Gradually the larger districts were reduced in size to
a maximum of five members, and since 1969 most have been three-member
districts. The number of parties contesting elections declined to a highly stable three-party system in which the third party typically wins less than half
as many seats as the second party. O'Leary calls these parties "majority-bent
parties with an eye to power" (1979, 98–99, 110–13).

Some social choice theorists have criticized proportional voting procedures because of a theoretical possibility that changes in individual order-
ing of preferences could alter the outcome of such elections in ways that
negate the "true" choices of voters (Doron and Kronick 1977; Fishburn
and Brams 1983). This possibility, a condition called "non-monotonicity,"
suggests that the opportunity exists for strategic voting (often called insin-
cere voting or manipulation) to determine the winner or winners of such
elections.

However, strategic voting is possible in all electoral systems, and strategic choices may actually reflect a voter's true preference. For example, in
a plurality election with several candidates, a voter who knows that her
first choice cannot win may vote for a less preferred candidate in an effort

e.g. Voting for Clinton instead of Perot to keep Dole from ↑ winning

to keep an even more disliked alternative from winning. Her true preference, then, is to keep the least liked candidate out of office. Successful
strategic voting depends on understanding how the voting system works,
as well as knowing something about the choices other voters are likely to
make. The knowledge required to vote the PR/STV ballot strategically is
far more intricate than with plurality voting (Reeve and Ware 1992,
160–61). Hence the STV ballot is more "resistant to manipulation" than
other methods of voting that are more widely practiced (Still 1984,
261–62; Merrill 1988, 66; Austen-Smith and Banks 1991; Bartholdi and
Orlin 1991). In *Making Votes Count*, Gary W. Cox has analyzed strategic
voting in mass elections in a variety of electoral systems, producing both
mathematical models and empirical evidence of strategic voting practices
and their consequences for parties and representation (1997, chaps. 3–7).
Where democratic elections are the basis for governing, strategic voting
will be practiced.

Summary and Conclusion

Electoral systems are a little-recognized link between the voters' acts of
choice in democratic systems and the kind of representation that they win.
Electoral systems have political consequences. Plurality voting systems,
whether at-large or in small districts, tend to overrepresent the majority
or plurality and underrepresent or exclude the minority. While malapportionment and gerrymandering may exacerbate this outcome of plurality
voting, a majority is commonly manufactured in the absence of such egregious tactics simply through the effect of the winner-take-all decision rule.

Semiproportional systems, the most common of which are limited voting and cumulative voting, are based on at-large or multimember district
voting and can be used with either partisan or nonpartisan ballots. By preventing the electoral sweeps of plurality voting systems, these decision
rules are likely to result in some representation of a minority party or
group. The principal disadvantage of LV and CV is that in the absence of
well-organized nominating and voting, minority candidates may lose
because their support is either diffused among too many candidates or
wasted in surplus votes.

Full proportionality can be achieved by true proportional systems, with
ballots organized by party list or by STV. While PR/PL is necessarily associated with a partisan ballot, PR/STV is adaptable either to partisan or to
nonpartisan elections. In order to prevent a large number of very small
groups from each electing its own representative in a decision-making

body, most PR/PL systems today set a minimum percentage of the vote that is required for a small party to gain any representation at all. This is not a major issue in PR/STV elections since the number to be elected in a district or a jurisdiction is usually no greater than nine, and this sets a minimum of 10 percent to elect a representative.

The choice of electoral systems has real consequences both for voter behavior and for governance. In systems governed by plurality elections, the winner-take-all result forces candidates and parties to build coalitions in the electorate before the election, if victory is the goal. This is one reason why two-party systems are generally associated with plurality voting patterns. In proportional systems, although coalition building before an election is useful and may indeed produce a working majority in the elected body, it is also possible to build a majority coalition in the policy-making body after the election. For this reason, proportional systems may encourage the formation and persistence of more than two parties in partisan polities and produce more diverse representation in nonpartisan bodies.

The electoral system is only a part of the larger system of representation that is supposed to make democracy a government of, by, and for the people. Recruitment of candidates, organization of parties and interests, and electoral campaigns are other inputs into the process of creating a representative government. Structures of government and decision rules within those structures shape the policies produced as outputs, but the electoral system is a critical and often unrecognized link between the more visible forces of politics in a democracy and the actual governing of a society. The choice of an electoral system should be made deliberately and with full understanding of its consequences for representation and governance.

4

Tales of Five Cities

THE PERIOD FROM 1915 TO 1960 when twenty-two American cities adopted PR/STV was a time of rapid social change and growing cultural pluralism. In the late nineteenth and early twentieth centuries, as cities absorbed millions of European immigrants, political party leaders held the reins of power, securing votes in exchange for minimal provision of services. Operations were financed through payments by businesses seeking franchises and favors. The resulting paradigm of power appeared wasteful, particularistic, and inefficient to growing numbers of activists who called themselves reformers.

Five of these PR cities were in Ohio, where revision of the election system was one feature of a reform attack on "boss rule" and its attendant corruption and mismanagement. Three large industrial cities—Cleveland, Cincinnati, and Toledo—were governed by deeply entrenched Republican machines. The two smaller cities, Ashtabula and Hamilton, had less centralized structures of power, but the political parties were significant actors in their daily political life. Republicans made most of the policy decisions in Ashtabula, while Hamilton was one of the few cities in the state where the Democratic Party ruled. Although there were unique circumstances undergirding the adoption of PR/STV in each of these cities, common factors outweighed the differences. Revelations of graft and fraud in the operations of government and public dissatisfaction with the level of services provided—from electric power to sewers, streets, parks, and recreation—explain the rejection of the status quo.

In Cleveland and Toledo, reform efforts were rooted in the independent mayoral regimes of Tom Johnson and Samuel "Golden Rule" Jones. Although Johnson was a Democrat and Jones was a Republican, both had advocated electoral reform as a means of facilitating broader representation of the citizens of their respective cities. Both Cleveland (1913) and

Toledo (1914) had adopted charters providing for nonpartisan elections of municipal officeholders. As noted in chapter 2 above, both cities had retained their ward-based councils but experimented with nomination by petition and preferential voting for both council and mayor on the nonpartisan Bucklin ballot.[1]

In Ashtabula, Cincinnati, and Hamilton, Progressive victories represented more drastic political change. These three cities were still using partisan ballots for local elections until they adopted PR/STV. They had some experience, however, with at-large elections, since their councils were a mixture of ward and at-large seats, with ward members in the majority.[2]

Ohio was fertile ground for experimentation in electoral systems. The adoption of home rule by state constitutional amendment in 1912 cleared the path for new municipal charters, an opening for city autonomy that had been closely watched by both the National Municipal League (NML) and the Proportional Representation League (PRL). The choice of PR/STV as the preferred alternative to existing electoral systems in these cities is attributable to the tireless efforts of both local and national activists who were committed to diversity of representation. Their choice of proportional representation was tied to support for the city manager plan, a connection that was neither accidental nor enigmatic. An impartial city manager was to sweep away the waste and fraud practiced by the bosses and by successive inept mayors; in a democracy, they believed, this efficient administrator required policy guidance by a truly representative city council.

In spite of the persistent power of the political machines, the politics of the time revolved more around issues than around parties. Coalitions bent on changing the rules of the political game were willing to experiment with new ideas. In all five of these Ohio cities, Progressives became committed to PR/STV. Augustus Hatton, a political scientist at Western Reserve University in Cleveland, drafted three of the five Ohio PR/STV charters. Hatton became a national expert and consultant for the NML on charter revision. He also won two terms on Cleveland's city council, elected by PR in the 1920s. The national PRL chose Ashtabula as an experimental site, apparently at the suggestion of the local labor leader, William E. Boynton. Ohio PR advocates coordinated testimonials to advance the spread of PR elections. For example, in 1919 five Ashtabula community leaders who had initially opposed PR wrote statements for the Coshocton (Ohio) Charter Commission, then considering electoral system reform, testifying that PR was working well to the benefit of their city (*Equity* 1919, 21:76–78).

Evidence suggests that each city in turn looked to the experience of the other Ohio cities in choosing its new electoral system (*PRR* 1928, 85:17). Although Toledo's 1934 adoption followed repeal of PR/STV in Ashtabula and Cleveland, its reform leaders were captivated by the continuing success of PR in Cincinnati and Hamilton. Members of the Toledo Citizens' Charter Committee looked upon Cincinnati in particular as a model for what they hoped to achieve by adopting a council of nine, to be elected at-large by PR (Stinchcombe 1968, 40).

The support of labor for Ohio PR campaigns was a significant source of strength. The participation of labor leaders in Ohio's Progressive movement was, if not unique, at least unusual in the early twentieth century. In the adopting period (1915–34), labor organizations in these five Ohio cities were not unanimous in support of PR elections, but in each city some unions, and in Cleveland an organized Union Labor PR Club, provided notable support for PR elections. These labor groups published and distributed pro-PR literature and turned out voters for adoption campaigns and against repeal initiatives.

Because Ohio was seen as a national leader in reform efforts and at the same time a typical state politically, the Proportional Representation League and the National Municipal League, both headquartered in New York City, involved themselves in the Ohio charter campaigns. Beginning in 1912, Clarence Hoag, secretary of the PRL, and his successor, George Hallett Jr., made numerous trips to Ohio by train, meeting with Augustus Hatton and arguing the PR case before charter commissions and councils. From then until 1960, when Hamilton voters approved the last repeal of PR in Ohio, PRL and NML staff traveled tirelessly to assist in campaigns, not only to promote adoption of PR but also to prevent repeal. Reform regimes were more persistent in some cities than in others. Cleveland's PR charter lasted only eight years, a brief span compared with the sixteen years in Ashtabula and Toledo and thirty-four years in Cincinnati and Hamilton.

Contemporary sources generally give credit to the PR-elected councils and their city managers for effective government. In these reformed cities, improved and expanded public services were delivered, and fiscal responsibility was achieved. Only in Cleveland, where the Republican organization managed to retain its power and perquisites throughout the decade of reform, and Ashtabula, where prohibition-related violations were linked to a council member, was serious misfeasance uncovered and punished in the PR-elected councils.

However, local political party leaders who lost power in the PR period fought back with repeated attacks on the reform package. In all five cities, the rise of ambitious aspirants to power, both inside and outside the old parties, helped to topple reform regimes. Although the city manager and the small at-large council were targets as well, PR/STV was singled out for the most persistent repeal initiatives. In four of the five cities, PR was repealed only when it was separated from the city manager plan; only in Cleveland was the entire reform charter discarded. By 1960 this advanced electoral system was abandoned in the five Ohio cities.

PR may have been more vulnerable than the other reform features in part because of its complexity, but careful examination of election results in the context of the times shows that more fundamentally it was vulnerable because the minority groups that gained representation at the table of public policy making were not welcomed there by the majority. Furthermore, the reformers themselves flagged in their efforts, failed to organize political support among PR's beneficiaries, and in many cases simply joined the tide of suburbanization and left the cities.

Expectations for Change

The PR experience in the five Ohio cities has been explored in detail by Ronald J. Busch (Ashtabula), Kathleen L. Barber (Cleveland), Robert J. Kolesar (Cincinnati), Leon Weaver and James L. Blount (Hamilton), and Dennis M. Anderson (Toledo). Coordination of the research enabled the investigators to test common hypotheses about adoption and repeal of PR/STV, voting turnout, characteristics of council members elected, the significance of transfer votes, and the extent of consensus or conflict in council operations. For comparative purposes, each case study included outcomes from three elections prior to adoption of PR/STV ("pre-PR"), the PR elections, and three elections under the systems adopted to replace PR ("post-PR"). Accounts of the five cities related in this chapter rely primarily on the findings of these comparative studies.[3]

When PR/STV electoral systems were introduced into the Ohio cities, voter turnout was expected to change. Proponents anticipated a rise in turnout because the new opportunity for representation would draw previously hopeless voters to the polls. Opponents expected a decline as voters faced a new and complex ballot.

Among turn-of-the-century advocates of proportional representation, voter turnout was an important concern. John Commons, citing the decline he observed in state and local voting in the 1890s, attributed growing disinterest in politics to the hopelessness of voters who faced a choice between the candidates of two machines. Unable to get their candidates elected, he argued, they rationally chose not to vote. PR in his view would bring out a "full" vote because the present "hopelessness" would be dissipated. He noted that some Progressive reformers favored compulsory voting, but the "real problem," he maintained, "is not how to compel unwilling voters to vote, but how to give effect to the votes of those who are willing" (Commons 1907, 153–62).

Commons's observation that voting turnout began to decline in the 1890s is generally accepted today, although the reasons for the decline are in dispute.[4] Legal and institutional reforms such as personal registration, residency requirements, and the secret ballot were tactics by which reformers fought the dominant party organizations, making it more difficult for the bosses to turn out their loyal followers. At the local level, nonpartisan elections conducted in the off year, at-large elections for city councils, and the city manager plan were additional reforms that displaced the old, more militant, participatory partisan politics (W. D. Burnham 1981; J. F. Reynolds 1988). In the reformed city, the disappearance of mayoral elections, which had traditionally focused on personalities, was said to weaken the links between citizens and politics. The resulting shift from political to administrative power, with its emphasis on bureaucratic expertise, was itself believed to reduce political participation (Skowronek 1982). Although PR elections were adopted within the context of these more widely known and implemented institutional changes, their core purpose—to ensure diverse representation for policy making—was intended to stimulate participation. ✓

The shrinkage of the electorate that occurred with the party realignment of 1894–96 is often attributed to the collapse of competition that accompanied the rise of a sectional party system in which Democrats dominated the South while Republicans captured a firm hold on the industrial Northeast and Midwest. Plurality voting systems left little incentive for minority party voters to go to the polls in either the South or the North. Most of the turnout decline occurred between 1900 and 1920, but the addition of women, then a large, relatively apolitical body of voters, to the electorate in 1920 contributed modestly to this trend (Kleppner 1987, 44–77).

The New Deal realignment of the early 1930s stimulated a national upsurge in electoral participation that peaked in 1960. Economically disadvantaged voters were mobilized by New Deal policies and by the growth and activity of labor unions, at least for presidential elections, a pattern interrupted only temporarily by the dislocations of World War II (Kleppner 1982, chap. 5). The relationship between PR elections and local turnout in Ohio must be evaluated in light of these larger trends.[5]

Characteristics of Council Members

Changes in the characteristics of council members were foreseen with the adoption of PR/STV. Proponents expected "better men" to be elected, as well as a wider representation of significant groups in the electorate. Opponents who held office feared that they would lose position and status, but they argued publicly that the average person would lose power when neighborhoods lost their voices, a concern that was based as much on the at-large feature of the system as on the STV ballot. Both political and demographic variables were examined to ascertain the nature of the changing composition of these five city councils over three electoral periods. The investigation included party affiliation, incumbency, race and ethnicity, gender, education, and occupation of council members.

Party affiliation. Partisan change occurred in the larger context of state and national party tides as the dominant Republican Party experienced first the Progressive split of the early twentieth century and then the sharp blow of the Great Depression. In the late 1920s and early 1930s, Ohio's generally weak, fragmented, and often co-opted local Democratic parties grew into effective electoral organizations as the Republican machines disintegrated. The nonpartisan ballot was more effective in some cities (Ashtabula and Cincinnati) than in others (Cleveland and Hamilton) in separating the local political sphere from its larger partisan context.

Opponents of PR argued that the two-party system would be damaged beyond repair by the adoption of PR, since minor parties would be among the minorities that could more readily elect their candidates. Under plurality-based electoral systems, from early in the twentieth century up to World War I, Socialists were occasionally elected in Ohio to both city councils and school boards. Before World War I, when the Socialist Party was growing nationally, its leaders endorsed proportional representation at the national and state levels. By the 1920s, shrunken by its opposition to the war and by the postwar "Red scare," the party took no position on electoral systems even as its candidates continued to run for local office, as did Communist Party candidates.

Incumbency. Under any electoral system, incumbency is expected to be an advantage for candidates seeking reelection. It is difficult to identify clear expectations about the impact of PR on the likelihood of voters returning incumbents to office. Some advocates argued that electing "better councilmen" with the interest of the whole city in view would lead to long-term commitments to public service. Other advocates claimed that bringing unrepresented groups inside would add stability to council membership. Opponents, who feared fragmentation from the representation of many small groups, cast doubt on such an outcome.

Quality of candidates. The Progressive reformers who engineered electoral change in the first half of the twentieth century were eager not only to enact their policy agenda but also to secure "better men" in positions of power. Generally "better" was understood to mean independent of party control and more educated than the council members traditionally elected from small wards, therefore drawn from the ranks of business and the professions. In communities that switched to PR/STV, this was to be achieved in three ways: by self-nomination through petitions, eliminating the primaries where parties were powerful even in nominally nonpartisan systems; by multicandidate rank-order choices on the ballot, making independent and minority candidacies more viable; and by enlarging the scope of the election to the city as a whole or, in the case of Cleveland, to large districts, making a wider range of candidates available for selection. "Quality" is measured (where available) by education and occupation, both measures that were significant to the reformers.[6]

Still, PR leaders appear to have understood that there was a difference between the often-used phrase "better men" and representativeness. Augustus Hatton, for example, author of several Ohio PR charters, would later analyze Ashtabula's first PR election for the *New Republic:* Rinto, a "young Finnish attorney," ranked sixth in first-choice votes but was edged out in the final count by the incumbent, saloonkeeper Corrado, "representing the wet interests as well as the Italian vote." Rinto's election over Corrado, Hatton wrote, "would have improved the quality of the council but would have made it less representative." On the whole, he concluded, the new council would "contain more ability than the present one elected on the ward plan . . . and be more representative of the entire body of voters" (Hatton 1915, 97–98).

Ethnicity, race, and gender. The representation of minorities previously excluded by winner-take-all elections was a frequently articulated goal of the electoral reformers. Ethnicity was less an issue for the descendants of the older, pre–Civil War immigrants to the Midwest, the Irish and the Germans, than for more recent arrivals from southern and eastern Europe. Yet even these newer Americans often found their way into politics through the integrative nominations that the bosses used to extend and consolidate their influence. All five cities used some wards for council elections before the adoption of PR, and two, Cleveland and Toledo, were entirely ward-based. Still, proponents of reform argued, PR elections conducted at-large would give opportunities to ethnic groups which were not residentially clustered to win their own representation. Opponents feared that this very opportunity would emphasize the role of what they called "racial and religious blocks" in city government.

While the reformers spoke and wrote generally of increased diversity as a goal, the election of women and African Americans was seldom explicitly promoted. Yet the Civic (later Citizens) League of Cleveland urged citizens to recruit and organize campaigns for "men and women of standing and influence," and maintained stoutly that "the council of a city of a million population calls for men and women of character, training, experience, ability, and capacity for leadership" (GC 1925, 2.2:4; 2.6:2). This same civic organization, which rated candidates for its members and for the public, listed selected black candidates as "preferred" or "well-qualified," sometimes modified as "a satisfactory representative of his people," as distinct from preferred white candidates who would "make a satisfactory councilman" (GC 1923, 1.1:5; 1925, 2.6:2ff.; 1927, 3.8:37–41; 1929, 5.7:35–45).

Fragmentation or Cooperation in City Governance

The model of city government most widely portrayed in turn-of-the-century debate over reform encompassed a small council, elected at-large by plurality vote, which would elect a ceremonial mayor, make policy, and hire a city manager who would administer the city efficiently and economically. The goal was purportedly to serve the interests of the city as a whole, not the interests of its component parts, whether neighborhoods or groups of citizens. Yet the official voice of the reform movement, the National Municipal League (later the National Civic League) actually called for PR/STV elections as the electoral system of the *Model City Charter* from 1915 through successive editions until 1964. The representative quality to be attained in the policy-making body was key to the recommendation.

Given this commitment of the reform leadership, perhaps the outcome to be explained is not the adoption of PR/STV in a few cities, but the failure of reformers to get it adopted more widely or to retain it where it was adopted. Perhaps the NML was ineffective; at least it was less effective than the opponents of PR/STV, who attributed European qualities to its practice. The only European country to use PR/STV, however, was Ireland, where it was adopted to ensure representation of the English minority in the Irish Dail. From the 1930s on, the system most often cited by opponents of PR was that of Germany under the Weimar Republic, whose electoral system was not PR/STV but proportional representation/party list (PR/PL), instituted without a threshold requirement for a minimum percentage of the vote for a political party to secure seats in the parliament.

Because of the many small groups represented in the Weimar Republic, arguably facilitating Hitler's rise to power, PR became vulnerable in the United States to the charge of causing political fragmentation leading to destructive conflict. The existence of stable European democracies that had elected their parliaments by PR/PL for decades, such as Belgium, Finland, Sweden, Denmark, and Norway (in some cases longer than Germany had), was not persuasive to opponents of PR, nor were explanations of the differences between PR/STV and PR/PL effective. Although proponents were confident that better policy would be developed by councils that reflected the true diversity of the city, opponents imagined fragmented public bodies racked by controversy over every issue to come before them.

To test the purported relationship between electoral systems and divisive behavior of councils elected by this system in the five cities, data were gathered on nonunanimous votes on substantive issues (both ordinances and resolutions) in selected years over three electoral systems.[7]

The historical record documented in the five-city research project supports some of the expectations of the reformers. Although municipal turnout was not demonstrably affected in most of the cities, characteristics of council members did change, especially with respect to the representation of minorities, as will be seen below. Little evidence can be found to support the fear that PR/STV would cause fragmentation of council behavior; indeed, improved consensus building was observed and appears to be linked to the electoral system. Findings drawn from the investigation will be summarized for each city, in chronological order of PR/STV adoption.

What Really Happened

Ashtabula

A small Lake Erie port city of about 20,000 population, Ashtabula was ethnically but not racially diverse. Originally settled by "Yankees" from

New England and New York State, the city attracted Irish immigrants from the building of the Erie Canal to the Civil War. Its location on the underground railroad made it a transit point for slaves escaping from the South through Ohio and across Lake Erie to freedom in Canada, but only a few settled there and by the PR period the African American population did not exceed a few hundred. With the development of the steel industry in Youngstown, Ohio, and Pittsburgh, Pennsylvania, the city became an important port for iron ore, shipped from the shores of the upper Great Lakes to Ashtabula and sent on to the mills by rail. Between 1870 and 1910, the city absorbed waves of immigrants from Finland, Sweden, and Italy. By 1910, a substantial majority of the population was either foreign born or had at least one foreign-born parent.

Ashtabula was governed by a mixed (ward and at-large) council and mayor, nominated in partisan primaries and elected on a partisan ballot. The council comprised four ward representatives and three members elected at-large. The Republican Party and the "native whites," citizens of Anglo-Saxon origin who constituted 43 percent of the population in 1910, were solidly in control of political life.

In 1912, a split in Ohio between regular Republicans and Progressives opened up political debate in Republican-dominant communities such as Ashtabula. At the same time, the Home Rule amendment to the Ohio Constitution ignited local initiatives for reform. Democrats and Socialists, distinct minorities in Ashtabula politics, joined Progressive Republicans to elect a local charter commission.

The political climate in Ashtabula was restive over issues of waste and fraud, and reform success seemed likely. Labor leader William E. Boynton was elected to the charter commission and chosen to be its first vice president. He worked hard, along with an equally enthusiastic chamber of commerce, to persuade the commission to recommend PR/STV as a way of improving representation in city government. However, a majority of the commission voted to propose retaining the existing electoral arrangements. The Ashtabula reform charter of 1914 was adopted without PR, but Boynton and his allies did not give up. In 1915, the pro-PR commission members succeeded in putting on the ballot a separate PR amendment to the new city charter, to go into effect before the November municipal election. Its advocates frankly promoted its adoption on the democratic ground that the city's diversity called for some assurance of minority representation in city policy making. Actually, there was no ethnic majority in Ashtabula, either native or immigrant, during this period, but the more recent immigrant groups were considered to be the minorities. The city's labor unions actively promoted PR and believed themselves instrumental in winning a majority vote. In August 1915, PR was incorporated in the city charter by winning 60 percent of the vote in a special election.

Ashtabula's voters would elect its city council by PR for sixteen years. Both the pre-PR and PR periods fell entirely within the nationally low turnout cycle before the New Deal, while the substitution of plurality at-large voting in 1931 coincided with a national upsurge in voting in the early 1930s. Although national trends cannot be entirely discounted, neither do they fully explain the changes in turnout under successive electoral systems. Pre-PR municipal tur   ed 66 percent of those registered, dropping s   ing the PR period. The decline actually set in, h   of women to the electorate in 1920, not with t   A post-PR rise in average turnout to 73 percent   panied the Great Depression and a growth in uni   actors not attributable to the electoral system. I   cal candidates seemed to drive turnout.

The characteristics of successful co   , changed significantly with the new electoral sys   h Republicans retained their council majority t   systems, the PR period saw a significant drop in Republican hegemony and a rise in independent representation. When plurality voting was reinstituted after the repeal of PR, Republicans more than regained their previous strength at the expense of both Democrats and independents, and incumbents experienced a dramatic rise in reelection success.

As in the other Ohio PR cities, minor parties failed to thrive. Before World War I, Socialists were organized and vigorous participants in Ashtabula politics. In the first PR election in 1915, Ashtabula's voters did elect to council R. W. Earlywine, a leading citizen and a Socialist who had served on the charter commission, the only instance of minor party success in all Ohio PR elections. The small size of the Ashtabula council—seven—meant that support of about one-eighth of the voters was required to elect a member. After World War I, the minor parties apparently could not muster such support for one candidate. The Socialists themselves split over doctrinal questions, particularly in the large Finnish community, and they grew even weaker electorally.

Ethnicity was an important factor in Ashtabula politics, in part because of the historic political and social dominance of the native white population. This group lost its majority status on the city council with the introduction of PR elections. Irish Americans were the leading beneficiaries of PR, because they were not numerous enough to win plurality at-large elections, and their residences, scattered throughout the city, prevented their success in any single ward of the old council. Finns, Swedes, and Italians also gained representation through PR. Italian Americans tended to live in more concentrated residential clusters, and they had achieved some representation by ward in the pre-PR mixed council, but they gained an additional seat by PR. These ethnic successes dissipated with the introduction of plurality at-large voting in 1931; only the Finnish representatives had become sufficiently accepted politically to maintain, and indeed increase, their presence on the council.

The cleavage between Protestants and Catholics in Ashtabula was more pronounced than that defined by ethnicity. The PR period (1915–31) encompassed Ohio's most heated local disputes about prohibition, the role of religion in public schools, and Sunday closing laws. In this small community, ethnic differences reinforced religious cleavages, while a watchful Ku Klux Klan operated on the shadowy edge of political life. Catholics more than doubled their membership on the council, reaching almost a third of the total. When plurality voting returned in the post-PR period, their electoral strength was diluted and Catholic representation dropped to its pre-PR level.

In Ashtabula, the black community was too small (less than 1 percent of the population in 1920 and 1930) to play a significant role in the city's politics. Although women must have been numerous enough, and they won the vote during the PR period, they apparently played a traditional apolitical role. From newspaper accounts it does not appear that either black candidates or women even ran in local elections under any of the three electoral systems.[8]

It is difficult to measure the impact of PR elections on the decision-making patterns of the council. Did diversity bring conflict to the table? Or did the ranking of candidates, with its incentive to soften sharp lines of attack in campaigns in order to win second- or third-choice votes from competing candidates' supporters, result in more moderate debate after the election? Would bringing previously excluded groups into the decision process encourage mediation of their demands? Conflict, so prominently covered by the press in Ashtabula, actually rose but slightly during the PR years. Most ordinances and resolutions passed unanimously, as they had before PR and would again after repeal. Analysis of the workload shows that while 12 percent of the ordinances were passed by divided votes in the pre-PR period, 17 percent were nonunanimous during the PR period, a proportion that dropped marginally to 16 percent in the post-PR era. The adoption of resolutions shows a similar pattern.

Since PR was implemented during a period of great national, statewide, and local debate over prohibition, the minority representation won by "wets" on a council previously dominated by "drys" could well explain the modest increase in nonunanimous votes. The selection of six city managers in thirteen years was contentious because the manager was responsible for enforcing the prohibition laws. Yet the repeal of the electoral system left the city manager plan undisturbed. Voters seemed to blame the representation on council of previously excluded religious and ethnic groups through PR as the cause of the turnover of managers. Furthermore, in 1929 the conviction, imprisonment, and removal from council of an Italian American councilman (a saloonkeeper originally elected from a ward under the old system) for violation of federal prohibition laws generated negative opinions that opponents succeeded in turning against PR. From newspaper accounts it would appear that repeal of PR was intended to exclude the minority group representation that had been achieved under PR. The post-PR council majority was native white, Protestant, and Republican, representing less than a majority of the population. Incumbents flourished, as their share of successive councils increased from 39 percent under PR to 71 percent of the total post-PR membership.

In the repeal campaigns, while conflict on council was presented by Ashtabula newspapers as the most negative aspect of PR elections, a technical issue relating to the count was a troubling element. In Ashtabula, the surplus for transfer was required to be taken proportionally from each of the precincts, but ballots were transferred "as they may happen to come in the different [precinct] packages, without selection" (Ashtabula City Charter 1915, as amended). This was believed to be a random draw, eliminating any possibility of favoritism, but it enabled chance to play a role in the outcomes. Instead of amending this obvious procedural flaw, the voters repealed the entire PR method of voting in 1929, with 58 percent of the voters approving council elections by plurality at-large.

After sixteen years of PR elections, Ashtabula, the first city in the United States to adopt PR/STV, became the first to repeal the system. Two repeal attempts, put on the ballot in 1920 and 1926 by Republican organization leaders who had seen their power slip away over time, were unsuccessful, but in 1929, in a low turnout election, their third initiative succeeded and plurality at-large elections became the rule. Policy-making power in Ashtabula returned to a council composed overwhelmingly of Protestant Republican incumbents, representing a plurality (the largest minority) of the city. The contribution to diversity made by the PR system was rejected.

Cleveland

At the time PR/STV was adopted for council elections in Cleveland, the city was Ohio's largest, its leading commercial, industrial, and financial center. With close to 800,000 people in 1920, Cleveland ranked fifth in population in the country. Moreover, to the reformers, Cleveland posed a special challenge. Its population was brimming with immigrants whose poverty, illiteracy, and lack of experience with democracy were believed to threaten democratic institutions' ability to work. Although Cleveland had been settled by New Englanders, significant numbers of Irish and German immigrants arrived before the Civil War. Between the Civil War and World War I, hundreds of thousands of immigrants came from southern and eastern Europe to work in the city's factories and steel mills. During World War I, labor shortages led the managers of major Cleveland companies to recruit black workers from the Deep South. These new migrants and their families augmented Cleveland's small black population, which had moved north largely from the border states before 1900.

By 1920, over two-thirds of the city's people were either foreign born or of foreign parentage. Although European immigration declined during the 1920s as a result of the national quotas of the 1924 Immigration Act, the number of black residents would double again before 1930 to 8 percent. Population growth also brought annexation and suburbanization. While Cleveland was still growing by annexing adjacent communities, the new residents of outlying areas maintained control of their core public functions by incorporating. By 1929, reformers would note regretfully that the "best citizens who should afford the political leadership of the community" had moved to the suburbs.

In the city itself, a Republican machine had consolidated power in the late nineteenth century, operating through traditional practices of patronage, graft, and favoritism in the granting of city contracts and utility franchises. Reform initiatives rose within the dominant Republican Party before 1900, but it was a Democratic mayor, Tom L. Johnson, a former business leader and congressman, who overthrew the Republican machine in 1901 and governed the city in a reform mode through four terms. Johnson and the Cleveland Municipal Association led the movement for home rule in Ohio, which was adopted in 1912 and which provided the framework for successive waves of reform. "Boss rule" was the principal target of the reformers.

In 1913, Cleveland adopted the state's first home rule charter, which decreed nonpartisan elections and increased the power of the mayor, but retained its ward-based council. The major reform introduced was the

Bucklin preferential ballot, permitting voters to express first, second, and "other" choices for their local council members (see chap. 2). Democratic reform mayor Newton D. Baker, author of Ohio's home rule provision and Cleveland's first home rule charter, was elected twice, but he was unable to dislodge Republican control of the council. The Republican organization adapted to the new electoral system with ease, instructing its voters to mark one choice only, while independents, often casting multiple preferences, helped elect party candidates over their own first choices by marking them as second or third choices. In 1915, the Republicans recaptured the mayor's office, and the reformers began drafting yet another charter. By this time, PR/STV had been incorporated into the National Municipal League's *Model City Charter* and adopted in Ashtabula. ⌐

Adoption and repeal of PR/STV. Many Cleveland advocates of the PR/STV ballot saw it as merely correcting the flaws of the Bucklin ballot. Clevelanders seemed to like preferential voting, and with the STV system, second or subsequent choices on a ballot would be counted only if the voter's first choice was already elected or trailed hopelessly at the bottom of the list. Peter Witt lost the 1915 Cleveland mayoral election because on the Bucklin ballot his supporters marked second and "other" choices for his principal opponent. Witt then chaired the Committee of One Hundred formed in 1921 to support a new charter that included PR/STV elections for Cleveland's council. The plan called for four large multimember districts to elect twenty-five city councilmen. Each district was to elect five, six, or seven members. Although smaller than Cleveland's then-existing council, elected from thirty-three (single-member) wards, the proposed PR council was large in contrast to Ashtabula's seven members elected citywide. Of the five cities in the United States that had adopted PR/STV by 1921—Ashtabula, Boulder, Kalamazoo, Sacramento, and West Hartford—only the small community of West Hartford used districts, electing fifteen council members from four districts (Moley 1923, 652).

Hatton fashioned Cleveland's district plan as a realistic compromise between the old ward-based council and a small at-large council. As an active participant in Cleveland politics, he recognized the deep roots of neighborhood loyalties in this largest and most cosmopolitan of Ohio cities. For the sake of winning reform, he wanted to avoid the bruising political battles of an earlier decade between white native Protestants and Catholic ethnic groups over ward versus at-large elections for the city's school board. The politics of religious and ethnic representation were familiar to Cleveland voters, and the stakes were high.

A city manager plan was closely tied to the adoption of PR/STV. Since the manager would be in charge of administering the city, the charter's sponsors considered it critical to ensure a broadly representative council that would appoint the manager and make the policies that guided administration.

A vigorous campaign to adopt the proposed charter was launched by the Committee of One Hundred, the Union Labor PR Club, the new Cleveland League of Women Voters, the *Cleveland Press*, and the Socialist paper, the *Cleveland Citizen*. Powerful forces opposed the charter, including the *Cleveland Plain Dealer*, both political parties, the Chamber of Commerce, and the Cleveland Federation of Labor.

Given this sharp division of opinion among the city's leaders, the charter's approval in November 1921 by 57.2 percent was startling. The charter passed in twenty-nine of the city's thirty-two wards, with support strongest in wards populated by native-born whites with high levels of school attendance and high voter participation. Since the parties were targets of the reform rhetoric, it was not surprising that support was weak in wards where the parties were well organized, foreign stock and black voters lived, and levels of school attendance were low (Mingle 1974, 81–88).

Victory in a city the size of Cleveland was celebrated by election reformers across the country. Political scientist and advocate Chester C. Maxey wrote, "If Cleveland, with her 800,000 people of every race, color and creed, can accomplish such a thing, what may not democracy dare to hope!" (Maxey 1922b, 13).

Cleveland governed itself through the 1920s under this reform charter, conducting five municipal elections by PR/STV. Four repeal initiatives, fueled by political ambition, were defeated between 1925 and 1929. The first, initiated by both parties, attacked only the PR sections of the charter and was narrowly defeated in a small turnout. Harry Davis, the former Republican mayor of Cleveland and a one-term governor of Ohio, sponsored three more repeal issues, aiming to restore the office of popularly elected mayor, which he believed he could win. These too went down to defeat. By 1931, although PR's advocates argued that the electoral system was gradually increasing the independence and ability of council members, its critics attacked both PR and the manager plan as "the boss plan" and urged its repeal "to return the city's government to the people," ironically the same theme used in the 1921 campaign to adopt the PR charter. Ray T. Miller, the crusading Democratic county prosecutor who had earned his fame by sending Republican (PR-elected) council members to the penitentiary in the late 1920s, was a prominent leader of the successful 1931 charter repeal campaign.

In 1931, Cleveland was heavily burdened by unemployment, hunger, and radical unrest, and a popularly elected mayor and ward council members who could provide city jobs for their constituents were strong attractions. Their appeal was concrete and practical, not abstract and theoretical. More significantly, the historic national shift in electoral strength from Republican dominance to a newly energized Democratic Party occurred in Cleveland between 1928 and 1932. As the Democratic Party approached majority status, its leaders lost interest in the PR/STV ballot's ability to ensure minority representation. Plurality voting, which would assist a new majority to consolidate its power, became more attractive. Both Davis and Miller were elected to the mayor's office for a term in the 1930s under the new (unreformed) charter, and Miller ultimately became the boss himself.

The only Ohio city to repeal PR in the depths of the Depression, Cleveland replaced its reform institutions with a large, ward-based council elected by plurality and a popularly elected mayor. The single reform element retained, the nonpartisan ballot, was at most a facade, since the parties had survived all manifestations of reform at little cost. Throughout the PR period in Cleveland (1923–31), the Republican organization had maintained its majority control of council, and its leader, Maurice Maschke, had selected the city managers. Indeed, the defeat of PR in Cleveland marked also the defeat of the old Republican machine, weakened by the scandals that reform had failed to prevent.

Although the large-district compromise had facilitated the 1921 adoption of PR/STV in Cleveland, it became a source of dissatisfaction to reform leaders in that city as well. The districts were aggregations of the old wards, which operated unchanged as the building blocks of the party organizations. The demise of the reform charter in Cleveland was hastened by the tepid support it received in 1931 from its natural constituency, the reformers, who were then distracted by efforts to promote what they thought would be a better PR/STV electoral system. Significant segments of the reform leadership advocated a smaller (nine- or fifteen-member, PR-elected) at-large council, undermining support for the existing system.

Impact of electoral system change. Within the context of these complex factors associated with adoption and repeal of PR/STV in Cleveland, we can now examine the impact of three electoral systems on turnout, representation, and consensus among council members.

As in Ashtabula, Cleveland's pre-PR and PR periods fell entirely within the low turnout cycle before the New Deal, whereas the abandonment of

PR coincided with the national upsurge in voting in the early 1930s. In Cleveland, however, the average turnout for municipal elections in both the pre-PR and PR periods was relatively high, at 77.5 percent of registered voters. Elements of continuity that may have contributed to consistent turnout patterns through the two periods include the earlier adoption of the nonpartisan ballot and preferential voting in Cleveland, and the Republican machine's uninterrupted control. The number of voters who went to the polls increased significantly in the last PR election (1931), which was also the occasion of the hotly debated fifth repeal initiative. Average turnout for the post-PR period dropped by 10 percentage points, to 67.6 percent, but the significance of the decrease is blurred by a change in the registration law of Ohio. It is difficult to show a clear impact of changing electoral systems on turnout in Cleveland.

Political tides sweeping Ohio and the nation from the aftermath of World War I through the Great Depression make it difficult to ascertain the partisan impact of electoral system change. Cleveland's long-entrenched Republican organization retained control of election outcomes in the transition from ward-based preferential voting to PR/STV. The Republican majority on the council grew marginally under PR at the expense of Democrats; independents earned almost 10 percent of the seats, replacing both Socialist and Democratic ward-elected members. The return to a large ward-based council in the 1930s was marked by a decline in the Republican majority to a plurality only, with a strong and rising Democratic minority and a shrinking independent presence.

Although the city had a significant history of minor party activity, minor parties did not appear to benefit from the PR/STV ballot in Cleveland. Between 1910 and 1920, Socialist Party candidates won not only in preferential ward elections for city council but also in plurality at-large elections for the school board. In a highly publicized confrontation in 1918, however, two elected Socialists (who had defeated incumbents in 1917) were expelled from the council for "disloyalty to the United States" because of their opposition to American participation in the war. The charged wartime atmosphere apparently deterred Socialist Party candidates from running for council in 1919, but in 1921 they returned to the electoral arena. During the PR period, there were small party candidates, including Socialists, Workers, and Communists, on the PR ballot in all four Cleveland council districts. But in these five-, six-, or seven-member districts, the minimum vote required to win a seat (one-sixth, one-seventh, or one-eighth of the total vote) was too stiff a barrier to surmount, and no minor party candidate was elected, in spite of some ratings of "qualified" from the reformers.[9]

Continuity and change in council members' characteristics. There is little evidence in the Cleveland case of an election system effect on incumbency. The firm control held by the Republican organization through pre-PR and PR elections and the continuity of the old wards, which were clustered to create large PR districts, help to explain the continuity of incumbent success through two electoral systems. Almost two-thirds of council members were reelected under both systems. However, in Cleveland's post-PR system less than half of the incumbents were reelected. Although ward lines remained unchanged through all three systems, the post-PR council was created at a time of party upheaval. Republican dominance was crumbling as Democrats _____ in the city, and incumbent officials were on the vulnerabl _____ sition. The independents, hailed in 1925 as th _____ no would be brought into public service by refo _____ pursuits (or out of the city) after a term or tw _____ small groups, hoped for by some and feared by _____ ed.

But had the "quality" of candi _____ red by the traditional variables of education _____ hanges in the expected direction are observed _____ ce. Knowledge of the extent of change is limit _____ ion levels of 30 percent of pre-PR Cleveland c _____ be ascertained. During the PR period, the proportion know.. _____ attended college increased from the pre-PR 44 percent to 60 percent. A further rise in education levels in post-PR, when the council was elected from thirty-three small wards, to almost 64 percent who had attended college suggests that the measure reflects a linear rise occurring in educational attainment over time among the population generally, and therefore among candidates and especially among successful ones. Some changes in occupational status could also be observed. The shift to PR was accompanied by a 10 percent increase in professional members, a corresponding decrease in business occupations, and a smaller decline in blue-collar representation. In post-PR, with the council elected from wards, the share of members from the professions (mostly lawyers) did not change, but business representation dropped again more than 10 percentage points while the blue-collar share rose by that amount. This was hardly surprising in light of the growing strength of the Democratic Party.

In Cleveland, ethnic representation was not an issue. A wide array of ethnic groups already had distinctive voices on the council in Ohio's most diverse city. In the pre-PR period, ethnically clustered neighborhoods, ward elections, and the preferential ballot combined to facilitate diverse representation. Furthermore, the Republican organization had absorbed and elevated prominent men in the nationality groups as ward leaders, positions that enabled them to be or to recruit candidates and required them to get their voters to the polls. Cleveland's Republican organization adapted comfortably to the PR/STV ballot, losing power only in the economic crisis of the early 1930s, as ethnic voters began to transfer their allegiance to the rising Democratic organization. With post-PR's ward-based council, Cleveland's many ethnic pockets retained their representation even as their residents switched parties.

In Cleveland, women ran as candidates but were unable to win in the ward elections of both pre- and post-PR. Women were elected, however, in each of the PR elections (1923–31), making up 6.4 percent of the total PR council members. The multimember districts of the 25-member PR council may have facilitated women's victories; but the cultural context of Ohio's Western Reserve was also supportive, as organized women worked first for suffrage, then for PR, and subsequently for the candidates they trusted.

African American representation grew in proportion to the city's black population growth, from one to three members in the PR period, although initial access had been achieved earlier. The Republican organization had promoted and secured the election of Thomas W. Fleming, a black barber and later an attorney—known as "the Negro ward boss"—since 1911. He was easily elected from his ward on the pre-PR council and continued to win election on the PR ballot from his multimember district in 1923 and 1925. In 1927, two additional black candidates won election and three African American seats became the norm on the 25-member PR council. When PR gave way at the depths of the Depression to a thirty-three-member ward-based council, black candidates were able to hold their own because of the residential segregation that had intensified during the 1920s as the black population grew. Indeed, African Americans were proportionally represented on the Cleveland council under all three electoral systems (1917–37), but through distinct channels.

Conflict and consensus. In the Cleveland experience there is little evidence of unusual conflict in the way its council did business, even though it reflected the diversity of the city's population. Most ordinances and resolutions passed unanimously under all three electoral systems. The percentage of nonunanimous votes on substantive issues rose slightly over time, from pre-PR (1.4 percent) through PR (2.2 percent) to post-PR (3.7 percent). The highest percentage of nonunanimous votes in any single year occurred in 1936 (7.5 percent), in the post-PR ward-based, plurality-

elected council. A leadership contest that erupted in the partisan transition of the 1930s from Republican to Democratic control was the major
source of divided votes. The fears of fragmentation of power through the
workings of PR proved to be unfounded.

Although prohibition-related corruption and self-dealing by council
members in the sales of public land were uncovered (and punished) in the
PR period, significant public improvements were initiated and completed,
public services were expanded, and taxes were lowered. City Manager
William R. Hopkins believed to the end that the city manager plan, not PR,
had dragged down the reform charter in the estimation of voters, and in
1935 he would advise a New York City charter commission to adopt
PR/STV for council without the city manager plan. The post-PR council,
absorbed in arranging patronage to alleviate hardship among friends and
relatives, seemed unable to stem the deterioration of services and the
decline in revenue brought on by the Depression. Former opponents of PR
joined its advocates to call for restoration of the PR–city manager charter.

Such a proposal for the city did not reach the ballot, but reformers
found a wider arena for their ideas, promoting a county charter to improve
metropolitan governance. In 1935, a countywide charter commission proposed a charter incorporating a county manager and a nine-member
county council to be elected at-large by PR/STV. To ensure fair representation from all parts of the county was believed to be essential, both to
pass the charter and to govern effectively when it was implemented. This
charter was approved by Cuyahoga County's voters in November 1935,
with Cleveland, the largest of sixty cities in the county, casting a significant margin of votes for its adoption. Before it could be put into effect,
however, the Ohio Supreme Court invalidated the entire charter on a
technicality unrelated to PR.[10] And so the "great experiment in democracy" ended, later to be referred to by local historians as "the city manager
years" (C. P. Miller and Wheeler 1990, 120).

Cincinnati

Within a year of Cleveland's first PR election, Cincinnati voters
adopted a reform charter that, like Cleveland's, provided for city council
elections by PR/STV. Cincinnati's charter movement was empowered by
opposition to the traditional machine-style practices of the Republican
organization, led by the legendary George B. Cox and his successor,
Rudolph K. Hynicka. Accustomed to controlling local politics for decades,
the organization seemed to be disintegrating by the second decade of the

twentieth century under the pressure of investigations of corruption and indictments for perjury (Z. Miller 1968, 205–8, 239–40). In 1924, close to 70 percent of Cincinnati's voters approved a "good government" charter, drafted by reform activists and built on a city manager plan and PR elections. Three decades of reform government ensued (1925–1955), transforming the city's reputation in civic-minded circles.

The longevity of PR elections in Cincinnati, surpassed in Ohio only by its northern neighbor, Hamilton, may be attributed to the political skills and persistence of the reform coalition, which brought together Democrats and independent Republicans in a virtual political party. The Charter Committee recruited candidates, conducted campaigns, defined coherent platforms, and mounted opposition to five repeal initiatives, defeating four of them. In 1957, the fifth repeal initiative succeeded, ending the PR period.

The second-largest city in the state, Cincinnati grew relatively slowly from 401,247 residents in 1920 to 503,998 in 1950. Although Irish and German immigrants had settled in the city in the nineteenth century, it seemed homogeneous in the twentieth, with only 11 percent foreign born by 1920 and 7.5 percent African American residents. While the percentage of immigrants in the population would steadily decline through the PR period, the black population grew slowly to 15.6 percent in 1950 and 21.6 percent in 1960. Suburbanization was also slow. In contrast to Cleveland, where many professional and business leaders had moved out of the city by 1930, Cincinnati's middle and upper middle classes were more firmly rooted in city neighborhoods.

Cincinnati's pre-PR council, composed of twenty-six ward representatives and six elected by plurality at-large, was dominated by the Republican Party. In the three pre-PR elections, the victory of thirty-one, twenty-nine, and thirty-one Republicans on the thirty-two-member council fueled the drive for reform. A home rule charter, adopted in 1917, had made few changes in the local government structure, but it provided a footing for further change. A fiscal crisis in 1923 jolted the community into action. The charter presented to the voters and adopted in 1924 featured a council of nine members elected at-large, with administration by a city manager. Independent Republicans of the Charter Committee had insisted on the city manager, while the Progressive Democrats of the coalition successfully bargained for PR elections. The large multimember districts of Cleveland's charter, originally drafted for Cincinnati as well, were dropped from the final version presented to the voters (R. A. Burnham 1992, 209). Republican Murray Seasongood insisted that the Cincinnati charter "avoided the objectionable features of the Cleveland charter which, by requiring only 2,000 or 3,000 votes for election, made racial, geographical, religious, and other blocs possible" (Seasongood 1933, 25). PR was meant to provide an opening for opposition to the Republican machine, Seasongood contended, not to introduce factionalism into government.

Still, proponents viewed the city as a "pluralistic entity composed of separate but equally legitimate and interdependent groups and classes, which deserved, among other things, a voice in city government" (R. A. Burnham 1997, 132). Although most black voters, as loyal supporters of the Republican organization, voted against the proposed charter, one group, the political branch of the local Universal Negro Improvement Association (founded by Marcus Garvey), backed the charter because of its PR component. In the early PR council campaigns, its chairman, William Ware, urged black voters to cast their first choice vote for an independent black candidate and then mark Charter Committee candidates as their second, third, and subsequent choices on the ballot. Not until the late 1930s did the Charter Committee integrate its own ticket.

In 1931, however, Cincinnati's first black council member, Republican-endorsed Frank A. B. Hall, was elected, after running twice unsuccessfully as an independent. Competition for the fifth seat on council appears to have forced the endorsement. In 1937, the Charter Committee changed its strategy. Instead of conceding the black vote to the Republican organization, the Charter group began to include a black Republican candidate on its council ticket. Not until 1949, however, with the endorsement of a black Democrat, attorney Theodore M. Berry, did the Charter Committee's African American candidate win. Berry, recent past president of the Cincinnati NAACP and a leader in the growing civil rights movement, quickly established a major role in Cincinnati politics, winning reelection and ultimately displacing Jesse Locker, the Republican organization's black council member.

By 1957, owing to Berry's popularity and the council's practice of electing the top vote-getter in the council race to be mayor, the possibility emerged of a black mayor. Indeed, Berry was poised to become mayor in 1957 when the fifth repeal initiative appears to have been pushed over the top by a racist whispering campaign against PR.[11] Of the reform features of Cincinnati's local government, only the PR ballot was repealed; the small at-large council and the city manager were not challenged. In the next two elections, Berry lost in the plurality at-large (9X) contests, and in the third post-PR election he chose not to run. Although Berry would run again in the 1960s, would win, and would even be elected mayor by his fellow council members, the defeat of PR/STV in Cincinnati in 1957 can be attributed to what would today be its greatest strength, the ability to facilitate the representation of minorities.

Impact of electoral system change. Evidence of electoral system effect on the turnout of Cincinnati voters is unclear. The pre-PR and early PR years fell within a low national turnout cycle, while most of the PR years were played out during a time of generally greater political activism, including voting. The post-PR years followed the 1960 national turnout peak, into another era of decline. With no registration data for pre-PR Cincinnati, turnout under its pre-PR mixed systems is difficult to evaluate. The system was partisan, with a separately elected mayor, often believed to encourage turnout. The change to PR/STV also converted the system to a citywide election on a nonpartisan ballot without a popular mayoral election, all conditions believed to discourage turnout. During the thirty-four years of PR/STV, however, Cincinnati turnout averaged 62.4 percent of registered voters, with a range from a high of 75.8 percent to a low of 51.7 percent. The fluctuations in turnout under PR in Cincinnati did not follow national voting trends, but appeared instead to be shaped by local issues and candidates. With the change to plurality at-large (9X) elections in 1959, turnout dropped to an average of 56.9 percent for the post-PR period. This dip in average turnout did coincide with a post-1960 decline in voting turnout nationally, but it was interpreted by some contemporary observers to result from the loss in representation experienced by Charterites and African Americans under plurality at-large voting.

Continuity and change in council members' characteristics. Changes in the likelihood of incumbents' reelection were clearly associated with changing electoral systems. Although traditionally high, incumbent safety increased with each innovation. Perhaps because of effective control by the Republican organization in the wards of the pre-PR years, 61 percent of council members were reelected. With PR, the proportion rose to 67 percent, and when PR was repealed, it rose again to 81 percent. Plurality at-large voting seemed to provide the greatest advantage to incumbents.

The paucity of educational data for council members before 1925 makes it hazardous to draw conclusions about the impact of PR elections on the status of those elected. Occupational data, more generally available, indicate that a majority (55.2 percent) of the pre-PR ward-elected members were in small business, while professional (15.6 percent) and blue-collar (14.6 percent) occupations accounted for most of the others.

With the implementation of PR, occupational status was clearly altered. The majority for the PR period was professional (52.8 percent), whereas the business presence dropped to 27.1 percent and blue-collar fell to 6.3 percent. The plurality at-large council of post-PR continued these trends, with 55.6 percent professional, 25.9 percent business, and no blue-collar members. PR/STV seemed to represent a midpoint between ward elections and at-large plurality elections, since with PR/STV candidates ran citywide but could win with a strong appeal to a limited constituency.

Of the five Ohio PR cities, Cincinnati experienced the most dramatic partisan change. The mixed pre-PR council, which was 95 percent Republican, gave way to a Charter Committee majority in nine of the sixteen PR elections. Although the Charter majority was composed of independent Republicans, Democrats, and independents, it was a coherent and integrated coalition that rightfully earned the label of political party. A stable local two-party system functioned effectively throughout the PR period. Although independents were occa ' ~ollv elected, minor party candidates were unsuccessful under all thr   With post-PR plurality at-large elections, the Repu   trol, as its leaders had anticipated in their repe   R elections. For more than a decade after repe   y fractured into Democratic and Charter mino   r 1998, 46).

Because of the relatively ho   Jincinnati's white population, ethnicity seems n   cant political role in this era. The city's principa   man origin, but by the 1920s German immigrar   ent of the population (R. A. Burnham 1992, 7   ultural distinctiveness, German Americans were po....   nd held leadership roles both in the major party organizations and in the reform movement.

The experience of African Americans was quite different. Prior to PR, no black candidates had been elected in Cincinnati, which was in many ways a southern city. They won representation on the PR ballot, however, an advance that was lost in the post-PR plurality at-large elections. In Cincinnati, black candidates on the PR ballot first ran unsuccessfully in the 1920s and 1930s as independents, then, having demonstrated some electoral strength, were endorsed by their respective parties for the next election, which they won. Party competition clearly enhanced their prospects, since both Charter and Republican organizations were striving to capture at least five seats on the nine-seat PR council. But they were not recruited by a party, as had happened much earlier in Cleveland in pre-PR elections. It would appear that the opportunity structure provided by PR—the ability to appeal citywide to a black constituency, which needed to number only one-tenth of the voters plus one—was the underlying factor in their self-recruitment. Furthermore, party support was not sufficient to elect African Americans to the plurality at-large council in the post-PR period. Yet on eleven of the sixteen PR councils and on every council from 1941 through 1955, one or two African Americans were elected.

Women had experienced a political triumph in Cincinnati before the adoption of PR. In a victory symbolic of the newly attained right to vote, in 1921 two women were elected to at-large seats on the mixed pre-PR council. Women played an important organizational role in Charter Committee activities leading up to and throughout the PR period, but they were elected only three times in sixteen PR elections. Although women were nominated, it appears that Charter forces did not actively promote their candidacies. In fact, in 1927 Charter leader Murray Seasongood assured an audience in Atlanta that PR would not mean women's "control." Although they were important workers in the PR movement, he said, they "have been thoroughly unselfish about it, not even aspiring to positions as women and effacing themselves as candidates in the forthcoming election" (Seasongood 1960, 76). A female candidate won a single term in 1943, but not again until civic leader Dorothy Dolbey was elected in 1953 and 1955 on the PR ballot and was reelected on the plurality ballot in 1957 and 1959. Her visibility as a two-term incumbent and as vice mayor under PR undoubtedly assisted her successful transition to plurality at-large elections.

Conflict and consensus. Since the impetus for PR had been to introduce opposition into the operation of local government in Cincinnati, conflict would be an expected behavior on the PR councils. Yet a thorough contemporary study of the Cincinnati council votes found that most tallies were unanimous. Little evidence of conflict is identified even when an independent served as one of the nine members. The election of the mayor and the filling of council vacancies provided the occasions for most divided votes (Straetz 1958, 62–96). Numerous studies of Cincinnati's PR-elected government (the most studied of its kind) have shown that the election of a working party majority facilitated decision making. Moreover, the electoral pressure to appeal for second- and subsequent-choice votes from supporters of other candidates appeared to reduce tension on the council once the election was over. This pattern of operation persisted in the post-PR period. While machine control had provided stability in the large ward-based council of the pre-PR years, the small at-large council facilitated the election of incumbents, which in turn provided stability in the PR and post-PR years.

Hamilton

Hamilton is a small industrial city just north of Cincinnati that grew from 39,675 in 1920 to a peak of 72,354 in 1960. PR/STV was used for seventeen city council elections over more than three decades in Hamilton, the most extended experience with PR in the United States other than in Cambridge, Massachusetts. Before adoption of PR in 1926, Hamilton was governed by a popularly elected mayor and a mixed council composed of a council president and three members elected at-large, plus six members elected from wards. Candidates were chosen in a partisan primary and elected on a partisan ballot. Unlike the power structure of the other Ohio PR cities, the ruling organization was Democratic and the boss was the mayor himself, Harry Koehler.

As in the larger "boss-ridden" cities, a strong reform movement was actively engaged in city politics. Earlier reform regimes had been elected in 1913, when a Socialist mayor and majority of council were elected, and in 1923, when the local Republicans gained control. Both reform regimes lasted but a single term, swept away by the Democrats, whose hold on power was deeply rooted in the political culture of rural southern Ohio. Hamilton was reputed to be a "wide-open town" where liquor interests, gambling, and prostitution operated under the shelter of the Democratic organization.

The 1926 reform charter introducing the city manager plan and PR/STV elections was adopted in Hamilton, as in Cleveland, Cincinnati, and Toledo, its advocates maintained, to "restore power to the people." A Charter Commission, elected in 1925 as the new PR charter was being implemented in nearby Cincinnati, unanimously recommended a similar plan, but with seven council members for this smaller city instead of nine. The class conflicts that seemed to characterize politics in Hamilton were evident in the business, professional, and Woman's City Club leadership of the charter campaign. Significant opposition arose in two low-income wards where Appalachian in-migrants were beginning to weigh in politically. However, the president of the Trades and Union Council joined the fray on the side of the charter, and even Mayor Koehler endorsed it. The charter passed narrowly.

During the three decades of PR/city manager government, local politics seemed insulated from state and national trends as Hamiltonians split their political loyalties. In the early years, Republicans, running without their party label, gained a working majority on the city council while the voters supported Democratic candidates for state and national office. By the 1950s, with memories of the Koehler regime fading, the voters were returning a Democratic, labor-endorsed majority to the council on the nonpartisan PR ballot, while the growing presence of Appalachians among the voters shifted the city to the Republican column in the winner-take-all state and national elections. The extraordinary longevity of the reform regime in Hamilton may be attributed to its cohesive and programmatic character, while the opposition, known as antiestablishment, was diverse and conflictual. Antireform forces included those who favored the old ways of the "wide-open city," labor groups critical of their own leaders, and the politically active Ku Klux Klan. ⟍

Hamilton's PR-elected government survived four repeal attempts, the first three initiated by the displaced Koehler faction of the Democratic Party, a group that by 1933 had been unable to get even one candidate elected on the PR ballot. The fourth repeal initiative, in 1944, was a flawed measure that required the election of a new council at the very (national) election in which the question of repeal was to be decided. The fifth attempt, however, in 1960, after thirty-four years of PR elections, was a different matter. The 1957 repeal of PR in Cincinnati was fresh and close at hand, and all the other Ohio PR cities had abandoned PR. All but Cleveland had kept their city managers, so the administrative element of the reform plan appeared secure. Hamilton had twice as many voters as when PR was adopted, and many of PR's original proponents had died or moved to the suburbs. The electrifying element of the 1960 repeal campaign, however, was its leadership by a disappointed candidate, AFL-CIO president Robert Westfall. Westfall had ranked sixth (of seven) on first-choice votes in the 1959 election, but dropped to eighth in the transfer process, while a reform slate candidate, Jack Blumenthal, won the seventh place by transfers, securing a reform majority. When a vacancy occurred early in 1960, the majority appointed not Westfall, the runner-up, but the top losing candidate of its own slate. Using the appointive discretion provided by the charter was not illegal, but this was a political mistake that probably sealed the fate of PR in Hamilton.

Over more than three decades, Hamilton conducted seventeen PR/STV elections, and it had been sixteen years since the last repeal attempt. Few issues related to the electoral system can be identified in Hamilton. Race was not publicly articulated as an issue, although the small black community had achieved representation through the PR ballot. It appears that a disapointed runner-up was able to defeat the election system by exploiting the community's unease about the majority's appointment of its own candidate to the vacancy. The presidential year with a close election provided the largest turnout any repeal issue had seen. Sixty-six percent of eligible adults voted on repeal, although typical turnout in Hamilton's local elections was about 40 percent of eligible adults under all three electoral systems examined here. PR was voted out by a greater number of Hamiltonians than had ever voted in a local PR election.

An additional irony was to be observed in the post-PR years that followed. Westfall ran for council in 1961, received the highest vote of any candidate, and automatically became mayor under a provision of the amended charter. Republicans won a majority in the second post-PR election (1963), Democrats in the third (1965). But the council elected in 1965 broke into three factions unable to assemble a majority to make important policy decisions, an outcome that had not occurred in three decades of PR elections. Moreover, in post-PR, despite Westfall's dramatic win in 1961, the blue-collar presence on council had shrunk to half its late-PR share.

In spite of Democratic machine dominance in pre-PR Hamilton, voters were rather evenly divided between the major parties, as demonstrated by volatile swings from Democratic to Republican and back to Democratic majorities on council. Over th   ies tied, each gaining an average of half of the   ly PR period, Republicans carried a majority of   ction; by late PR, Democrats just as consistentl   gradual partisan shift in the community. Pl   the post-PR period brought back the unstabl   experienced before PR, with the Democrats h   iod.

Because of the lengthy period   from pre-PR through post-PR (1926–1965),   les could be advanced as explanations for char   least the tides of national politics that ebbed and   in local elections appears to have increased and dropped with local candidates and local issues, both within election system periods and between them, leaving no pattern to explain. *Hamilton*

The stability of membership on the council did change with electoral systems, with less turnover occurring in each successive electoral system. The instability of the pre-PR election outcomes have been noted, with the partisan swings of the electorate's close division in party voting. Only 23 percent of incumbents were reelected in the pre-PR period. This incumbent success rate more than doubled with PR elections, to 57 percent reelected, and increased again but less dramatically, to 67 percent in the plurality at-large voting that followed PR. Over the years of PR elections in Hamilton, many council members appear to have built stable citywide constituencies over time. An additional factor was the combination of at-large elections and the nonpartisan ballot, common to the PR and post-PR periods, calling for greater visibility for successful candidates than the pre-PR ward-based portion (six of ten members) elected with party labels from small districts.

The most notable changes resulting from Hamilton's PR elections were found in the occupations of council members. The pre-PR council was composed of industrial workers (60 percent) and men in small business, sales, and clerical positions. The proportion of blue-collar council members dropped in the early PR years to 19 percent, but rose through three decades to 33 percent in the late period of PR. Business representation increased with PR, and one professional member was generally elected. In the post-PR period, blue-collar representation dropped again to the early PR level, but the business sector fell also to 19 percent. With a slight increase in professional members, the post-PR council showed the most diverse array of occupations to be found in the entire span of three election periods.

Women's political activity was growing in Hamilton as elsewhere in the mid-1920s. Women were elected to the partisan office of treasurer as well as to the nonpartisan school board. In pre-PR council races, one woman was an unsuccessful candidate. As in Cincinnati a few notable women played visible political roles as advocates for a home rule charter, for PR, and as candidates for council. Also as in Cincinnati, only three times were women elected by PR/STV, in 1943, 1945, and 1951. This feat was not to be repeated, however, until the post-PR elections of 1961 and 1963. The PR system with nomination by petition rather than by partisan primary may have helped these women make their mark in local politics, but their successes were few.

Hamilton's population was the most homogeneous of the PR cities of Ohio, with less than 7 percent foreign born in the 1920s and less than 4 percent African American. Although the population almost doubled between 1920 and 1960, its predominantly native white character did not change. The black population grew only slightly, to 6 percent of the total, while the foreign-born presence shrank. The major change in composition of the population was cultural, resulting from the in-migration of

Appalachian whites seeking jobs in Hamilton's burgeoning industries. Because they were native whites, their access to representation in their new community is difficult to measure.

The opportunities for self-starters through nomination by petition brought the black community into organized politics. The first black candidate ran in the first PR election, but not until the late 1940s did this small minority win representation. The pattern established in Cincinnati was the key to success. A Hamilton dentist, Dr. L. L. Hunter, ran unsuccessfully as an independent in 1947, a race that led to his recruitment by the reform slate in 1949 when he was elected. A second black candidate, Fred Grant, was appointed to a vacancy on the council in 1957 because he had placed eighth in the final count of the 1955 election. In November, running as an incumbent and a member of the antiestablishment slate, he was elected to a full term. Like Dr. Hunter, Grant became a transfer loser when he ran again as an independent. A place on a slate seemed essential for a minority smaller than the PR threshold, 12.5 percent of the total vote for a council of seven. These limited successes, however, brought leaders of the black community into the pro-PR coalition, and they worked for its retention throughout the repeal initiatives. Their judgment proved correct in the post-PR years, when no African Americans were elected to council.

A major difference in council behavior developed during the PR period in Hamilton. In the pre-PR era, 75 percent of the substantive roll call votes were nonunanimous, showing that discord was the most common result of discussion and debate. With the PR-elected council, split votes dropped to less than 10 percent in the early years, and rose only to 11 percent in the late years of PR. With the new plurality-elected regime in the 1960s, conflict rose again to 19 percent nonunanimous votes on substantive issues. Under all three electoral systems, conflict arose over enforcing the gambling laws and choosing council's leadership. But social conflict seemed to subside under PR. Contemporary newspaper accounts suggest that the PR-elected councils operated with a high degree of consensus to improve city services, achieve financial accountability, and extend public power.

The transfer process in Hamilton tended to benefit candidates from the reform slate who seemed to perform an integrative function, coming to the public policy table with broader backing than the candidates who had placed ahead of them on first choices. If the representation of voters' values and preferences provided by PR "vented" conflict through the council, then PR operated successfully, and its demise is owed not to its failure but to the political leaders who were displaced and sought a return to the familiar ways of the old politics.

Toledo

Toledo's proportional representation elections came embedded in a 1934 home rule charter that was itself the culmination of a long series of Progressive reform efforts. Toledo experienced eight PR elections before repealing its new electoral system in 1949 when the fifth and successful repeal initiative left the charter's other reform elements in place—nonpartisan ballots, the city manager, and a small at-large council.

A large manufacturing city at the western end of Lake Erie, Toledo had a population of 290,718 in 1930, with 12 percent foreign born, 27 percent foreign stock, and a 4.6 percent African American presence that would grow to 8 percent by 1950. A home rule charter, adopted in 1914, was the result of many years of colorful reform advocacy by Samuel M. "Golden Rule" Jones, mayor from 1897 to 1904, and his associate and successor, Brand Whitlock, Progressive mayor from 1905 to 1913. The innovations of that charter were the provisions for nonpartisan primaries and nonpartisan elections for the mayor's office and the twenty ward council members. By the 1920s, however, the Republican county organization, chaired by Walter F. Brown, had gained informal control of the city government. The City Manager League was formed to initiate further institutional reform measures. Four charter amendments reached the ballot, two in 1928 and two in 1931, but all were defeated by the voters. Of these, a charter commission proposal for a small PR-elected council and the city manager plan was the most popular, winning 41 percent of the total vote in 1928.

This was the plan chosen by the City Manager League to bring back to the voters as a charter amendment in 1934, at the depth of the Great Depression when the city's economy was in ruins. The city's civic leaders steered the effort to success at the polls; University of Toledo students campaigned from door to door on its behalf. The Central Labor Union fought the very idea of at-large elections; the Republican organization was ready to accept the city manager plan but called PR "un-American," sounding a theme that would resonate the following year in the first campaign to repeal the newly adopted form of government before an election for the new nine council members could even occur.

This and three more repeal initiatives in 1937, 1945, and 1946 were beaten back by an amorphous reform coalition that was severely weakened by the City Manager League's decision in 1941 to withdraw from its political partylike activities and to become a research organization. This decision was a turning point, marking the decline of an active reform movement in Toledo. The opposition was organized by a variety of sources. Josephine Guitteau, an anti-PR activist, led the 1937 and 1946 repeal campaigns to return to a twenty-one-member ward-based council. Arguing that a large council was more representative and therefore more democratic, she attacked PR as a system under which minorities would "dominate" the council. Her deputy's reputation as a former Ku Klux Klan leader lent an ominous overtone to the debate. The 1945 repeal effort was initiated by the CIO-PAC with a starkly different goal: to retain the city manager and the nine-member council elected at-large, but by plurality, not by PR. Even dissatisfied reformers found this flawed because the plan lacked a primary.

As the minority party in Lucas County until the mid-1940s, the Democrats had benefited from PR elections. Increasing links between local, state, and national politics aided the growth of the Democratic Party, which in 1947 for the first time won control of the Toledo city council. Yet its chairman, John P. Kelly, opposed PR as unfair and too complex, claiming, "I never could get the point of it." Kelly objected also to a technical flaw in the method of transferring surplus votes, similar to Ashtabula's problem. The count was conducted at the board of elections. As the votes were counted, once candidates reached the quota their ballots were set aside; all surplus transfers came from the ballots not yet counted. Hence the order in which precinct ballots arrived at the board might affect the final outcome. The charge of "lottery" was not totally unjustified.[12]

It was Kelly who led the final challenge to PR elections in 1949, adding to the CIO-PAC plan of 1945 a nonpartisan primary to select eighteen council candidates, nine of whom would be elected by plurality vote. The language of the campaign was captured by PR's opponents. Both the ballot and the media defined plurality at-large voting as "Popular Voting," and the pro-repeal slogan became "PV versus PR."[13] Sixty-five percent of the voters chose to repeal PR. The 1949 repeal vote by ward showed that support for PR had eroded to 38 percent in the upper-income wards, which had previously returned the largest majorities for PR. In the Polish and Hungarian wards, which had initially opposed PR but then supported it after "their" candidates were elected, favorable votes also evaporated. It was only in Ward 8, with its concentration of black voters, that PR retained its constituency, 56.4 percent voting against repeal.

Unlike the other Ohio PR cities, where turnout of voters rose and fell with local issues and candidates rather than in a pattern associated with the electoral system, Toledo experienced a modest but measurable decline in local voting during the PR years. The entire pre-PR, PR, and post-PR periods in Toledo fell within a high national turnout cycle. Local elections showed a different pattern. While an average of 47.3 percent of the adult population voted for the old ward-based city council in the pre-PR period, the average voter turnout for the eight PR elections fell to just under 40 percent. However, by the last PR election, turnout had increased to 47.3 percent, the average of the pre-PR elections. Turnout dropped significantly in the first post-PR election, to 38.6 percent of eligible adults, but the average turnout for the post-PR period showed a slight increase over PR-era voting to 43.8 percent of the adult population. The dislocations of population associated with World War II could be expected to explain the drop in turnout during the PR period (1935–49), but at the same time the turnout was rising in congressional and presidential voting. In Toledo this was a period of growing Democratic and union political activity, which may have had a more significant impact on turnout in partisan races than in the nonpartisan local elections.

Local elections in Toledo had been nonpartisan since 1914, but the pre-PR ward-based council was predominantly Republican, a pattern replaced by more competitive outcomes under PR. Party affiliations became better known because of candidate slates. The Republicans won 64 percent of the council seats elected by PR, but the party's margin narrowed gradually over time, until the Democrats gained a majority in the last two PR-elected councils. Occasionally in the pre-PR period Socialists and Communists had been elected to the city council. Independents were elected in four of the eight PR elections, but, as in most other Ohio PR cities, no minor party candidates won. In the first winner-take-all post-PR election, eight Republicans and one Democrat were elected, but in the following three elections the Democratic majority was restored and independents disappeared. Toledo's relatively late partisan shift to the Democrats, a shift that other northern Ohio urban industrial areas had experienced during the Great Depression, was reflected in these local nonpartisan contests.

The continuity of membership on Toledo's council increased after the changeover to PR elections. In the first PR election, only one of the twenty incumbents won under the new system, but for the remaining PR elections, the incumbent success rate rose from an average of 42 percent of pre-PR council members who were reelected from the wards every two years, to an average of 73 percent, almost three-quarters of all PR-elected members. The sharp partisan swings of the post-PR winner-take-all elections, in contrast, reduced the power of incumbency, and the likelihood of reelection fell to just over 50 percent of the council members.

Changes in socioeconomic status were more clearly tied to the electoral system. The wards of the pre-PR council sent a majority (56 percent) of small business people as representatives, with blue-collar occupations second in importance (19.5 percent). In the PR period, representation became more diverse. The blue-collar presence was maintained (20.8 percent) but professional occupations rose from 2 to 42 percent, replacing many of the business representatives, now down to 34.7 percent. In post-PR, blue-collar representation disappeared altogether, while professional and business occupations held their own. Since education levels rose dramatically in each of the reform periods, what seems to have happened is that at-large elections, requiring greater resources for campaigns, raised the status of winners in all occupational categories. In the at-large setting, PR saved representation for organized labor. With the loss of the PR ballot in post-PR, even union leadership disappeared.

The PR ballot was significant also in facilitating the representation of ethnic and racial minorities. Polish Americans comprised the ethnic group least residentially concentrated in Toledo and were unable to win representation by ward. Residing in two different neighborhoods, the Polish community, although originally opposed to changing electoral systems, gained the presence of one or two members on each PR-elected council by using the transfer process to support its candidates. In 1945, the first African American to be elected, James B. Simmons Jr., was able to win in spite of the fact that blacks constituted only 7 percent of the population at that time. With a 10 percent threshold to win a seat on the nine-member council, Simmons had to gain white support and apparently did so through the transfer proce[...]d 1949 on the PR ballot, Simmons lost in 1951[...]lity voting in spite of endorsements by the pres[...]the United Labor Committee, and reform lead[...]er League. Public-ity about his 1951 loss and t[...]in the community appear to have enabled him t[...]plurality elections of post-PR.[14]

Politics was still a man'[...]h-century Toledo. Women were absent from the[...]ugh the City Man-ager League had a Women's A[...]rvives that women participated in reform efforts.[...], who championed the old order in PR repeal campaigns, was conspicuous. In the PR period, only four women ran for council positions, and none ranked higher than eighteenth place. Without the mobilization of support, even an electoral system designed to diversify representation cannot manufacture results. In post-PR, women disappeared even as candidates.

The changes in representation brought by PR elections did not lead to the factionalism predicted by its opponents. In fact, as measured by divided roll call votes on substantive issues, conflict was reduced even as the workload of the council increased in the PR period. The twenty-one-member council elected from wards in 1933, for example, cast nonunanimous votes on 26 percent of all ordinances, a degree of division that dropped sharply to 7 percent on the first PR council, 4 percent in the middle years of PR, and 9 percent on the last PR-elected council. The first post-PR council maintained a low level of disagreement, with 4 percent nonunanimous votes on ordinances coming before it. Votes on amendments, where the most disagreement would be expected as the details of legislation are worked out, followed a similar pattern. The small council and its citywide election may have contributed to this phenomenon, but it is at least clear that the diversity produced by minority representation did not result in the feared polarization of the council.

Common Threads in the Abandonment of PR

The stories are legion of the achievements of PR regimes, including expansion of services and the building of infrastructure for cities that were both growing and diversifying, but they are difficult to quantify. The comparative history of urban policies is obscured by the aberrations of the politics of place. But the progress that was said to be made has usually been credited to the city managers, not to the electoral system. In all but Cleveland, when PR was repealed the city manager was retained, along with the small at-large council; the only major change was the substitution of plurality voting for the PR/STV ballot. The old political bosses had lost power under the reform charters. Republican organizations in Ashtabula, Cincinnati, and Toledo and the Democratic organization in Hamilton were displaced from power, producing avid leaders of repeal efforts. Their struggle to regain the old perquisites of municipal control drove the repeal initiatives. Whereas Cleveland voters were disillusioned because so little had changed under the reform charter, a new alignment of forces in the other cities galvanized the old into opposition. Although eventually the reform leaders tired of the struggle and moved to the suburbs or died, nevertheless, for a time city politics provided an arena in which contests between reform and reaction were lively.

Only in Cincinnati did reform leaders build, nourish, and sustain a constituency for PR elections. Although Scandinavian and Irish Americans in Ashtabula, Polish Americans in Toledo, and African Americans in Cleveland, Cincinnati, Hamilton, and Toledo gained significant representation by the PR/STV ballot, the proponents of PR did not use these gains in minority representation as organizing tools for their cause. Because they did not organize the beneficiaries, reform leaders lacked practical local support to fight against repeal in time of need. What looks today like a failure to play from strength actually may have been a defensive strategy to downplay the success attained by ethnic, religious, and racial minorities through the PR ballot, precisely because the system was vulnerable to the unpopularity of such representation. In repeal campaigns, minority success was often alleged to contribute to divisiveness in the community.

In all five cities, opponents of PR used the complexity of the tally and transfer of the STV ballots as their lead point. Defenders used the PRL's argument that telling time and buying insurance were common human activities easily conducted without understanding how clocks, watches, or actuarial tables worked. It was a fact that the counts were time-consuming; opponents criticized the delay, while defenders praised the drama of public observation of the transfer process.

The repeated challenges to PR may themselves have had a cumulative effect. Although each repeal attempt grew out of specific ambitions, resentments, and concerns, the general impression of unpopularity emerged from the constant attacks. In three cities—Ashtabula, Cleveland, and Cincinnati—46 percent or more of those voting favored repeal every time the issue was put on the ballot. In Hamilton and Toledo, lower rates of opposition were recorded, but the vote for repeal did not fall below 27 percent of those voting anywhere in Ohio.

Like adoption of PR/STV electoral systems in Ohio, the rejection of PR reveals common problems in addition to the factors unique to each city. First, displaced political leaders sought a return to winner-take-all elections as a means to regain control of public office. Second, reform forces failed to organize the minorities that gained representation under PR/STV into effective advocates of its retention. Finally, and perhaps most significantly in the long run, the political climate of the first half of the twentieth century did not favor the outcome that PR/STV was designed to produce—precisely, the representation of minorities.

The Significance of Transfer Votes

In most PR elections in the four Ohio cities where transfer data are available, the leading candidates on first-choice votes were the ultimate winners of the election. Although transfers at subsequent stages of the count frequently changed the rank order of the winners, only about 10 percent of the total seats on PR councils in Ohio were won or lost by transfers.[15]

A "transfer winner"—a candidate who did not place among the leaders on first-choice votes but moved up in rank to winner through the transfer process—was an integrating candidate with fairly broad support in the electorate. In contrast, a "viable loser" (or "transfer loser")—a candidate who placed among the leaders on first-choice votes but failed to gain the minimum required vote by the last transfer—had a substantial but narrow base of support that was not broadened by second-, third-, or subsequent-choice votes from the supporters of other candidates.

The advantage of reform endorsements was clear in Cleveland, Cincinnati, and Hamilton, where transfer winners were more likely than transfer losers to be reform-endorsed professionals with higher levels of education. They were also more likely to be Democrats in Cleveland and Charterites in Cincinnati. Transfer losers were conversely more often Republican and were significantly less educated. This combination of attributes probably indicates that they were candidates of the old Republican machines. Only in Cleveland did a woman fall into either of these categories; she was a transfer winner.

African American candidates tended to win on first-choice votes, and occasionally had surplus votes that were often (but not always) transferred to other minority candidates. However, about a fourth of the transfer losers in Cincinnati and Hamilton were black candidates who started in the top circle and, because of insufficient transfer ballots, dropped too far to win. In both Cleveland and Toledo, all transfer winners and transfer losers were white.

Toledo results show a less distinct pattern than the other cities. Reform and labor endorsements were found equally among transfer winners and transfer losers. Polish Americans, a significant minority in Toledo politics, were also present in both categories. The impact of the rejected ancien régime was also muted, as the former (apparently discredited) mayor was a transfer loser in the first PR election, although two of his henchmen won with relative ease in the first two PR elections, and each became a transfer winner in two subsequent races. Individual candidacies and idiosyncratic political factors appear to have shaped these outcomes in Toledo.

Overall, the transfer process of PR/STV appears to have made a modest difference in electoral outcomes. The limited vote aspect of PR (each voter ultimately supports one candidate instead of seven or nine) shows a more significant impact on African American representation. It is clear that in a PR election, as in any multicandidate contest, effectively promoted slates assist both partisan and nonpartisan groups to achieve their goals. Ranked voting on the PR ballot, however, with subsequent transfers during the count, ensured that minority candidates would not defeat each other and the majority would not capture all the seats.

Analysts often relied on the transfer option to explain the greater consensus in the operations of PR councils. In order to win transfer votes, candidates needed to appeal for second-, third-, and other choice rankings from voters whose first choice was committed to another candidate. Personal attacks among candidates therefore became a dysfunctional campaign strategy. As a result, less friction seemed to carry over from the campaigns into the operations of the council, and less was introduced in anticipation of the next campaign.

Conclusion

The struggle for proportional representation begins to make historical sense in the context of competing yet overlapping political cultures, one based on ethnic roots and communitarian values, the other on rational functions and individualism. The representational theory in which PR is grounded bridged the gap between these contrasting worldviews by allowing for self-defined identities—whether ethnic, racial, political, or unaligned—to integrate themselves into the policy-making function of local governments.

Indeed, diversity of views *within* the PR movement itself reflected (in a narrower band) the pluralism of the reform movement generally. At one end of the ideological spectrum were individualists, such as Murray Seasongood, who feared a low threshold of election lest religious and ethnic groups gain too much power. At the other end were Tom Johnson and Jane Addams, who valued PR for its very ability to bring such groups into governing structures. Yet all agreed that more representative policy making should result in the efficient implementation of public policies that would serve social justice.

The history of PR in the cities examined here—an experience barely mentioned in major works of urban history—illuminates a far more complex set

[handwritten margin note: does PR integrate these ~~functions~~ approaches or simply impose one on another?]

[handwritten note at bottom: increased representativeness = efficiency?]

of values motivating both reformers and bosses than was previously recognized. Many of the most powerful bosses of the early twentieth century
were Republicans who operated in the interest of private entrepreneurs
who held economic power. They were supportive of reforms, like the city
manager plan, when they could control the choice of managers, as Maurice Maschke did in Cleveland. Maschke supported PR as well in two of
the five repeal efforts, a positio   pport for "his"
city managers, and by the contin   dates for council. Many of the reformers were   onomic justice
through passage of labor legislat   scope of governmental services, as well as ch   rnment.

   The motives of PR proponer   e similar: the
reformers sought to wrest power f   turn it to ordinary people whose diversity they   xtent appreci-
ated. Most PR advocates shared   ves the desire
to equalize the burden of taxatio   n favor of the
wealthy; to expand public service   eation, parks,
and sewage treatment; to regulate local labor practices; to extend public
ownership to private utilities; and to promote efficiency in the delivery of
these public services. They were committed to the city manager plan as
the means of introducing efficient public administration into American
communities. Unlike many of their fellow Progressives, however, they
understood policy making as the critical function of a broadly based and
diverse council, representative of all important groups in the city. They
saw "free" voting and "full" representation, both attributes of PR, as tools
for achieving these substantive goals.

   The proportional representation movement and its sponsors may have
been largely absent from either traditional or revisionist accounts of the
period because they failed to fit into the prevailing analytical dichotomy.
PR/STV now appears to have been a political reform launched ahead of
its time. What it did best was to facilitate the representation of both the
majority and substantial minorities in the governing process. Although
this quality was important to the advocates of PR, it was not a major concern in the broader local politics of the first half of the twentieth century
in the United States. In fact, the election of previously unrepresented or
underrepresented minorities was often cited by PR's opponents within the
reform movement as a weakness, because it undermined the dominant
faith that there was an objective interest of the "city as a whole" that could
be represented through correctly structured elections.

   The pluralist view that the city was a mosaic of interests and groups, not necessarily geographically based but entitled to participate in the making of public policy, was held by too few to sustain this particular reform. Even with the backing of the National Municipal League and its model charters from 1915 on, PR advocates were forced into a defensive position as early as 1920, when the initial repeal issue reached the ballot in Ashtabula, the first PR city. Although the pluralist vision was articulated in the PR literature of the day, it did not capture either the mainstream of the reform movement or—because of its antiparty thrust—the old political establishment.

The analysis of what actually happened in five Ohio cities that used PR/STV elections between 1915 and 1960 tells us that this electoral system was neither as powerful a tool of governance as its proponents hoped, nor as damaging to the polity as its opponents claimed. As only one of a group of reforms introduced into the structure of urban government—nonpartisanship, the at-large election of a smaller council, and the city manager plan were the better-known components—the change in electoral system had limited impact. The professional and educational levels of council members rose; minorities gained representation where they had been underrepresented or not represented at all before.

Myths that have obscured the understanding of proportional representation for many years should be dispelled. The conventional wisdom came to be that the PR/STV ballot was too complicated for people to understand, causing turnout to decline. In four of the five cities this turned out not to be true. Turnout rose and fell with local issues and personalities in each of these cities. Although some voters may have been deterred from going to the polls, others were encouraged to vote because of their improved chance to win some representation. Overall turnout was not demonstrably shaped by the electoral system.

Another myth that has persisted through the years is that PR produces fragmentation of the political system because of the more accurate representation of segments of society. In none of the Ohio cities using PR elections was there a significant increase in conflict among council members. In fact, it appears that the electoral pressures of ranked voting led to greater consensus as campaign styles changed. Although comparative urban policy studies have yet to deal adequately with important substantive areas, such as education, parks, labor practices, and public works, with which Progressive Era reformers were concerned, the five cities appear to have "worked" during their PR years.

In these five Ohio cities, PR/STV was demonstrated to be an electoral system technically capable of facilitating public decision making in complex communities as well as producing fair representation. Four decades have passed since the last repeal of PR/STV in Ohio. These passing years have witnessed rapid political and societal changes in the expectations and aspirations of Americans and in the ways they relate to their governments at every level. The pursuit of fair representation continues even as the definition of "fair" has shifted from the representation of self envisioned by John Stuart Mill to the representation of groups, increasingly self-conscious and determined to be heard. As an electoral system capable of channeling the expression of diverse values and policy preferences, PR/STV is once more, at the turn of the millennium, becoming the subject of public debate about who is entitled to participate in decisions and how they might do so.

5

The Voting Rights Act
and the Right to Representation

THE FUTURE OF PROPORTIONAL REPRESENTATION in the United States may be very different from its past. Demographic and political pressures are opening the political system to fresh ways of looking at the meaning of democracy. As the population becomes more diverse, better educated, and at the same time less participatory, citizens, lawmakers, and judges are seeking new ways to implement political values that are as old as the nation. The meaning of equality continues to evolve.

In the first half of the twentieth century, intense political battles were fought in the United States over voting and representation. The difference between the right to vote and the right to representation, however, was not widely understood. The right to vote spoke to the suffrage question: who should vote, an issue that depended on legislative majorities and on judicial interpretations of federal and state constitutions. The right to *representation,* nowhere constitutionally specified, depended on electoral systems that translated those votes into power.

Plurality ballots and geographically based districts have traditionally been used in the United States, in spite of the fact that winner-take-all elections, whether conducted in single-member districts, multimember districts, or at-large, render large numbers of ballots ineffective and may leave significant groups unrepresented. Those with resources have formed interest groups to perform the representative function indirectly on their own behalf, while those without resources have increasingly withdrawn from politics, polarizing the American system. Although the gridlock of interest groups and the decline of electoral turnout cannot be attributed to only one cause, the skewed system of representation is clearly a contributing factor.

Only since the right to vote was virtually settled by its federal enforcement under the Voting Rights Act of 1965 has the right to representation been directly addressed. As underrepresented plaintiffs asserted that a right was being violated by their exclusion from a fair share of seats at the public table, the legal and constitutional concept of "minority vote dilution" took shape. Attempts to remedy practices that restrict the ability of minorities to speak for themselves on city councils, in legislatures, and in Congress have shaken electoral systems to their roots. In the 1990s, controversies over apportionment and districting, the number of officials on a governing board, and the appointment of a key federal election law enforcement official erupted in public debate. The central, often unstated question at the turn of the twenty-first century is whether the country will continue to accept the winner-take-all rule as its guiding principle of representation.

This chapter will trace the development of both a constitutional and a statutory right to representation, note common remedies for violations of the right, and explore new developments in the use of alternative electoral systems to facilitate fair and effective representation. Finally, it will be argued that since winner-take-all elections polarize the electorate and exclude significant numbers of voters from representation, the right to be represented can only be fully secured by some type of proportional representation.

Minority Vote Dilution and Proportional Representation

The context of the American debate about representation has changed significantly since the end of the Ohio experiments with PR in 1960. The black civil rights movement and the heightened consciousness it generated among other underrepresented groups led to cases in the federal courts and to congressional legislation that, step by step, expanded the right to vote to encompass the right to representation. Although this fuller right remains ill-defined, it includes the right not to have one's vote diluted by an electoral system that denies a fair opportunity to elect candidates of one's choice.

Before 1960, the right to vote meant access to casting a ballot; by 1982, it required evaluation by the results of elections. In adopting results as a standard, however, courts and Congress specified that proportional representation is not required. Minorities previously excluded from power by a winner-take-all system are entitled to a remedy, but how much representation (less than proportional) is enough remained unclear. In 1994, the U.S. Supreme Court conceded the validity of proportionality as a standard by which fair representation could be measured (*Johnson v. DeGrandy*). These developments are significant for the future of electoral systems. Although proportional representation is not *required* under current judicial interpretation of the laws and the Constitution, neither is it prohibited. Could its time at last have come?

Constitutional Roots

The concept of vote dilution is not limited to the underrepresentation of minorities. In fact, it was the underrepresentation of the *majority* in the majority-rule system that gave rise to the first finding of unconstitutional vote dilution. In 1964, the malapportionment of state legislative bodies that gave the rural minority of voters greater representation than the urban majority was held to be unconstitutional. This condition existed in virtually all the states. The urban majority gained protection when the U.S. Supreme Court held that "diluting the weight of votes because of place of residence impairs basic constitutional rights under the Fourteenth Amendment just as much as invidious discrimination based upon factors such as race or economic status" (*Reynolds v. Sims* 1964, at 566). The Court's analysis focused on the individual right—each person is entitled to an equally weighted vote—but the political impact of the ruling was anticipated by groups: rural voters who would lose their privileged position, and urban voters who would gain their fair share of power.

Even before *Reynolds*, the Court had observed the element of unfairness in winner-take-all election results. Invalidating one of the more egregious voting arrangements that degraded the value of urban votes, the Supreme Court struck down Georgia's county unit system by which a candidate for statewide office gaining the most votes in a county would win the entire "unit vote" assigned to that county (*Gray v. Sanders* 1963). The number of unit votes assigned to each of the many counties of Georgia was not proportional to the county population. Foreshadowing the outcome of *Reynolds*, the Court found the fatal violation of the Fourteenth Amendment in the inequality of the population ratio to unit votes. Moreover, in a little-noticed note, the Court pointed out that "even if unit votes were allocated strictly in proportion to population," the losing candidate's votes were counted "only for the purpose of being discarded" (at 381, n.12). The Court failed to observe, however, that this flaw exists in every winner-take-all election system and would be remedied only by proportional representation

(J. Still, 389–90). This critical insight failed to take root in the Court's thinking about representation, or among voting rights activists, and became a passing anomaly.

The purpose of the Court's remedy for unequal populations was presented as "fair and effective representation," a goal defined only by the simple numerical standard of one person, one vote. In *Reynolds*, the Court allowed remedial choices of either multimember or single-member districts as long as the population criterion—equal numbers of representatives for equal numbers of people—was not violated (1964, at 577).

Plurality voting in multimember districts, however, raised the probability of shutting minorities out in winner-take-all sweeps. In 1965, in a challenge to Georgia's new multimember state senate districts, the Court ruled that such districts, although not in themselves unconstitutional, might be invalid if they "operate to minimize or cancel out the voting strength of racial or political elements of the population" (*Fortson v. Dorsey* at 439). In 1973, this discriminatory effect led the Court to reject a multimember district plan for the Texas legislature by which minorities, although able to cast votes, were denied access to representation. The Court cautiously pointed out, however, that invalidating a plan that discriminated against minority voters was "not the same as declaring that every racial and political group has a right to be represented in the legislature" (*White v. Regester* 1973, at 769).

Single-member districts have generally been the preferred remedy for such discriminatory effects. For minority groups that are residentially clustered, single-member districts may produce the desired relief. But districting is not a neutral activity. Whether the impact on representation is deliberate or accidental, district lines help some groups and handicap others. Racial gerrymanders were for many years a key tool for the exclusion of African Americans from representation, either by dividing a cluster of minority voters into several districts where they were nowhere a majority, or by concentrating them into one district where, as a supermajority, their votes were wasted.[1]

Evidence of such racially discriminatory districting led the Court to support what came to be called the affirmative gerrymander. Here, political boundaries are drawn deliberately to create single-member districts for minorities that previously experienced discriminatory exclusion from a legislative body. A New York State districting plan that created two new majority-minority state legislative districts for black and Hispanic voters was challenged by Hasidic Jews whose community was formerly concentrated in one majority-white district. The Court upheld the plan splitting the Hasidic community between the two new districts on the ground that the minority groups gaining representation had been denied representation in the past, whereas Hasidic Jews would be fairly represented in the legislature as a whole by whites elected from other districts (*United Jewish Organizations of Williamsburgh, Inc. v. Carey* 1977). This approval of "virtual" representation for the Hasidic Jews (representation by someone they did not elect who was presumed by race to share their values) would return to haunt the racial gerrymander cases of the 1990s.

This decision highlights the power of districting authorities to assign value to different groups and to shape the dimensions of political conflict. In the 1970s, the Burger Court's working theories about representation placed "group political access" above the individual voter's right to be equally represented (Maveety 1993, 221). Partisan groups as well as racial minorities gained protection. In *Gaffney v. Cummings*, the Court upheld a Connecticut legislative districting plan that protected incumbents and therefore could be expected to perpetuate the existing division of power between the two major political parties. "Rough proportional representation of the statewide strength of the two parties" was found to be a legitimate state goal, not a violation of the Fourteenth Amendment Equal Protection Clause (1973, at 738, 752). This decision gave constitutional approval to incumbent protection. Today, as a result of over a quarter century of incumbent-controlled line-drawing, sitting legislators choose their constituents at redistricting time, in clear violation of democratic theory's assumption that constituents choose their legislators.

Although reluctant to open its doors to all claims of unfair partisan gerrymandering, the Court grew more willing to look at electoral arrangements that "consistently degrade a voter's or a group of voters' influence on the political process as a whole" (*Davis v. Bandemer* 1986, at 132). Still, in this Indiana case, the Court showed its anxiety about entering such a political thicket. While finding the plaintiffs' allegation of a partisan gerrymander to be appropriate for court review, when it came to the merits of the case the justices were not persuaded by fairly blatant evidence that a gerrymander had occurred. A "mere lack of proportional representation," whether for a partisan or a racial group, could not prove unconstitutional vote dilution (at 121–37).

Statutory Enforcement: The Voting Rights Act

The Voting Rights Act of 1965 (42 USC § 1973 [1994]) was passed to enforce the right to vote that is implicit in the Fifteenth Amendment. Evidence of continuing discrimination in voting practices and even outright exclusion of African Americans from the polls led Congress to strengthen earlier attempts to protect voting rights. Some violations were so egregious that Congress required states in which discriminatory practices were serious and persistent to get permission from the District of Columbia federal district court or from the civil rights division of the Justice Department before changing voting regulations (§ 5). In sustaining this unprecedented restriction of state power, the U.S. Supreme Court held that "the right to vote can be affected by a dilution of voting power as well as by an absolute prohibition on casting a ballot" (*Allen v. State Board of Elections* 1969, at 569). This proved to be a significant step on the path to a substantive right to representation.

In 1967, for the first time since 1929, Congress required the states to use single-member districts for congressional elections. This measure was taken to prevent the states covered by the Voting Rights Act from using statewide winner-take-all elections to diminish the electoral opportunities of newly empowered black voters (2 USC § 2c 1994).

In 1970 and again in 1975, Congress extended the Voting Rights Act, each time expanding its coverage and adding new federal protections to the right to vote. The 1975 renewal (for seven years) broadened the act to reach language minorities, specifying Hispanics, Alaskan natives, Native Americans, and Asian Americans as protected classes. This provision, which relied on congressional power to enforce the Fourteenth Amendments equal protection clause, also expanded the geographical scope of the act to wherever significant concentrations of these language minorities are identified (§ 4).[2]

In 1982, Congress found that minority vote dilution continued to exclude some Americans from full political participation. It extended the Voting Rights Act again, this time placing the entire country under federal protection against minority vote dilution for twenty-five additional years. Moreover, a new standard was defined for judging violations (§ 2). The courts had required a showing of *intent to discriminate* in order to prove a constitutional violation (*City of Mobile v. Bolden* 1980), but intent was difficult to prove. Congress provided an alternative statutory path for minority vote dilution cases by substituting *results* of elections as probative in section 2 cases.

Illegal vote dilution is now defined as any "voting qualification or prerequisite to voting, or standard, practice, or procedure" that "results in a denial or abridgement of the right of any citizen of the United States to vote" on account of racial or language minority status. A violation can be proven by showing that "the political processes leading to nomination or election" in a state or locality "are not equally open to participation" by these minorities and that their members have "less opportunity than other members of the electorate . . . to elect representatives of their choice." The statute permits consideration of "the extent to which members of a protected class have been elected to office," but stipulates that "nothing in this section establishes a right to have members of a protected class elected in numbers equal to their proportion in the population" (42 USC § 1973(a) [1994]).[3] Here Congress added its weight to the Court's denial that minority vote dilution requires proportional representation as a remedy.

Judicial Application of Standards

In the decade after passage of the 1982 amendments, hundreds of cases challenged plurality at-large or plurality multimember district elections on the grounds of minority vote dilution in elections for city councils, county commissions, state legislatures, and the U.S. house of Representatives. In 1991, state judicial elections were subjected to federal review as well (*Chisom v. Roemer* 1991; *Houston Lawyers' Assoc. v. Atty. Gen. of Texas* 1991; E. Still 1991).

Until 1986, the federal courts required plaintiffs to show that the "totality of circumstances" in the political process of nominations and elections created unequal access to power for minority voters, a standard drawn from an earlier federal court of appeals decision (*Zimmer v. McKeithen*, 5th Cir. 1973). Since 1986, claims have been decided by a more rigorous three-part test put forth by the Supreme Court to determine whether such elections prevent minority voters from electing candidates of their choice. First, the plaintiff minority group must be "sufficiently large and geographically compact to constitute a majority of a single-member district." Second, the minority group must be "politically cohesive" enough to be able to elect a candidate in such a single-member district. Third, it must be shown that "the white majority votes sufficiently as a bloc to enable it . . . usually to defeat the minority's preferred candidate" (*Thornburg v. Gingles* 1986 at 50–51, 56).

[margin handwritten note: Gingles test]

The Court's criteria in *Thornburg v. Gingles* look to the remedy of single-member districts, yet, as demonstrated in chapter 3, single-member districts create difficulties of their own in achieving fair representation. Plurality voting leaves minorities within districts unrepresented. White voters placed in the new majority-minority districts have complained of becoming mere "filler people," voters who provide "numerical chaff to the representational wheat of another group" (Aleinikoff and Issacharoff

1993, 632). Members of minority groups may become filler people as well, as blacks and Hispanics found in contesting each other for majority status in Florida legislative districts (*Johnson v. DeGrandy* 1994, at 1023).

Additional complex issues include how small remedial districts must be and therefore how many are required in a statewide plan; how district lines are to be drawn to ensure majority-minority districts; how often lines must be redrawn to accommodate population mobility; and how concentrated a majority-minority must be to have a genuine opportunity to elect candidates of its choice without wasting minority votes in supermajorities (Grofman, Handley, and Niemi 1992, chap. 5; Morrison and Clark 1992). Mixed systems merely add to these districting problems the potential for vote dilution of a few at-large seats, a category in which minorities are most underrepresented in the nation generally (Engstrom 1992, 746–47).

On the level of practical politics, as distinct from constitutional theory, an obvious test for fair representation of minorities in a single-member district system is whether the share of majority-minority districts is proportional to the minority population. In spite of its earlier denial that proportional representation is required, in 1994 the Court actually applied this criterion as a benchmark in a Florida districting case. Evaluating a state legislative districting plan alleged to dilute minority voting strength in Dade and Escambia Counties, the Court refused to find illegal dilution because the number of districts in which minority voters (both Hispanic and African American) formed effective voting majorities was roughly proportional to their respective shares in the voting-age population (*Johnson v. DeGrandy* 1994). Proportionality meant equal electoral opportunity. Insisting that the Court was not recognizing a right to proportional representation, Justice Souter distinguished "proportionality," which he called "the political or electoral power of minority voters," from "proportional representation," which he defined as "a guarantee of electoral success for minority-preferred candidates of whatever race" (*Johnson v. DeGrandy* 1994, at 1014, n. 11). This distinction proved confusing at best, since proportional representation election systems, as the term is commonly used, actually provide only the opportunity, not the guaranteed result, of gaining representation.

The minority plaintiffs in *Johnson v. DeGrandy* had petitioned for the maximum possible number of majority-minority districts. This the Court rejected. Even though two more Hispanic districts for the U.S. House of Representatives could have been drawn, the state was not required to create them: "One may suspect vote dilution from political famine, but one is not entitled to suspect (much less infer) dilution from mere failure to guarantee a political feast" (*Johnson v. DeGrandy* 1994, at 1017).

The claim to a maximum possible number of minority districts raises the issue of losing districts in which minorities can influence (although not control) their representatives. In order to craft more minority districts, line-drawing authorities must draw minority voters out of integrated districts where they could *influence* the selection and actions of a representative. Arguably, minorities lose rather than gain power when this happens, especially if supermajorities that waste votes are packed into such districts.

Minority-Influence Districts

Conflicting political values are at stake in choices made between fewer safe districts with supermajorities of minority voters and more numerous racially diverse districts in which minorities may influence the outcome of elections and the subsequent policy choices of the representatives. "Descriptive" representation (that is, minority legislators get elected) may appear to be fair representation, but "substantive" representation happens when legislators actually respond to the needs of minority voters. Both of these qualities are important, but trade-offs are often made.[4]

This issue is not new to the Supreme Court; indeed, it lay at the heart of the challenge to a New York congressional district in 1964. A districting statute that concentrated black and Puerto Rican voters in one Manhattan congressional district, making it over 86 percent minority, was challenged as discriminatory because it segregated voters by race and place of origin. A neighboring district became almost 95 percent white. The plaintiffs were minority voters objecting to their exclusion from the white district and to the packing or wasting of minority votes in the minority district. The Court allowed the district's black representative, the Rev. Adam Clayton Powell, to intervene in support of the constitutionality of the act, a position noted by the Court when it rejected the challenge. The Fourteenth Amendment, the Court ruled, does not require the equal distribution of minority voters among congressional districts (*Wright v. Rockefeller* 1964, at 54). Liberals on the Court were divided: Justice Black wrote the majority opinion, whereas Justices Douglas and Goldberg dissented (*Wright v. Rockefeller* 1964, at 60). The dissenters argued that the outcome should be controlled by *Brown v. Board of Education:* racial segregation by law is inequality. Justice Douglas wrote:

> The fact that Negro political leaders find advantage in this nearly solid Negro and Puerto Rican district is irrelevant to our problem. Rotten boroughs were long a curse of democratic processes. Racial boroughs are

also at war with democratic standards. . . . The principle of equality is
at war with the notion that District A must be represented by a Negro,
as it is with the notion that District B must be represented by a Cau-
casian, District C by a Jew, District D by a Catholic, and so on.(*Wright
v. Rockefeller* 1964, at 62, 66)

At a time when few African Americans held public office, the Court's decision in favor of this racial gerrymander is hardly surprising, but the decision submerged the issue of minority influence for several decades.

Today, the issue is alive again, this time owing to a confluence of interests between minorities seeking more seats, and more secure seats, and
Republicans, often a political minority, pursuing control of state legislative chambers and the U.S. House of Representatives. Ohio was the setting for a minority representation case that was to bounce up and down
like a yo-yo in the federal court system for most of the 1990s. In 1991,
Ohio's Republican-controlled state apportionment board adopted a state
legislative districting plan that increased the number of majority-minority
districts in the state by subtracting minority voters from previously integrated districts that usually elected white or black Democrats, and concentrating them in heavily minority districts. Adjoining Assembly districts
were left more white and, given the proclivities of the excluded black voters to vote Democratic, more Republican. This was widely believed to be
part of a national Republican Party strategy to gain control of previously
Democratic legislatures (*New York Times*, 3 March 1993, A9).

Dissenting Democrats on the Ohio apportionment board challenged the
plan as a dilution of minority voting strength in violation of both section 2
of the Voting Rights Act and the Fifteenth Amendment. They claimed that
minority vote dilution was not only real but intentional, because it was carried out for the political purpose of maximizing Republican voting strength.
Voting was not racially polarized in Ohio, as even the Republican defendants conceded. Black plaintiffs who joined the suit showed that every
district in Ohio that was at least 35 percent black had elected a black representative. Packing these new majority-minority districts, the Democrats
alleged, led to fewer minority-*influence* districts, where black voters could
elect candidates of their choice with white support.

As in *Wright*, three decades earlier, black groups weighed in on opposite sides of the dispute. The Ohio NAACP backed the Republican plan,
while the Congressional Black Caucus filed an *amicus* brief opposing it,
arguing that "the Voting Rights Act was not intended to result in political
segregation of minority voters into a few districts, limiting their electoral

influence, unless absolutely necessary." The outcome of Ohio's 1992 leg-
islative election, held under the disputed plan on order from the U.S.
Supreme Court, was known even before oral arguments were heard in the
case. In that election, one additional black candidate was elected to the
Ohio House, while Republicans captured eight additional seats (*The Plain
Dealer*, 6 December 1992, 29A; 9 December 1992, 3A).[5]

A unanimous Supreme Court concluded that even though Ohio did not
have a history of racial discrimination in districting, the state was entitled
to create more majority-minority districts if it chose to do so, as long as
the overall effect of the plan was not to "diminish or abridge the voting
strength of the protected class." The Court refused to address the issue of
whether black voting strength was diminished by the loss of minority-
influence districts and ruled that the Republican partisan advantage was
irrelevant. Since the board had relied on proposals from the Ohio NAACP
and the Black Elected Democrats of Ohio (BEDO) in drawing the new
districts, the Court said, its intent could not be assumed to be discriminatory (*Voinovich v. Quilter* 1993, at 154, 160).

Twice more the three-judge federal district court rejected the 1991
Republican plan, once again for "packing" black voters unnecessarily into
the contested districts, and once for population disparities. Twice more
the Supreme Court sent the case back for reexamination in light of its new
rulings. By August 1997, the retirement of Democratic Judge Anthony
Celebrezze Sr. changed the composition of the three-judge court, which
then upheld the 1991 plan by a 2–1 vote. U.S. Circuit Judge Nathaniel
Jones, himself an African American, previously in the majority and now in
an angry dissent, called the districting plan "a scheme to contain, and will
most assuredly limit, the voting power of black electors." The board, he
wrote, was "doing a dance on the graves of Medgar Evers and other voting rights martyrs of both races" (*Quilter v. Voinovich* 1997, at 1052).

Influence districts fared better in Tennessee where a federal district
court recognized them as a source of political strength for minority groups
and speculated that "black voters might have more influence on the political process with two strong influence districts than they would with one
additional majority-minority district." Searching for a standard to evaluate
how much is enough to create influence, Chief Circuit Judge Gilbert S.
Merritt estimated that 25 percent of the voting-age population was a reasonable minimum minority to generate a political impact in the legislature
(*Rural West Tenn. African American Council v. McWherter* 1995, at 1101).

Justice O'Connor's majority opinion in *Voinovich v. Quilter* had stressed
respect for the state's responsibility in the federal system for state legislative

apportionment and districting (1993 at 156–57), but the Court's evolving theory of the racial gerrymander would soon weave together the strands of judicial interpretation shaping both legislative and congressional districting by federal standards.

Congressional Redistricting: Iguanas and Other Monstrosities

The 1990s witnessed dramatic court battles over strategies to improve the representation of minorities in Congress. Twenty-two African Americans had served in Congress between the Civil War and 1901, all Southern Republicans. The last was Representative George White of North Carolina, the only black member from 1897 to 1901. He is said to have left Congress voluntarily because racist attitudes made his service futile (Swain 1993, 21–28). In the 1990s, mandated by the Voting Rights Act to provide opportunities to minorities to elect representatives of their choice (the first round of redistricting following enactment of the 1982 amendments), state legislatures drew single-member districts for minority voters, using the traditional plurality-based, winner-take-all elections. These efforts succeeded in producing the largest number of minority representatives in the U.S. House in history. The number of Southern Republicans in the House also rose, as neighboring districts became more white and more conservative. The Bush administration's Justice Department supported this districting strategy by issuing directives to some states to "maximize the number of districts with black and Hispanic majorities," a policy which assisted in the Republican capture of the House majority in 1994. The Clinton administration continued support for this "bleaching" of districts in southern states because it led to increased minority representation (Yeoman 1998, 19).

The first round of this congressional redistricting produced seventeen new majority-minority districts in nine southern states; African Americans were elected in sixteen of these districts in 1992 and again in 1994. Nine additional Hispanic members were elected from districts redrawn to facilitate the representation of Spanish-speaking voters. Voters in these new districts succeeded in nearly doubling the number of minority members in the U.S. House. Opponents of race-based districting, for the most part white voters, went to court, invoking the Fourteenth Amendment equal protection clause to challenge these new districts as a violation of their rights. These plaintiffs were the "filler people" alluded to earlier, who won standing in court to vindicate their right to representation as individuals.

The first major Supreme Court decision on these race-based districts came from North Carolina, a state that had not sent a minority member to Congress between Representative White's departure in 1901 and the 1992 election. The 1990 Census, showing a 22 percent black population in the state, gave North Carolina an additional seat in the U.S. House for a total of twelve. The state legislature drew two new districts with majority-minority population. One of these, District 12, was the subject of *Shaw v. Reno* (1993), in which the Supreme Court agreed with the plaintiffs that this district was an unconstitutional racial gerrymander because it concentrated black voters "without regard to any other considerations, such as compactness, contiguousness, geographical boundaries, or political subdivisions" (*Shaw v. Reno* 1993, at 637). This "snake-like" district, which was 160 miles long and wound through ten counties, connected black communities along an interstate highway. Justice O'Connor, writing for the majority, warned of the "risk of lasting harm" posed to society because including in one district

> individuals who belong to the same race, but who are otherwise widely separated by geographical and political boundaries, and who may have little in common with one another but the color of their skin bears an uncomfortable resemblance to political apartheid. It reinforces the perception that members of the same racial group regardless of their age, education, economic status, or the community in which they live think alike, share the same political interests, and will prefer the same candidates at the polls. We have rejected such perceptions elsewhere as impermissible racial stereotypes. . . . By perpetuating such notions, a racial gerrymander may exacerbate the very patterns of racial bloc voting that majority-minority districting is sometimes said to counteract. (*Shaw v. Reno* 1993, at 647–48)

The Court compared the "segregation" of congressional districts to the former invidious separation of the races in southern parks and schools.[6]

This was the first of many decisions in the 1990s invalidating such plans and repeatedly requiring the revision of district lines. The constitutional debate grew bitter. In disputes from North Carolina, Georgia, Louisiana, Florida, and Texas, the Supreme Court rejected one congressional districting plan after another as "racial gerrymanders" that violated the Fourteenth Amendment right to equal protection of the white plaintiffs.[7] Majority-minority districts were labeled "bizarre" (*Shaw v. Reno*, at 644), "serpentine" (*Shaw v. Hunt*, at 906), and "iguana-like" (*Abrams v. Johnson*, at 89), but the harm to the plaintiffs remained ill-defined. By

1996 in North Carolina's revised legislative plan (holding firm for two minority districts), white voters (79 percent of the voting-age population) were still a majority in ten of twelve, or 83 percent, of the state's congressional districts. How were the plaintiffs harmed? Justice O'Connor explained, "When a district obviously is created solely to effectuate the perceived common interests of one racial group, elected officials are more likely to believe that their primary obligation is to represent only the members of that group, rather than their constituency as a whole"(*Shaw v. Reno* at 648).[8] The Court does not supply empirical evidence of this allegedly defective representation. Along with Justices Breyer, Ginsburg, and Souter, Justice Stevens dissented consistently, as in *Shaw v. Hunt* where he attacked the idea that "a State may draw unsightly lines to favor farmers or city dwellers, but not to create districts that benefit the very group whose history inspired the Amendment that the Voting Rights Act was designed to implement" (at 950–51).

The Court's rigid stance against consideration of race in districting was slightly modified in 1995. In the ongoing Georgia dispute, conceding that districting authorities are always "aware" of race, as they are of other demographic and partisan characteristics, the Court ruled that race could not be the *"predominant"* motive for drawing particular district lines (*Miller v. Johnson* 1995). Even so, the districts drawn to enhance minority representation, when challenged, were to be subjected to "strict scrutiny"—a kind of searching review that required the state to show a "compelling governmental interest" in the classification by race and to show that the means used were no broader in scope than absolutely necessary (*Adarand Constructors, Inc. v. Pena* 1995).[9] In *Miller* the Court refused to recognize compliance with federal antidiscrimination laws as a compelling state interest (at 921–22).

Among the congressional districts invalidated by the federal courts were Hispanic districts in northern cities. In 1996, the U.S. Supreme Court rejected Rep. Luis Gutierrez's Illinois Fourth District in Chicago, overturning a lower federal court decision that justified its "uncouth configuration" as a means to remedy past electoral discrimination against Hispanics. In 1997, a district drawn in 1992 to increase New York City's Hispanic representation in Washington was invalidated by a three-judge federal court. The legislature had pulled together Hispanic neighborhoods from Brooklyn, Queens, and lower Manhattan to create the new Twelfth District, a noncontiguous area split by the East River and described as "ink splotches from a Rorschach test." This newly created district in New York City facilitated the primary victory of Democratic Rep. Nydia M. Velazquez over nine-term incumbent Democratic Rep. Stephen J. Solarz (whose own district had been eliminated in New York's redistricting) and her subsequent election to the House. Velazquez's unsuccessful Republican (and Hispanic) election opponent, Angel Diaz, challenged the composition of the district. Like the African American plaintiffs in *Wright v. Rockefeller* (1964), Diaz argued that his ethnic group was "marginalized and segregated" by the majority-Hispanic district. The federal court concluded that his complaint fell so clearly within the pattern of *Shaw v. Reno* (1993) and its progeny that no trial was needed; summary judgment was granted and the district was invalidated on Fourteenth Amendment equal protection grounds (*New York Times,* 27 February 1997, A1, B2).

In 1996 and 1998, in spite of the court-ordered revision of district lines that had reshaped these two Hispanic as well as many black districts to majority white voting-age populations, black and Hispanic House members, now incumbents, were reelected from their revised districts (*CQ Weekly Report,* 7 November 1998, 3029, 3032).[10] These victories of minority incumbents in the now white-majority districts have been dismissed by proponents of race-based districting as mere evidence of the power of incumbency (Lublin 1997, 284), while some journalists have reported on these outcomes, especially for black representatives in the South, as signs of decreasing racial polarization in southern politics (e.g., *New York Times,* 23 November 1996, 1, 8).

By 1999, when North Carolina's Twelfth Congressional District bounced back to the Supreme Court for its third review (under the name *Hunt v. Cromartie*), its population was only 47 percent black. Its legislative sponsors maintained that their goal in delineating the district was not racial but political, to preserve the partisan balance of the state's congressional delegation, comprising six members of each major party. To reach this goal, they argued in the Supreme Court, the Twelfth District had to be Democratic. The fact that black voters tended to support Democrats and therefore were included in the district in significant numbers should not invalidate or "taint" the district (*New York Times,* 21 January 1999, A12). This argument was directed toward the Supreme Court's preference, clearly stated in earlier cases, for the use of "traditional" criteria for districting (*Miller v. Johnson* at 916, *Bush v. Vera* at 977–81). Protection of incumbents and partisan balance were among these criteria.[11] Representative Melvin L. Watt, the original (black) winner in the district invalidated in *Shaw v. Reno,* was now a four-term incumbent, twice-elected in the redrawn majority-white district. Would traditional principles protect him as an incumbent? Or had the Court painted itself into a corner where only the election of a white representative in that district would erase the racial "taint"? If so, would not such an outcome be retrogression in minority representation, violating the Voting Rights Act? In May 1999, the Supreme Court post-poned resolution of that incongruous issue by sending the case of North Carolina's now famous Twelfth District back to the lower court for another full trial.[12]

Justices on both sides of the issue of race-based districting find them-selves entangled in the very political thicket that Justice Frankfurter famously warned against decades earlier (*Colegrove v. Green 1946,* at 556). Traditional districting principles are among the brambles of that thicket. The power of incumbency, partisan patterns of voting, and racial polarization in voting are stubborn political facts that block the path to the goal of fair representation. Moreover, if such political constraints are to be respected, then demographic reality—the racial distribution of the state's population—thwarts the use of districting to achieve the outcome sought. A majority of black voters, both in North Carolina and across the South, live outside these specially drawn districts, yet neither the ruling majority nor the protesting minority of the Court alluded to the option of an alternative electoral system that would free the voters from the con-striction of single-member districts.

Judicial Elections and Minority Vote Dilution

The debate over districting was muted in judicial election cases, in part because of the perception that judges are above politics, chosen to make "right" decisions, not decisions responsive to the people who choose them, whether by appointment or election. Yet state judges are elected in thirty-eight states, and minority judges have been relatively rare on the bench. Mississippi was the first state in which the Voting Rights Act was enforced for judicial elections, in a federal district court opinion invalidating plu-rality at-large voting for state trial judges.[13] Similar challenges were brought in seven other states, and by 1991, the U.S. Supreme Court issued a ruling that applied the Voting Rights Act to judicial elections (*Chisom v. Roemer, Houston Lawyers' Assoc. v. Atty. Gen. of Texas* 1991).

A threshold question was whether judges were "representatives," and therefore their election should be brought within the ambit of the Voting Rights Act. In theory, judges are accountable to the law, not to the voters, nor to the litigants in a civil case, nor to victims and defendants in crim-inal cases which are brought in jurisdictions where crimes occur, not nec-essarily where the judge is elected. The judicial function is to apply the law impartially, even in defiance of public opinion. Finding that the word *representatives* "describes the winners of representative, popular elections," Justice Stevens wrote for the majority in *Chisom:* "If executive officers, such as prosecutors, sheriffs, state attorneys general, and state treasurers, can be considered 'representatives' simply because they are chosen by popular election, then the same reasoning should apply to elected judges" (501 U.S. 380, 399). Moreover, the Court has noted that, in their exercise of discretion, judges do in some sense engage in policy making, a representative function (*Gregory v. Ashcroft* 1991, at 466). Conceding in *Chisom* that judges could be appointed, thus escaping Voting Rights Act coverage, the Court found that a state's decision to elect them and thus subject them to popular will brings the state under the Voting Rights Act mandate not to discriminate.

How to remedy minority vote dilution in judicial elections raises more complex questions than those that arise in legislative settings. The most common remedy for VRA violations, the drawing of single-member electoral districts, is even more problematical for judicial than for legislative bodies, because of the disjuncture between jurisdiction and election district. The state's interest in "linkage" between the electoral base of a judge and the jurisdiction in which he or she decides cases has been held by the Supreme Court to be "substantial" (*Houston Lawyers Assoc. v. Atty. Gen. of Texas* 1991 at 426–27). Majority-minority subdistricts for electoral purposes within larger judicial districts have been adopted since 1991 in several jurisdictions, but it seems that appellate courts have not been supportive of what they see as violation of this linkage.

In Hamilton County, Tennessee, for example, a federal district court decision to establish judicial subdistricts for election of countywide judges was vacated by the court of appeals and remanded for more specific findings about the vote dilution claim. The district court affirmed the finding of a VRA violation, and ordered the state to submit a new election plan (*Cousin v. McWherter* 1995). After the legislature was unable to agree on a remedy, the district court ordered countywide cumulative voting for Hamilton County judgeship. Racially mixed residential patterns made compact remedial districts difficult to draw, the court pointed out, and minority voters living outside of possible remedial districts would be relegated to "virtual representation," flaws that would be corrected by CV elections (*Cousin v. Sundquist* 1996). The appeals court then rejected this new remedy, finding that CV, "like a subdistricting system, would encourage racial bloc voting" (*Cousin v. Sundquist* 1998). Since the appeals court also overturned the district court's finding of minority vote dilution in Hamilton County, no remedy was actually necessary. This judicial attack on CV appears gratuitous because it was not needed to decide the case. Even more troubling than the appellate activism shown here is the lack of understanding of alternative electoral systems exhibited by the judges. In CV elections, as explained in chapter 3, voters are free to choose candidates by any principle of selection; race may be relevant or irrelevant to the voter.

Protection of Language Minorities

Although race-conscious districting has facilitated African American representation, other less segregated minorities are unlikely to benefit. As the American population grows steadily more diverse, the justification for protecting only those classes defined in 1975 will inevitably wane. Immigration and differential birth rates are projected to change the face of the nation. The 1990 census reported that non-Hispanic whites constituted 75 percent of the population. By the year 2005, Hispanics are expected to be the largest minority group in the United States, approaching 36 million residents, surpassing 35.5 million African Americans.[14] The number of Asians, which doubled in the 1980s, will double again to about 15 million. The numbers of immigrants from the Caribbean and Africa, now a little over 1 million, are likely to grow to 3 million in the next two decades. The Census Bureau projects that by 2050 there will be no majority racial or ethnic group in the United States (Roberts 1993, 81–83, 246–55; Cohodas 1994, 704, 711).

How this diversity will be manifested in the electorate and in turn represented in political office is a key issue for the future of the democratic system in the United States. At present, Hispanic Americans are less likely than African Americans to be citizens, therefore less likely to be able to register and vote. The higher percentage of youth in the Hispanic population also shrinks its presence in the electorate. But the partisan stakes have defined the issue, initially the seemingly simple question of how or even whether these minorities are counted in the Census. The struggles of the 1990s over race-based districting led to harsh partisan debates in Congress, and between Congress and the executive branch, about how to conduct the 2000 Census.

The Census counts the population, but how? The Census Bureau reported that it missed 8.4 million people in the 1990 Census and counted four million others twice. The Bureau announced that it would use modern statistical sampling techniques, recommended by the National Academy of Sciences and the General Accounting Office of Congress, to achieve a more accurate count in 2000 (National Research Council 1994, 4; 1995, 37–43). The 1990 undercount disproportionately affected urban minorities who tend to vote Democratic.[15] The Bush administration acknowledged the undercount but refused to make a statistical adjustment.[16] Relying on the reference in Article I, sec. 2 [3] to an "Actual Enumeration," Republicans in Congress have opposed anything but a direct head count of the population as unconstitutional. The Clinton administration, in contrast, has consistently supported statistical sampling as a legitimate and widely accepted technique to achieve an accurate count. It is believed that sampling would find enough missing people to justify additional legislative and even congressional districts in New York and California, and could increase prospects for Democratic victories in marginally minority districts in Ohio, Illinois, and Texas (*New York Times*, 7 February 1999, E4).

Former Speaker of the House Newt Gingrich called statistical sampling "a dagger pointed at the heart" of the Republican majority in the House of Representatives. The issue was reduced to specific numbers of seats by then Republican National Committee chair Jim Nicholson, who in 1997 sent a memorandum to state Republican chairs, exhorting them to oppose sampling, which could, he alleged, endanger Republican control of 24 U.S. House seats, 113 state senate seats, and 297 state house seats. Suits were filed to halt any statistical adjustment. One of these resulted from a deal between the administration and the Republican majority in the House that the Census Bureau could spend money to develop plans for statistical sampling in 2000, but general tax revenues could also be used by the House itself to sue the Census Bureau to prevent its use. The inevitable litigation was resolved by the U.S. Supreme Court in 1999. In a 5–4 decision, the Court interpreted the Census statute to mean that statistical sampling could not be used for the population count that determines the 2001 apportionment of congressional seats among the states. The justices found, however, that the statute required the secretary of commerce to authorize the use of statistical sampling for all other purposes "if feasible" (a determination already made). These purposes would include distribution of federal funds to the states and the states' legislative and congressional line-drawing (*Dept. of Commerce v. U.S. House of Representatives*, 1999; *New York Times*, 26 January 1999, A1, A20; E. Still 1999, 8–9). As a result, the Census Bureau began planning for two counts, one accomplished with and one without the use of sampling (*New York Times*, 24 February 1999, A17).

However accurate the 2000 Census may be, its numbers will set the parameters for drawing legislative district boundaries that will shape minority representation for at least the first decade of the new century. Race-based districts have garnered the most attention, but as growing language-based minority groups seek representation in the future, section 4 of the Voting Rights Act will increasingly come into play. Yet defining minorities by language was dubious from the start. Neither all Native Americans nor all Asian Americans speak the same language, whereas Hispanics who have a common linguistic heritage are diverse by race, nation of origin, and political party. Critics of section 4 have identified significant differences in historic patterns of discrimination and assimilation between African Americans and the specified language minorities, patterns that critics believe make it irrational to apply similar standards to districting and representational issues (Thernstrom 1987, 51–62).

As the United States becomes more diverse, political alliances are rapidly changing. Voting patterns of Hispanics are diverging from those of African Americans as socioeconomic progress continues on an uneven path. Not only are new coalitions forming in large cities such as New York and Los Angeles (Beinart 1997), but growing numbers of people of mixed-race origin seek recognition of their diverse heritage. A lobbying group, the Association of Multiethnic Americans, failed to win a separate "multiracial" classification in the 2000 Census, but the government decided to allow people to identify themselves as members of more than one race ("check as many as apply"). After extensive internal and public discussion of how multiracial persons would be counted for redistricting and compliance with the Voting Rights Act, the government announced in 2000 that "those listing themselves as white and a member of a minority will be counted as a minority." This policy maximizes the count of the minority population, and was welcomed by the NAACP Legal Defense and Education Fund. Critics of affirmative action, on the other hand, attacked the "byzantine complexity" of the resulting proliferation of racial categories (*New York Times*, 30 October 1997, A1, A19; 11 March 2000, A7).[17]

In 1982, when Congress extended the Voting Rights Act for twenty-five years, its assumption was that the lawmakers would not need to revisit these difficult political issues before 2007. However, rapid social, economic, and demographic change has forced continuing reassessment of strategies to achieve fair representation. The reliance on a rigid delineation of named minorities was already breached in the 1980s in cases brought by coalitions of minorities, usually African American and Hispanic voters who combined to challenge plurality at-large elections.

Minority Coalitions and Competition

Coalitions were organized in cases where the minorities that alleged vote dilution were too small to meet the first requirement of the *Thornburg v. Gingles* test: to be populous enough to constitute a majority in a single-member district. Counted together, these minority groups could qualify by crossing the numerical threshold. The courts have held that whether two minorities could combine to become a new legally cognizable minority suffering from "minority coalition dilution" requires evaluation of their "political cohesiveness," the second requirement of the *Thornburg v. Gingles* test.

Such political cohesiveness has been successfully demonstrated by evidence that both groups were subject to discrimination in the past, that they share political goals, and that they vote together for minority candidates (*LULAC v. Midland Independent School District* 1987; *Campos v. City of Baytown* 1988; 1989). Minority coalition suits, however, have been rejected more often than accepted. In the U.S. Supreme Court's first case over single-member district vote dilution, a majority-minority state senate district which had been imposed by a lower federal court in Minneapolis was invalidated. The district was an "oddly shaped creation" drawn to combine black voters with three other "separately identifiable" minority groups. The Court found neither a showing of political cohesion within the "agglomeration" of minority groups, nor evidence of majority bloc voting in the city, to justify such a district (*Growe v. Emison* 1993, at 41–42). Judicial reluctance to hear such suits may be based on concern that expansion of the Voting Rights Act's protection to "politically cohesive" coalitions of minorities could quickly become a legal resource for any political coalition unable to win seats (Grofman, Handley, and Niemi 1992, 70–73).

Competition among minority groups that are clearly not politically cohesive also challenged judges to interpret "fairness" in representation in the context of the single-member district plans drawn up after the 1990 census. In the Florida redistricting case, *Johnson v. DeGrandy,* the African American and Hispanic groups in Dade County, far from forming a coalition, competed for control of majority-minority districts. The Supreme Court decided that it did not have to choose between them, however, since both groups held voting-age majorities in a number of districts "substantially proportional to their share in the population" (*Johnson v. DeGrandy* 1994, at 1024).

In a companion case from Georgia,[18] this standard of proportionality was attacked in a lengthy concurring opinion by Justice Thomas, who was joined by Justice Scalia, calling for a reversal of the whole idea of a "right to representation." Proclaiming the concept of minority vote dilution to be a "disastrous misadventure in judicial policy-making," Justice Thomas urged a return to the literal meaning of the right to vote (*Holder v. Hall* 1994, at 893). It is the individual right, he argued, to enter a polling place, cast a ballot, and have it included in the final tally of votes cast (at 922–23). The conversion of this right to a group right has resulted in the "segregation of voters into racially designated districts," which could "balkanize" the country. He objected to the political choices that the Court has had to make in order to devise remedies for minority vote dilution, noting that such choices could devolve only from theories of representation. He specifically attacked the remedy of single-member districts and the goal of proportionality as mere political choices. Other choices, he suggested, could just as well be cumulative voting or the single transferable vote (*Holder v. Hall* 1994, at 909–10).

Although Justice Thomas did not advocate these alternative electoral systems, he expanded a critical debate about representation that academics, civil rights lawyers, and electoral system specialists have tried for some years to bring to the public.[19] The original intent of the Voting Rights Act of 1965 may have been, as Justice Thomas asserts, unambiguous. Aimed at voting discrimination against African Americans, it was the culmination of a hundred years of struggle to overcome the political consequences of slavery and racism, especially in the South. The subsequent expansion of its reach across the nation and to other minorities has become entangled in the rapid social and political change of the past quarter century. However, it is not only judicial creativity that has stretched the scope of the act. Congress has consistently reenacted the statute, an action that is understood to validate and incorporate the intervening interpretation of the courts. Furthermore, Congress has increased the scope of the act to ensure that casting a ballot is not just a formality but an "effective" exercise. Moreover, although political choices are frequently required of judges in Voting Rights Act cases, such choices are also required in many other areas of constitutional interpretation.

The contemporary debate about electoral systems, growing out of this recently developed right of representation, moves well beyond implementation of statutes into questions about the nature of representation and the meaning of democracy itself. These are the compelling questions that led Condorcet, Andrae, Hare, and others to invent balloting techniques that would give both the majority and minorities their proportional share of power.

Geographic versus "Voluntary" Constituencies

As rulings in Voting Rights Act cases become ever more tangled, it is apparent that the single-member district system is incompatible with fair representation, except in the presence of residential segregation. This unyielding fact is kindling the current interest in proportional electoral alternatives. The familiar geographic base of representation also needs to be recognized as a political choice, rooted in a practice developed long ago when communities were more homogeneous and less mobile than today's fluid societies. A territorial basis for representation was assumed, and a mechanical formula based on numbers in the population was applied, unrelated to any right to vote and even less to a right to representation. Moreover, alternative election systems were unknown to the framers of the American Constitution, to the authors of the original state constitutions, and even to the members of Congress who in 1842 first adopted the requirement for single-member congressional districts (see chap. 1). Other innovations commonly used in political life today—radio and television campaigns, public opinion polls, and the Internet, for example, and more broadly constitutional interpretations of the right to vote—have been integrated into American politics over more than two centuries since the framers hammered out their notions of representative structures.

As the stories in this book have shown, PR/STV, cumulative voting, and limited voting are three electoral systems that give voters the option to choose how they wish to be represented, whether by a neighborhood voice, a common political interest, a political party, or a group identity. Racial and ethnic minorities were the principal beneficiaries of the PR/STV elections used in Ohio cities between 1915 and 1960, and this neglected history is relevant to the current debate. In a PR at-large system, voters can build coalitions across such categorical lines to form truly voluntary constituencies. The geographic base of representation is not totally abandoned, since at-large or multimember district elections have never been the true culprits in the exclusion of minorities. It is the practice of plurality voting that has perpetuated the overrepresentation of the majority, the concomitant underrepresentation of minorities, and the wasted votes of losers in both at-large and district settings. With a proportional system, the political community itself becomes the natural base of representation and voters form coalitions as they choose, not as preprogrammed by single-member districting into small fragments of the community.

Today, whereas plaintiffs, judges, and some commentators see in single-member district plurality voting only sensible accommodation to familiar practices (Grofman and Davidson 1992, 300–314), others—both conservative and liberal critics of the enforcement of the Voting Rights Act—see the spread of dysfunctional politics. Abigail Thernstrom of Boston University, for example, views race-conscious districting to achieve minority representation as divisive and destructive of important political values such as compromise and consensus building. Her complaint goes beyond Justice Thomas's objection to judicial decisions promoting group entitlement to representation. Like Thomas, she would define the right to vote as merely access to the polls. However, where Justice Thomas leaves open the path to alternative electoral systems—if only they are chosen by proper policy makers, that is, legislators, not judges—Thernstrom values the winner-take-all system *because* "common citizenship," she argues, is more important than group membership. In her view, over time race-based districts will institutionalize existing racial divisions in society (Thernstrom 1987, 242–43). This view echoes the traditional fear of faction in politics that can be traced back to the founders of the nation.

Other political analysts are more concerned about the substance of minority representation. In a study of black representation in Congress, Carol Swain argues that the promotion of substantive policy interests of African Americans hinges on building multiracial coalitions. Swain advocates the unpacking of districts that have supermajorities of minority voters in order to expand minority influence, as well as encouraging efforts by black candidates to compete in less than safe electoral settings (Swain 1993, 207–11). These solutions to the problem of minority underrepresentation may be constructive paths to pursue, but they are at least partially blocked by judicial decisions upholding partisan plans that create ever safer districts for incumbents who hold the reins of power (e.g., *Voinovich v. Quilter* 1993).

Lani Guinier also objects to race-based districting on the ground that creation of safe minority districts produces what she calls token representation. Legislators or council members elected from such districts, she argues, are recognized as token by minority voters, who may participate when first given an opportunity to elect one of their own, but who fall away as the early minority winners become incumbents without power to change policy. Furthermore, even this token representation depends on the perpetuation of residential segregation and pits minorities against each other in contests for the strongest claim to a district. Not only does segregation become the base for minority political power, Guinier argues, but black voters in new racially configured districts become isolated from potential allies—both minorities in other districts and the white majority. This isolation in turn inhibits coalition building in the legislative process, which is necessary to achieve policies responsive to minority needs (Guinier 1991). Urging the adoption of proportional election systems instead, Guinier writes:

> The principle of proportionality is molded by the hope that a more cooperative political style of deliberation and ultimately a more equal basis for preference satisfaction is possible when authentic minority representatives are reinforced by electoral structures to empower them at every stage of the political process. Ultimately, however, representation and participation based on principles of proportionality are also an attempt to reconceptualize the ideal of political equality, and so the ideal of democracy itself. (1992, 34)

Guinier's solutions to the problem of racial polarization address both the electoral system and legislative procedures for policy making. Proportional or semiproportional representation elections would help to bring minorities to the public table. Once there, she argues, they need access to legislative procedures that respond to minority influence as well as to minority presence in decision-making bodies. She points to such American practices as supermajority requirements for passage of specified measures (now, usually tax increases) as means to enable minorities to influence public policies (Guinier 1991).

This modification of majority rule derives from the principle of power-sharing, which can be applied to require rule by consensus in deeply divided societies. For example, shared authority was written into the constitutional arrangements that, combined with PR elections, made possible the Northern Ireland peace agreement of 1998. Major decisions by the 108–member Northern Ireland Assembly, elected by PR/STV in June 1998, were required to win majority support from both Protestant and Catholic blocs to become law. In 1999, however, distrust between the Protestant majority and the Catholic minority led to a breakdown in implementation, underscoring the obstacles to minority power-sharing, as distinct from minority representation (*New York Times*, 27 June 1998, A1, A5; 16 July 1999, A9).

Discussion of Guinier's theories of both shared authority and electoral systems was truncated by President Clinton's withdrawal of her 1993 nomination to be assistant attorney general for civil rights in the U.S. Department of Justice (*New York Times*, 4 June 1993, Al, A12; 3 April 1994, E5). Denied the opportunity to explain to the Senate Judiciary Committee the analysis of voting rights expounded in her law review articles, she has tried to expand the national debate about remedies for minority vote dilution beyond racial districting by speaking and writing, especially to advocate cumulative voting (Guinier 1994).[20]

Harbingers of Change

While this debate was percolating among political theorists and voting rights experts, voting rights lawyers and activists successfully implemented alternative election systems in many small communities around the United States in the 1990s and deepened public awareness of the issue by initiating ballot measures for electoral change. PR/STV (now often called preference or choice voting), cumulative voting, and limited voting have all gained momentum in the American political system. A comprehensive tally is beyond the scope of this book, but examples of initiatives will be discussed.

   PR/STV (choice or preference voting). True proportional representation elections (by single transferable vote) have the most extensive actual history among alternative election systems in the United States, as this book has shown. PR/STV and PR/Party List are the two ways of voting that provide the most complete representation to any voting population. While PR/Party List is adaptable to state legislative and congressional elections, the traditional American reluctance to recognize the role of parties in organizing political life makes this method less plausible for use in the United States than PR/STV, which can be used in partisan or nonpartisan elections, gives the voter the opportunity to choose candidates as well as parties, and assures the voter that a lower-ranked choice cannot defeat a more preferred candidate. At present PR/STV is practiced only for electing the city council in Cambridge, Massachusetts, and school boards in Cambridge and New York City. Its use waned in the United States in the mid-twentieth century primarily because of the successful opposition of political party leaders displaced from power in most of the cities where STV ballots were used. Racism and cold war fears, in reactions to the diversity brought to local governments by PR elections, also helped to push repeal initiatives over the top.

   Today, civic leaders and voting rights activists are bringing PR initiatives to charter commissions and task forces considering ways to comply with Voting Rights Act requirements or, more generally, to improve representation. The Center for Voting and Democracy, the leading nonprofit organization in this political realm, has testified or assisted in organizing initiative campaigns for PR in sixteen states and the District of Columbia, as well as in a number of cities (Richie 1998, 94).

   San Francisco offers an instructive example of a community seeking to improve representation of minorities in local government by introducing a new election system. In November 1996, initiatives were placed on the ballot to convert city council elections from plurality at-large to either PR/STV or a district-based system. In what is viewed as a brief and under-funded campaign, a district alternative (Proposition G) was approved by 57 percent of the voters, while 44 percent supported PR/STV (Proposition H) (DeLeon, Blash, and Hill 1997). An exit poll exploring reasons for voters' preferences revealed that voters who supported PR/STV found it "more democratic," more likely to achieve representation of minorities, and likely to lead to less expensive campaigns than the current system. Those who voted "no" on PR/STV cited such reasons as finding the system "too complicated," preferring districts, or being satisfied with plurality at-large elections. The exit poll was accompanied by a simulated PR/STV vote that demonstrated the advantage of its ranked choices for committed candidates over candidates with wide name recognition but lacking a knowledgeable constituency (DeLeon et al., 28–33).

The impact of San Francisco's change to district elections in 2000 is of particular interest to voting rights watchers because, with the exception of Chinatown, the city's diverse population is not segregated residentially by race or ethnic group. This means that the utility of districts to provide minority representation will be significantly restricted by the Supreme Court's rulings on the racial gerrymander (DeLeon et al., 38). The residential integration of San Francisco's many minority groups was often cited in the initiative campaign as a powerful justification for choosing a PR/STV election system instead of districts.

In New York City, meanwhile, an attempt to switch community school board elections from PR/STV (its practice since 1970) to a limited voting plan was blocked by the U.S. Justice Department under its Voting Rights Act authority to prevent retrogression in minorities' opportunity to elect candidates of their choice (New York Times, 5 February 1999, A23). This event was significant because it was the first time that the Justice Department had been required to evaluate the effect on minority vote dilution of a switch from proportional to semiproportional voting. Attorney General Janet Reno informed the city that the proposed limited voting system, allocating four votes to each voter to elect a nine-member board in each of thirty-two community districts, would diminish minority opportunities to win in at least eighteen of these districts. With the PR/STV ballot and nine seats to be filled, one candidate can be elected by a minority of 10 percent; under the limited vote system (which is counted by plurality) a candidate would need at least 31 percent of the votes to win. If minority voters used all four of their votes, the threshold of representation would rise to 40 percent. Furthermore, not only would minorities face a higher barrier to election with limited voting than with the PR/STV ballot, but in majority-minority districts even a majority would find it difficult to elect a majority of the board, since each voter would be limited to four votes for nine seats. The Asian American Legal Defense and Education Fund (AALDEF), the Center for Voting and Democracy (CVD), and the League of Women Voters (LWV) had all protested the potential effect of the proposed change on African American, Asian American, and Hispanic representation in specific districts where minorities had gained roughly proportional representation under PR/STV.[21]

Cumulative voting. CV, a deeply rooted practice in Illinois legislative elections (1870–1980), is the object of a drive in Illinois to restore multimember districts and minority representation in the Illinois House of Representatives. The 1980 repeal of the 110–year-old three-member district system has left urban Republicans and suburban Democrats in Illinois feeling excluded from the political process by plurality voting in single-member districts. Both black and white former members of the lower house lament the loss of diverse viewpoints from all districts. Although CV provided only semiproportional representation (the three-member districts confined representation generally to the two major parties), it is viewed in retrospect as having "produced the most thoughtful, independent members of the legislature" (Editorial, *Chicago Tribune*, 30 May 1995). A citizens' group is working to restore CV legislative elections early in the twenty-first century.[22]

CV continues to be the election system of choice for city council elections in Peoria, Illinois, and it was adopted in Alamogordo, New Mexico; for the school board in Sisseton, South Dakota; and for a county commission, a school board, and several other local jurisdictions in Alabama (Engstrom 1992; E. Still 1992; *Time*, 25 Apr. 1994, 42–43). The most widespread current use of CV, however, has occurred in Texas where in 1995 a state law was enacted specifically permitting school districts to adopt CV (or LV) for election of members of local school boards (TX Ed.Code, sec. 11.054). Over fifty local jurisdictions in the state adopted cumulative voting in the 1990s (*Texas Observer*, 22 July 1994, 3–4; Richie 1998, 94). In 1999, Amarillo, a diverse city of close to 150,000 people where neither Hispanics nor African Americans served on the school board, became the largest jurisdiction in the United States to adopt CV. Settlement of a federal voting rights lawsuit, brought by the NAACP,

LULAC, and individual voters, provided for school board elections to be conducted by CV beginning in 2000 (*Reynoso et al. v. Amarillo Independent School District* 1999).

In most of these communities where CV elections have been held to date, one minority member has been elected to the three-, five-, or seven-member council or board. Minorities winning representation in these elections include African Americans and white Republicans in Alabama, African Americans and Hispanics in Texas and New Mexico, and Native Americans in South Dakota. CV's semiproportional character was evident in Centre, Alabama, where a black candidate was elected in the first CV election (1988), but because a second black candidate divided the vote in the 1992 election, both minority candidates lost (E. Still 1992, 185; *Time*, 25 Apr. 1994, 43). As minority candidates begin to win, it is not surprising that others are encouraged to run. Strategic voting and discipline in nominations will become increasingly important if CV is to fulfill proportional aspirations over time.

In Worcester County, Maryland, a federal district judge twice ordered the adoption of a CV plan for the five-member board of commissioners as a remedy for denial of voting rights to the African American minority. Twice the court of appeals reversed the decision, first on procedural grounds and later holding that neither party supported the remedy (*Cane v. Worcester County, Md.* 1995). In originally choosing the CV plan over a single-member district proposal, Judge Young pointed out that "cumulative voting, unlike single-member districts, will allow the voters, by the way they exercise their votes, to 'district' themselves based on what they think rather than where they live." The court called the CV remedy "less drastic" a remedy than single-member districts, because candidates would continue to run at-large. Furthermore, this remedy was viewed as less likely to "increase polarization between different interests since no group receives special treatment at the expense of others" (*Cane v. Worcester County, Md.* 1994 at 373).

While the issue's resolution lies in the future, what is noteworthy here is the district court judge's persistence in support of an alternative electoral system. Both the circuit court and the district judge noted Supreme Court Justice Thomas's recognition in *Holder v. Hall* (1994) that "there is nothing inherently radical or inappropriate about the judicial imposition of cumulative voting" to remedy a voting rights violation. Judge Young emphasized that the opportunity for voters to elect a candidate of their choice "will not come at the expense of geographical diversity, the division of municipalities, or racial segregation. Coalitions of voters will be free to cast their ballots on the basis of race, region, political issue, or any other consideration and have a real chance of electoral success while Board members will still be beholden to every county citizen" (*Cane v. Worcester County, Md.* 1995 at 694).

The experience of Chilton County, Alabama, with cumulative voting for its county commission and school board since 1988 has been well documented and illustrates both the potential of alternative voting methods to bring previously excluded groups to the table and the difficulty of gaining acceptance for unfamiliar ways of voting (Pildes and Donoghue 1995). Chilton County's previous election system, plurality at-large voting with residency districts to facilitate geographical representation, could not be ameliorated by single-member districts because the county's minority population was widely dispersed. Absence of black representation on the county's governing bodies was the exclusion driving the VRA case that brought about CV elections. The new system, however, enabled not only African Americans but also white Republicans and women to win seats on these boards. In the early years of CV, public attitudes toward the new voting system ranged from skeptical to hostile. Some voters believed that the system was unconstitutional because they thought it departed from the principle of one person, one vote, even though each voter had the same number of votes to allocate among candidates. Others when interviewed said they would have preferred single-member districts, even with a minority set-aside seat, a provision which would indeed violate the Constitution. But ultimately CV came to be accepted in Chilton County because it "worked" to accomplish the goal of minority representation (Pildes and Donoghue, 282–84).

Hispanic voters are more often residentially dispersed, especially in the southwestern states, where CV has also been implemented. In Alamogordo, New Mexico, a city of 24,000 population, 21 percent of the city's voting-age population was Hispanic at the time a mixed electoral system was adopted to settle a VRA suit. The new system provided for a seven-member council, with four single-member districts, and three members to be elected at-large by CV (Engstrom, Taebel, and Cole 1989, 480–81). In three successive elections (1987, 1990, 1994), one of the at-large seats was captured by a Hispanic woman (tabulation from the Center for Voting and Democracy, 1 Aug. 1994). Exit poll data from her first election showed that she could not have been elected without the support of some white voters, but the option available to Hispanic voters to demonstrate intensity by cumulating their votes carried her to victory. On the average, she received 2.6 votes from Hispanic voters (Engstrom, Taebel, and Cole 1989, 495). However, the system was more popular with voting rights experts than with the voters of Alamogordo, who voted in 1997 to convert council elections to all single-member districts in 2000 (Issacharoff et al. 1998, 746).

CV plans have also been proposed but rejected as remedies for the allegedly unconstitutional Twelfth Congressional District in North Carolina,[23] and at the local level for the Cincinnati City Council.[24]

Limited voting. In contrast to the relatively widespread publicity generated by cumulative voting plans in the past several years, limited voting (LV) has been implemented more quietly in current voting rights controversies. As explained in chapter 3, limited voting is conducted at-large and gives voters fewer votes to cast than the number of seats to be filled, empowering a minority to capture one or more seats. Voting rights cases have been settled by the adoption of LV systems for a few local councils, school boards, and county commissions in North Carolina, Georgia, and Arizona (Engstrom 1992, 759–62). Twenty-one towns in Alabama adopted LV elections as a result of an omnibus settlement of vote dilution claims in which the state's use of plurality at-large elections was found to be purposefully discriminatory by race (*Dillard v. Crenshaw County* 1986). These towns adopted either five- or seven-member councils, with voters limited to casting one or, in some towns, two votes. In both 1988 and 1992, in all but one of the municipalities where African American candidates ran, one or two were elected.[25] In all the Alabama LV communities in which minority wins occurred, the result was representation in proportion to the minority share of the voting-age population (E. Still 1992, 190–91; Engstrom 1992).

In North Carolina, where the racial gerrymandering cases gathered steam in the 1990s, a federal court upheld the constitutionality of limited voting as an "innovative" remedy for minority vote dilution in elections for county officials. The court concluded that LV avoids the problems the Supreme Court identified in the *Shaw* cases because in LV systems voters are not classified by race (*Cleveland County Ass'n for Government by the People v. Cleveland County Bd. of Comm'rs* 1998; Mulroy 1998, 350–51).

As these local advances in minority representation spread and take root, it seems reasonable to expect the traditional unquestioning acceptance of winner-take-all elections to erode. It is clear that in a range of elections from local to federal office, many voters want to renew and reinvigorate the political life of the country. Congress could be encouraged to clear away the statutory obstacle to alternative systems for congressional elections, the single-member district requirement for election to the House of Representatives. Repeal of that statute has become a key goal of election reformers. A repeal measure, the Voters' Choice Act (H.R. 3068, 105th Cong.), was first introduced by Representative Cynthia McKinney of Georgia, whose majority-minority district was redrawn twice by court order in the 1990s to a white-majority district (*Miller v. Johnson* 1995; *Abrams v. Johnson* 1997). In 1999, the repeal initiative was carried forward by North Carolina Representative Mel Watt, whose "bizarre" district spurred the Supreme Court on its hostile course toward race-based districting (*Shaw v. Reno* 1993; *Shaw v. Hunt* 1996; *Hunt v. Cromartie* 1999).[26] Inviting his colleagues to cosponsor the States' Choice of Voting Systems Act, Watt pointed out the severe cost of past litigation and the prospect of continuing court action in the 2001 round of redistricting. Moreover, he wrote, "Many people believe that the combination of having to create single-member districts and trying to create districts in which minority voters have a chance of electing representatives of their choice has resulted in increased racial polarization and has heightened racial divisions." Repeal of the single-member district requirement would empower the states to consider alternative voting systems (Watt, Letter to Colleagues, 23 February 1999).

The Supreme Court, too, may be persuaded by lower court acceptance and by successful if scattered use of alternative electoral methods to find a way out of its peculiar paradigm of representation. Because PR/STV, CV, and LV treat all voters alike, no voter is classified by race. In minority vote dilution cases, as Steven Mulroy points out (1998, 372–73), the Court's present test of the need for a remedy starts with the finding that the excluded minority is large enough and compact enough to justify creation of a single-member district (*Gingles* 1986, 50–51). This predicts the "potential to elect," which the minority group claims. In alternative election systems, the equivalent prediction can be based on the threshold of exclusion (the minimum number needed to elect): what percentage of the voters has the potential to elect a representative either at-large or in a multimember district (see chap. 3)? This minimum percentage is not a mandate or a quota but an opportunity for any self-defined group of voters to elect a representative. In Voting Rights Act cases, the second and third *Gingles* criteria of cohesiveness and racial bloc voting would still apply before courts would intervene to impose an alternative remedial system. Moreover, Mulroy suggests that the threshold of exclusion standard would outperform the present evaluation of compactness because it offers judges a "bright line" compared to the nebulous assessment of shape (bizarre) or appearance (ugly) presently applied to proposed race-based single-member districts (1998, 340–42).

To gain widespread support for full representation, however, alternative electoral systems need political support as well as legal justification. For this purpose, evidence is needed that representation translates into policy results.

The Policy Puzzle

As the American electoral system inches toward the right to full participation in the political process, the debate will expand beyond electoral systems themselves to their impact on policy. The psychological rewards, which voting brings to many and service in public office brings to a few, are not the ultimate goal of representation. Participation in policy making itself and influence on public policy outcomes are the intrinsic purposes of the exercise. This is called substantive, as distinct from merely descriptive representation. To link policy change to electoral system reform is a difficult challenge because of the complexity of political events that occur between elections and subsequent policy decisions. Still, when new ways of voting result in the election of officials with different partisan, racial, ethnic, or gender-based characteristics, new policies are at least anticipated. If previously excluded groups gain access to a system of governance, the assumption is that access will be used to modify existing policies and to address neglected needs.

A study of the connection between election systems and policy outputs was conducted by Louis Fraga in Dallas and San Antonio, Texas, over a period encompassing a shift from plurality at-large elections to a mixed single-member district and at-large system. In both cities, the new electoral system did result in greater minority representation. The changes found following implementation of the new electoral system were increases in minority shares of municipal employment, of appointments to city boards and commissions, and of city contracts. Nevertheless, although increased access to "positions of public influence" created the *potential* for influence on substantive policies, major social change had not occurred (Fraga 1991, 14–17). Closer examination of the politics of council interactions would be required to evaluate these findings, but these newly districted Texas cities appear to illustrate Guinier's theory that tokenism is produced by single-member district representation and by the resulting isolation of minority representatives in the policy process.

By opting for remedies for minority vote dilution based on single-member districts or on electoral systems partially districted and partially at-large, courts have made profoundly political choices in favor of descriptive over substantive representation. More than a quarter century of enforcement of the Voting Rights Act has successfully brought African Americans into the voting booth and into offices from which they had been effectively excluded. Less controversy has afflicted voting rights disputes than other efforts to overcome discrimination. Still, African Americans have not been able to win a proportional share of seats in most policy-making bodies, and Hispanics and other language minorities lag even further behind (Davidson 1992, 46; Cohodas 1994, 704, 711).

As seen in the post-1990 round of legislative redistricting, the cost of progress has been high. Significant examples of racial and political polarization show the concentration of minority voters in oddly shaped districts that have benefited white Republicans whose power in adjoining districts was solidified by the subtraction of minority voters (Graham 1992, 195–96; Guinier 1991, 1143; *Voinovich v. Quilter* 1993). Indeed, more than a decade ago, this result was predicted by electoral system experts (Piccard 1984; Zimmerman 1980, 1990). For these political reasons, housing segregation is likely to persist and even sharpen if Voting Rights Act violations are not remedied by alternative systems that expand the geographic base of representation and allow communities of interest to coalesce politically (Yates 1992).

The Supreme Court's erratic policy choices of the 1990s permitted gerrymanders for "traditional" purposes such as protection of incumbents and preservation of the distribution of partisan power, but rejected those where the "predominant" motive was believed to be racial (*Miller v. Johnson* 1995). Were it not for these decisions, the use of the gerrymander, identified by advocates of PR as a defect of district systems since the nineteenth century (McCrackan 1897; Hatton 1915; Stone 1915), could have grown from the traditional partisan power grab into a legal requisite. In developing this line of reasoning, the Court sustained the complaints of the "filler people" assigned to a district constructed for the purpose of providing representation not to them but to a different specific race or ethnic group. As noted earlier, the Court assumes (without evidence) that this *electoral* minority will suffer "representational harm" as individuals. Yet the Court fails to analyze either the nature of this harm or the political implications of its existence.

The Court's message can be reduced to the finding that representatives best represent those who vote for them, and losers are therefore constitutionally harmed. The harm of not being represented afflicted the Hasidic Jews who were told by the Supreme Court to rely on other whites elected in other districts to represent them in the New York legislature (*UJO v. Carey* 1977). The harm is experienced by Democratic voters in Republican-dominant districts drawn by Republican districting authorities (*Voinovich v. Quilter* 1993) and by Republicans in Democratic-dominant districts drawn by incumbents of the opposite party. When voting is racially polarized, the harm affects the black voters in white-majority congressional districts as well as white voters in the new majority-minority districts (*Shaw v. Reno* 1993). In fact, it applies to all voters who support losers in winner-take-all elections. If this logic is pursued, then clearly these voters, who are the electoral minority in every district, have a right to representation which can be vindicated only by proportional representation.

More than three decades ago, the Supreme Court recognized the individual right to an "equally weighted vote" (*Reynolds v. Sims* 1964), but when the Court corrected the evil of malapportionment the justices failed to see that a voter is not a "'member' of a 'group' comprised of all the voters in her district . . . the constituency is not a real group with shared interests and values" (Low-Beer 1984, 176). Voting for a losing candidate in a single-member district means casting a vote of zero weight. If votes are to be "equally powerful," then each voter should be represented in any policy-making body in proportion to the strength of like-minded voters in the electorate. Only proportional representation can resolve the apparent conflict between the individual right to vote and the group right not to be denied representation.

Conclusion

If democracy in the twenty-first century is finally to mean the full and substantive participation of all groups in political life, the electoral foundations for such change can be found in a variety of proportional systems. PR/STV is one of these that has been tried, as reported here. Its history does not sustain the fears of those who do not know about its earlier American practice. Turnout did not plummet; fragmentation of parties and groups did not grind the wheels of government to a halt. Minorities did make breakthroughs in representation. Shortcomings then attributed to the manual count would be eliminated today by the proven use of computers. Elections would be held at-large, but the STV ballot would enable both the majority and minorities to gain their fair share of seats. Minorities would not have to be defined by government edict, or squeezed into artificial small-district boundaries in order to gain representation, but would comprise voluntary constituencies and coalitions.

For election of single officeholders such as presidents, governors, and mayors, the instant runoff that allows ranked choices and transfer of losers' ballots to second and subsequent preferences would broaden the representation of voters in executive selection, decreasing the number of wasted votes in these elections as well. Accountability in executive offices should improve in the absence of plurality-win electoral contests.

The bias often expressed by lawmakers and judges against proportional representation is at least in part shaped by lack of knowledge about the variety of actual systems using PR and by the misunderstanding of the term itself. Advocates of PR face a stubborn belief by legislators and judges that proportional representation requires outcomes based on quotas assigned to racial, ethnic, or partisan groups. This belief is based on false premises. Election results are not predetermined when alternative election systems are used. Instead, these systems operate in areas larger than single-member districts in which voters can—voluntarily—choose how they wish to be represented.

The failure to understand how election systems work has led judges to entrap themselves between contradictory commands. On the one hand, they must require compliance with the Voting Rights Act to prevent dilution of minority voting strength, which in a territorially based election system demands race-based districting. On the other hand, they must support the Fourteenth Amendment equal protection rights of other voters whom the Supreme Court defines as mere "filler people" in racially drawn districts. Prevailing judicial theory holds that majority rights are protected if district lines are drawn by "traditional" principles which permit protecting incumbents and political parties but not racial minorities. On its face, this interpretation flouts the history of the Fourteenth Amendment, which was proposed and adopted specifically to protect the rights of the newly freed slaves. If a statute collides with the Constitution, the statute should give way. In the light of the Supreme Court's current jurisprudence, is the Voting Rights Act unconstitutional?

Justice O'Connor, a key figure in the development of the Court's current constitutional theory of voting rights, thinks not, because she sees the Voting Rights Act as "part of our national commitment to racial equality" (concurring in *Bush v. Vera* 1996, at 993), but the remedy of race-based districting still offends her. A majority of the Court—Justice O'Connor plus the four consistent dissenters in the congressional districting cases of the 1990s—may uphold the act. Still, reliance on a one-vote margin of the Supreme Court is shaky ground for so fundamental a political concept as the right to representation. Moreover, the Court has not yet found an acceptable principle of representation to guide the solution of minority vote dilution claims; ad hoc decision making prevails as the justices examine each challenged district for signs of invalidity.

The dilemma can be resolved and the act saved by the adoption of proportional election systems. "Free voting," Cleveland's Tom Johnson called it a century ago, attempting to capture in a phrase the fluid opportunities implicit in proportional representation. Under PR the voters decide which values or interests need representation. Rejecting the present territorial base for representation does not mean abandoning territorial interests. Localized interests would take their place among the range of issues of concern to voters and candidates. If the right to vote becomes the right to representation, as has been argued here, it is a right shared by minorities and the majority. Whether it is a group right or an individual right is inconsequential in proportional representation elections, since individuals are free to act independently or as participants in groups of their choice. The right to representation becomes the right to proportional representation.

In American communities where PR has been tried, proportional representation elections did not solve all social, economic, and political problems, nor should electoral systems be expected to bring utopia. A proportional election system can, however, enable representatives of most voters in a pluralist society to bring problems to the public table for debate and resolution. For individuals the promise of a fair and effective, equally weighted vote could be realized. For self-identified groups, adoption of the proportional principle for American elections would create opportunities for a more inclusive, less polarized democracy.

NOTES

Chapter 1

1. Called by French historian Françoise Mélonio "an aristocrat by instinct and a democrat by reason," Tocqueville appears to have understood the potential role of parties in democratic politics, but ever the intellectual, he was unable to exercise the political leadership or negotiate compromises that were needed to build a party. Mélonio writes: "His political failures, the oblique reading his work received, and the polite indifference given his parliamentary perorations pointed to the failure of the ideal of Reason promoted by the July regime" ([1993] 1998, 33, 213). Even Victor Considerant, whose proportional representation/party list system Tocqueville supported, opposed the idea of universal suffrage, which Tocqueville was promoting. "The education of the people," Considerant said, "has not been achieved. Before we allow them to exercise all their rights, we must wait for them to appreciate them better." Session of 15 June 1848, quoted in Mélonio, p. 54.

2. By 1921, proportional representation/party list systems had been adopted for parliamentary elections in Belgium (1899), Finland (1906), Cuba (1908), Sweden (1909), Portugal (1911), Bulgaria (1912), Denmark (1915), Iceland (1916), The Netherlands (1917), Romania (1918), Switzerland (1918), Austria (1919), Germany (1919), Uruguay (1919), Luxembourg (1919), Hungary (1919), Italy (1919), Czechoslovakia (1920), Norway (1920), Yugoslavia (1920), Estonia (1920), Lithuania (1920), Latvia (1920), and Poland (1921). Many of these countries had adopted PR/PL earlier for municipal and/or provincial elections. In 1916, Russia elected its constituent assembly under Kerensky by PR/STV, and Armenia, Georgia, and the Far Eastern (Siberian) Republic elected national assemblies by this method between 1918 and 1920 when they became part of the USSR (Hoag and Hallett 1926, 280–87).

3. Recently translated medieval works written by theologian-mathematicians in Latin, Arabic, and Catalan reveal earlier roots of collective decision theory. Ramon Lull (1235–1315) recommended a "Condorcet" method of indirect election of their abbess by nuns who would make pairwise comparisons of all reasonable candidates to choose the best. Nicholas Cusanus (1401–64) proposed a "Borda" selection process in which the Holy Roman Emperor would be chosen by electors who would allocate points in descending rank order of their preferences (McLean 1990).

4. It might seem obvious that John C. Calhoun of South Carolina would be discussed in this context. As philosopher of the slaveholding faction, he criticized political parties as centralizing forces, riding roughshod over minority needs and interests. Although early in his political life he had shared Madison's view that the diversity of interests in a large republic would tend to check majority tyranny, the failure of this check in the tariff controversy of 1828–33 led him to revise his thinking. He blamed party discipline in Congress, supported by patronage practices, for damage to Southern interests. However, Calhoun was not a proportionalist, and he did not question the assumptions of plurality voting. Because the slaveholders were geographically concentrated, by limiting suffrage they were able to secure representation in the territorially based national elections of the American system. Calhoun wanted a policy veto, not mere representation. He worked out his theory of the concurrent majority in the context of governing, not in the context of choosing who would govern (Calhoun 1851, *A Disquisition on Government*).

5. This simple formula was later refined to prevent the unlikely outcome of a tie vote among all candidates. The establishment of a "threshold," the minimum number of votes required to win, is discussed in chap. 3, infra.

6. Mill and Tocqueville shared ideas in an extended correspondence and in person when Tocqueville visited England in 1835. Both believed in the inevitability of political equality, and both feared the future degeneration of democracy into despotism. Mill reviewed both volumes of *Democracy in America* in the *London and Westminster Review* (1835, 1840) and wrote the introduction to its Schocken edition. Tocqueville wrote to Mill (3 October 1835) that Mill was "the only one who has entirely understood me," and he considered Mill his "prime confidant" during the writing of vol. 2 of *Democracy in America* (Lamberti 1989, 26, 135, 177).

7. From 1928 to 1944, the wives of business owners were also entitled to an additional vote in the districts of their husbands' enterprises. In the period between the two world wars, the university vote was 2 percent and the business vote 1.5 percent of the total vote. These plural votes were eliminated in 1948 (Reeve and Ware 1992, 47–49, 63).

8. Mill reprinted Hare's text in an article published in *Fraser's Magazine* (1859, 59:489–508) and in his *Thoughts on Parliamentary Reform*, 2d ed., 1860 (Mill 1972–88, 19:491–95).

9. Mill's championship of "Mr. Hare's plan," which he later conceded could also be called "M. Andrae's plan" ([1865, 1910] 1947, 275n. 1), led to the common use in both Britain and the United States of the expression "the Hare system of voting" to denote PR/STV. Since technical improvements in the calculation of the winning threshold and in methods of allocating surplus votes (see chap. 3) have not changed the basic purpose or concept of "Hare's" electoral system, the terms are still used as equivalents.

10. Limited voting (LV) is used within a plurality at-large system with more than one seat to be filled; each voter casts fewer votes than the number of

seats. In Mill's day, the parliamentary proposal was limited to three seats to be filled, with voters permitted to cast votes for two. Members of minorities, by casting their votes for one candidate, might secure representation. Some proportionality is achieved by this restriction on the winner-take-all feature of plurality at-large voting. The principle may be applied in larger multiseat districts as long as the voter is limited to casting fewer votes than the number of seats (see chap. 3).

11. Cumulative voting (CV), which also may be used in a plurality at-large system with multimember districts, gives the same number of votes to each voter as the number of seats to be filled, but the voter may express intensity of support by casting all votes for one candidate or by dividing the votes among two or more candidates. In a three-member district, by casting all three votes for one candidate, a minority of one-third of the voters could elect one of the three members (see chap. 3).

12. Hare's leading example of these "vagaries of the traditional method of voting" pointed to the constituencies of Liverpool and Glasgow, each of which elected two members. In these constituencies, political opinion was fairly evenly divided. Plurality voting, however, delivered both Liverpool seats to the Conservatives and both Glasgow seats to the Liberals, shutting out the minority party in each city (O'Leary 1979, 1–2).

13. From 1929 until 1967, Congress failed to renew the single-member district mandate. Its renewal in 1967 (PL 90–196) followed the implementation of the *Voting Rights Act of 1965*, to prevent southern states from reverting to at-large elections in order to exclude minority racial representation (Mast 1995, 38). This issue will be explored in chapter 5.

14. In 1803, the Ohio Assembly passed laws requiring blacks to carry federal court papers (and produce them on demand) certifying their free status. Negroes were not allowed to testify in the state's courts or to attend public schools. Although blacks were less than 1 percent of the population through the Jacksonian era, repeal of these laws was a contentious issue. Democrats generally opposed repeal, while Whigs, especially those living in the old Western Reserve in the northeast part of the state, strongly supported repeal. It was in 1849 that the legislature finally repealed the "Black Laws," when a majority of both Whigs and Democrats voted with the Free-Soilers for repeal (Maizlish 1983, 7–16, 134–36).

15. Examples include Mill's letter to Boston architect Charles A. Cummings urging the adoption of PR/STV in America (23 February 1863; Mill 1972–88, 15:842–43). Mill also corresponded with Australians (whose experience with Rowland Hill's PR/STV dated from 1840) about encouraging publicity in America, where the plan was "making its way" (letter to Henry Samuel Chapman, 24 February 1863, 1972–88, 15:844). An American publication appeared in 1862 with Hare and Mill listed as joint authors: *True and False Democracy: The Representation of All and the Representation of the Majority Only; a brief synopsis of publications on this subject* (Boston: Prentiss and Deland).

16. The senator's influence was felt in his own state, however, where in 1871 cumulative voting was adopted for the election of town councils (Buckalew 1872, 228–45).

17. The resolution expressing the sense of the convention stated that a system of cumulative voting would give the 60,000 taxpaying voters of the state "proportionate representation in the Legislature . . . with the 90,000 voters who pay no taxes." The convention's Committee on Suffrage and Elections estimated that this "just, wholesome and equitable provision" would "give the white people about forty members" in the lower house, and "always one member of the Board of County Commissioners" (J. S. Reynolds 1905, 166).

18. This account of the unsuccessful effort to introduce cumulative voting for South Carolina's legislature during Reconstruction corrects an error in Barber 1995, 31–32. Further research in the Archives of South Carolina proved that the proposal was not adopted.

19. See 44th Cong., 2d sess., U.S. Senate Committee on Privileges and Elections. 1877. Report No. 704: Inquiry into [Fraud and Violence in] the Elections of 1874, 1875, and 1876; 45th Cong., 3d sess., U.S. Senate Committee to Inquire into Alleged Frauds and Violence in the Elections of 1878. 1879. Report No. 855, with the Testimony and Documentary Evidence. Washington, D.C.: Government Printing Office.

20. Pennsylvania statutes for "reformed voting" provided for LV for election inspectors (1839), jury commissioners (1837), and delegates to the state constitutional convention of 1872 (Buckalew 1872, 228–45).

21. The 1870 Illinois Constitution was approved by 79.1 percent of the voters, while the CV amendment passed by a 58.5 percent margin (calculated from G. S. Blair 1960, 8–10).

22. After 110 years of CV legislative elections in Illinois, an initiative to repeal cumulative voting passed in 1980. It was linked to a reduction in size of the Illinois lower house prompted by a purportedly outrageous pay raise, which the members had voted for themselves. Since the voters had "decisively" approved the retention of cumulative voting in 1970, the reasons for abandonment of this semiproportional system in 1980 are at best clouded (Weaver 1984, 198–99; Everson and Parker 1983).

Chapter 2

1. Differences between Madison's interest group theory and twentieth-century pluralism are explored in Morgan 1974 and Bourke 1975.

2. It appears that the Congress was called by the Chicago Proportional Representation League, described in the first issue of the *Proportional Representation Review* as "a temporary organization effected for the purpose of preparing the way for a national society." *PRR* 1 (September 1893): 2–3.

3. Proposed article 18 would have eliminated the personal electors and apportioned the electoral votes of each state to each candidate according to

the vote won. Because the plan retained the two "senatorial" electoral votes for each state, regardless of population, the result would still have been skewed in favor of the small-population states and therefore not truly proportional. The PR League did not invent the idea of a proportional division of the electoral college vote. In the early presidential elections under the Constitution, practices for counting and aggregating votes varied widely among the states, but by 1836 all states had adopted the "unit rule," casting all their electoral votes for the winner of the popular vote. In 1848, the first proposal to divide each state's electoral vote in proportion to the popular vote was introduced in Congress. Many constitutional amendments for this purpose have subsequently been proposed. A proportional plan was approved by the Senate in 1950 but soundly defeated by the House, largely because of fears of encouraging minor parties to enter the presidential race. For discussion of the issues involved, see Wayne 1980 and Longley 1972.

4. The National Municipal League's *Model City Charter* incorporated the city manager plan and PR/STV in its 2d (1915), 3d (1925), 4th (1933), and 5th (1941) editions. In the 6th edition (1964), the NML noted PR/STV's vulnerability to repeal referenda in a number of cities that had adopted the system, and proposed PR/STV as "Alternative C." Alternatives A and B were variations of a mixed electoral system, with four at-large and three district representatives. The 7th edition (1989) recommends PR as one of five alternative electoral systems, noting that "concern for representation of minorities and the possibility of technological improvements that will simplify the counting process have renewed interest in PR" (NML 1989, xv).

5. This recommendation was retained through the 5th edition of the NML's *Model State Constitution* (1948) but was dropped without explanation (although the single legislative chamber was retained) in the 6th edition (1963).

6. Telephone interview with David Lampe, editor of the *National Civic Review,* 24 February 1992. Also see Hallett 1940, 166–67; Cassella 1990.

7. Constitutional home rule, allowing cities to choose their own form of government, was first adopted by Missouri in 1875. Between 1875 and 1974, forty-one states would adopt home rule provisions in their constitutions. Peaks of home rule adoptions occurred in response to intense Progressive activity around 1912 and 1923–24 (Glendening and Reeves 1984, 138–39).

8. A significant cleavage in the Ohio Republican Party between Liberals and Regulars can be traced back to the post–Civil War struggle over tariffs and temperance. Many of the liberal Republican leaders in Ohio were pre–Civil War antislavery Democrats. They shared the goal of industrial development with the regulars, but sought to achieve it through free trade rather than protectionism. Primarily urban, with a significant infusion of German Americans, these liberal Republicans opposed temperance laws and resisted the monopolies that they saw developing in the rapidly expanding cities. The tight grip of Republican machines on Ohio cities precluded electoral success

for these deviant Republicans in the 1880s and 1890s. More than half of the liberal Republican leaders in Ohio had joined (or rejoined) the Democratic Party by the end of the century, giving Democrats "wealthy and respectable new leaders and thus assur[ing] a more even partisan division among the upper class" (McGerr 1982, 323). The independent Progressive movement in Ohio was undoubtedly strengthened by this willingness of old-line Republicans to switch parties.

9. The number of members in the Ohio legislature was not fixed but was determined by population ratios (the total population of the state divided by 100). Fractional representation allowed for additional representation of counties with a population that was one-fifth or more above the ratio of representation. Such counties would gain an additional representative for one, two, three, or four biennial sessions of the decade of an apportionment. Rural counties were accorded the advantage of one seat for half a ratio of representation. When the Hanna amendment was adopted, only ten counties fell below the half-ratio minimum and therefore gained their own representatives after 1903. By 1960, forty-eight of the eighty-eight counties in Ohio lacked the half-ratio required before 1903, and seventy-one counties fell below a single ratio but still had a representative because of the Hanna amendment. The Senate apportionment remained relatively equitable, since three-quarters of a ratio entitled a district of one or more counties to one senator. As in the Ohio House, additional senators were allocated to populous counties, including fractional representation where justified by population. By this method of apportionment, gerrymandering was avoided (Barber 1981, 257).

10. In the nineteenth century, Ohio was a stronghold of the temperance movement and the birthplace of organized state-by-state prohibition efforts. The Women's Christian Temperance Union was founded in Cleveland in 1874. The Ohio Anti-Saloon League, founded in Oberlin in 1893, grew quickly into a national organization, headquartered in Westerville, Ohio; the league's top priority was to force political candidates to reveal their position on prohibition (Knepper 1989, 277).

11. In the Progressive Party's state convention of 1914, the "drys" among the delegates succeeded in persuading a majority that it was important to attract "dry" voters to their candidates for governor and other statewide offices. A plank supporting prohibition was written into the platform. A large and vocal minority still saw the liquor issue as a mere distraction from important matters of economic equity (Warner 1964, 483–87).

12. Herbert Bigelow of Cincinnati, president of the Direct Legislation League and later a leader in the PR movement, was elected president of the convention. Calling for a "new social compact" in his speech nominating Bigelow for that office, John D. Fackler of Cuyahoga County said, "Overshadowing all other questions and almost to the exclusion of every other issue, the question of this Convention's leaving in the hands of the individual citizen a greater and more direct control over the legislation of the state was para-

mount in the minds of men . . . elected to this Convention" (Ohio, 1912, *Proceedings*, 26).

13. The Progressives were most disappointed by the defeat of two amendments for which they had campaigned strenuously: women's suffrage and the abolition of capital punishment. Both highest turnout and closest margins were returned on these controversial amendments (Warner 1964, 341–43, and 353n. 76).

14. The Bucklin ballot was first used in Grand Junction, Colorado, in 1909 and adopted by more than sixty other cities, including San Francisco, Denver, Jersey City and Newark, N.J., in addition to these three Ohio cities (Kneier [1934] 1957, 365–70).

15. Pennsylvania was a case in contrast. In 1922, a state constitutional amendment had allowed home rule for the state's cities, but only if the legislature passed enabling legislation—and it never did, apparently owing to adamant opposition by the Republican state organization, which held secure majorities in both houses. Thus any local charter initiatives, either proposal of a new charter or adoption of a new electoral system, were vulnerable to the disapproval of the state legislature (Hallett 1940, 165).

16. With Augustus R. Hatton, by 1932 at Northwestern University, as president and with three vice presidents (one of whom was John R. Commons), the PRL continued a "separate corporate existence and . . . separate officers," operating "through" the NML. A section on PR, edited by George H. Hallett, appeared in each issue of the *National Municipal Review* for several years (*NMR* 1940, 29:217–18).

17. Upholding New York City's PR elections for community school boards against a Fourteenth Amendment equal protection challenge, District Court Judge Jack B. Weinstein ruled that PR does not deny equal protection because it does not discriminate against any identifiable group of voters. Furthermore, the legislature could reasonably have concluded that representation of minorities in school board decision making would assist in resolving differences and building support for needed changes. *Campbell v. Bd. of Educ.*, 1970.

Chapter 3

1. A majority is defined here as at least 50 percent + 1 of the total vote cast. A plurality is composed of the most votes for a candidate of those cast, if less than a majority, hence the largest minority.

2. In a multiseat plurality at-large election, not all voters make choices in all contests, so that winners may be chosen by different pluralities.

3. Efforts to measure and predict the partisan bonus delivered by plurality/single-member district electoral systems include Kendall and Stuart 1950; Tufte 1973, 1975; Niemi and Deegan 1978. Tufte's rule of thumb estimates that the majority party will gain 2.5 percentage points in seat shares for every

percentage point gain in vote shares (Tufte 1973, 546). These measures are analyzed in Barber 1983.

4. Voluntary strategic voting differs from formal systems of limited voting (LV), which are purposefully adopted to secure minority representation. See below, Semiproportional Voting Systems.

5. Voting is compulsory in Australia and voters are required to rank-order every candidate on the ballot. The alternative vote or instant runoff is adaptable, however, to voluntary voting, and voters can make as many or as few choices of candidates as they wish when ranking their preferences (Bogdanor 1984, 34).

6. Under federal law, stockholders of national banks are required to use cumulative voting for directors, a provision adopted by Congress in 1933 "to give, in case of controversy or division of interests, some representation to minority interests" (U.S. Senate, 73d Cong., 1st sess., 1933, *Cong. Record*, vol. 77, pt. 4, p. 3731). This provision, however, can be avoided by the use of a holding company structure. Corporations that allow their shareholders to elect directors by CV today include Abbott Labs, Hewlett Packard, Toys R Us, and Walgreen.

7. As noted earlier, currently popular terms for PR/STV are *preference voting* and *choice voting*. This system is currently used by a number of nongovernmental groups in the United States, such as the Motion Picture Academy (for selecting Academy Awards), American Mensa, and various faculty and student government bodies for electing officers.

8. Refinements of the rules described here are suggested by election system experts to streamline the count or to deal with special situations, the "what if?" questions (Newland 1982, 71–74).

9. In most PR/STV systems, a single X is accepted as the equivalent of a numeral one. Such a ballot is then "exhausted" after the first count. A ballot with more than one X is, however, invalid because neither the first choice nor subsequent rank-ordering can be ascertained.

10. If the threshold were set at 100 in this example, instead of 101, then a tie could ensue among ten candidates with 100 votes each. Although such a tie is extremely unlikely in an actual election, it is theoretically possible and is avoided by the addition of 1 to the threshold. Robert A. Newland, a British analyst of electoral systems, has argued that the final "+1" is not a necessary component of the formula, and it is sometimes dropped today, as in elections to the Irish Dail (Newland 1982, 66; Rae 1967, 36). Macklin treats the difference between the two formulae as insignificant (1989, 6). All electoral systems require a method to deal with ties. In a two-candidate tie with plurality voting, the usual tie-avoidance mechanism is a coin toss (Reeve and Ware 1992, 177n. 7). Ohio law provides for several other tie-breaking devices as well, such as drawing straws, picking cards, and throwing dice. A recent example occurred in a three-way single-member district plurality race for council

in Vermilion, Ohio, when the two leading candidates each received 161 votes. A coin toss broke the tie (*The Plain Dealer* (Cleveland), 22 November 1991, 2B). If the instant runoff (IRV) had been used, the third candidate, who received 146 votes, could have been dropped and his ballots redistributed to the second choices his supporters had marked. By this means, voter preference rather than chance would have determined the outcome.

11. For a comprehensive presentation of the count for a PR/STV election to fill six seats in an eleven-candidate contest, see Lakeman and Lambert 1959, app. 4, pp. 247–75.

12. A PR/STV ballot is termed "exhausted" when every candidate designated by the voter in order of choice is either already elected (i.e., has reached the threshold and does not need more votes) or already eliminated (i.e., has no chance of election and his or her ballots have been transferred to second or other choices).

13. The development of software for the PR/STV count was anticipated for some years (Piccard 1984, 520; Macklin 1989, 1) and was promoted by the Center for Voting and Democracy (CVD). In 1994, with the support of the Seasongood Foundation of Cincinnati, the Center conducted a computer recount of the 1991 city council election in Cambridge, Massachusetts, using its PRMaster program on a personal computer with manual data entry. In two minutes, the outcome matched the actual results. This demonstration propelled the city to accept computerization (Richie 1994). The tabulation system recommended by the Technical Working Committee for Computerization of Cambridge Elections and adopted by the city is adaptable to all Cambridge elections, PR/STV (municipal and school board) as well as plurality (state and federal), using precinct-based optical scanning of Marksense paper ballots. *Report of the Technical Working Committee*, 3 January 1996, 1; www.ci. cambridge.ma.us/city_hall

Chapter 4

1. Cleveland's council grew from twenty-six to thirty-three ward members under the pre-PR charter; Toledo's council had twenty ward-based members and expanded to twenty-one after 1930. In both cases, population growth led to the addition of new wards.

2.

City Council	Ward Members	At-Large Members	Total Members
Ashtabula	4	3	7
Cincinnati	26	6	32
Hamilton	6	4*	10

*Includes council president, separately elected at-large.

3. Busch, "Ashtabula: The Pioneer Community," 83–115; Barber, "PR and Boss Rule: The Case of Cleveland," 116–59; Kolesar, "PR in Cincinnati: From 'Good Government' to the Politics of Inclusion?" 160–208; Weaver and Blount, "Hamilton: PR Defeated by Its Own Success," 209–40; and Anderson, "PR in Toledo: The Neglected Stepchild of Municipal Reform," 241–81, all chapters in Barber 1995. The reader is encouraged to consult these full reports for detail and election statistics and, in a few cases where it was available, transfer data.

4. The complexity of measuring historical voter turnout is highlighted by nineteenth-century problems with fraud and census errors. Examining the measure "percent voting of those eligible to vote," Shortridge argues that reports of nineteenth-century turnout were falsely inflated by two factors: practices such as the stuffing of ballot boxes inflated the number of votes counted; and very large undercounts of the population, especially in poor urban areas, decreased the base number of eligible voters on which the calculation of turnout depends. Untrained census takers and overcrowded, even hostile, living conditions in urban neighborhoods are cited to explain the undercount. If these findings are accepted, then the alleged decline in voting from 1896 to 1931 disappears owing to public (instead of party) control of the electoral process and to improved census techniques (Shortridge 1981, 137–48). Most analysts of voting statistics, however, find an authentic decline in turnout associated with Progressive reform (J. F. Reynolds 1988).

5. Measuring turnout for local elections in pre-PR, PR, and post-PR periods is complicated by the failure of the census to report members of the population twenty-one years of age and older, by city, for the early years, necessitating the use of percentage of registered voters as the measure of turnout in Cleveland and Cincinnati. This measure itself lacks consistency over time because of a change in Ohio electoral law in 1930, when annual registration was replaced by "permanent" registration. With annual registration, there were generally fewer registrants in the municipal election year, providing a lower base number for calculating local turnout. When permanent registration was instituted, those who registered for the statewide and congressional election of 1930 remained registered as long as they voted at least once every two years, so that municipal turnout from 1930 on is calculated on the higher registration base of the previous state and federal election year.

6. "Better educated" is defined as council members having some college, a college degree, or postgraduate work. "Less educated" includes those who were educated through high school or less. Educational data were not available for Hamilton or Ashtabula. Occupations were classified as "professional," "business," "blue-collar," and "other."

7. The measure used to identify "conflict" is a broad one, since even one dissenter places an issue in the nonunanimous column. If factionalism were to be measured as a group phenomenon—such as on a nine-member council, splits of 5–4 or 6–3; on a seven-member council, 4–3 or 5–2; or on Cleve-

land's twenty-five-member council, 13–12, 14–11, or even 22–3—then "conflict" in Ohio's PR councils would be a rare event indeed.

8. A fire in the Ashtabula courthouse destroyed ballots and all official election records of the period.

9. J. G. Willert, one of the Socialist council members who had been expelled in 1917, was regularly rated "qualified" by the Citizens League, as was Socialist candidate Joseph Martinez in 1929. Transfer evidence from the 1929 Cleveland election shows that support was not often transferred from one minor party candidate to another, in part explaining their weakness in the final tally: 79 percent of the ballots giving Socialist candidates first-choice votes were transferred to non-Socialists, with antiboss candidates (independent, Republican, or Democratic) benefiting from the transfers. *PRR* 1930, 93:8.

10. Although the county charter with PR elections was passed by a majority of voters in both Cleveland and the county as a whole, it was invalidated by the Ohio Supreme Court for lack of two other majorities required by the Ohio Constitution: a majority in the county outside of the largest city, and a majority of the municipalities in the county (*State ex rel. Howland v. Krause*, 1936).

11. National and local events of racial significance coincided with Cincinnati's September 1957 repeal initiative. Federal troops were in Little Rock, Arkansas, enforcing court-ordered school desegregation over the defiance of the state's governor. Locally, interstate highway construction and urban redevelopment in Cincinnati's West End combined to displace a large concentration of black residents who were forced to seek replacement housing in previously white areas (R. A. Burnham 1997, 152).

12. In contrast, in Cleveland, Cincinnati, and Hamilton, the surplus was drawn systematically from the entire pool of a winning candidate's votes, so that the order of counting precincts would not affect the final outcome. If 10 percent of a candidate's total first-choice votes were above the minimum number needed to win, every tenth ballot from his total pool of ballots would be drawn for transfer.

13. The ballot defined a vote "FOR THE AMENDMENT" as one that "provides for the election by popular vote and eliminates proportional representation (PR)"; the alternative box "AGAINST THE AMENDMENT" was simply explained, "retain proportional representation (PR)."

14. Simmons was later elected vice mayor by the city council. Tradition called for succession to mayor. Stinchcombe reports that "Toledo voters and community leaders were willing to sanction Negro representation on the city council, but a Negro vice mayor and the thought of a Negro mayor were cause for alarm." Simmons was defeated "easily" in 1961, and in 1963 a charter amendment was passed restoring the pre-PR popular election of the mayor (Stinchcombe 1968, 194). These events in Toledo followed the comparable racial polarization that accompanied the repeal of PR in Cincinnati and the subsequent defeat of council member Theodore Berry.

15.

	No. of Transfer Winners (= No. of Transfer Losers)	Percentage of Seats
Cincinnati	15	10.4
Cleveland	12	9.6
Hamilton	8	6.7
Toledo	9	12.5
Total	44	9.6

Chapter 5

1. An example may be drawn from South Carolina legislative districts at a time when the state's population was 60 percent black. In 1882, a gerrymander was adopted "so as to make certain that the Republicans would control but one of the seven congressional seats. It provided for a colored majority of 25,198 in one district, slight colored majorities in four, and white majorities in two" (Simkins 1932, 548). Most Republican voters in the South at that time were black (see chap. 1). In the twentieth century, discriminatory racial gerrymanders were invalidated in *Gomillion v. Lightfoot,* 1960; *Perkins v. Matthews,* 1971; and *Connor v. Finch,* 1977. For a history of the racial gerrymander, see Parker 1984.

2. In the 1975 amendments, the trigger introduced for coverage, in addition to low voter turnout, was a finding that ballots or other voting materials were provided only in English in an election district where more than 5 percent of the voting-age citizens belonged to one of the specified language minorities. 42 U.S.C. §1973b(f)(3). For a legislative history of the VRA, see Issacharoff et al. 1998, 274–76, 411–34.

3. The substitution of a "results" standard for the "intent to discriminate" was debated extensively in the Senate Judiciary Committee when the 1982 amendments were considered. If a showing of fair "results" were required, Senator Orrin Hatch of Utah feared that minority vote dilution could be evaluated only against the standard of proportionality. To alleviate these concerns, the stipulation that no right to proportional representation is established by section 2 was proposed by Senator Robert Dole of Kansas on the Senate floor and adopted in the final act. For Dole's own explanation of his "proviso," see Issacharoff, Karlan, and Pildes 1998, 433–34.

4. A continuing debate among political scientists elicits conflicting conclusions about the relative merits of majority-minority districts and influence districts. See, e.g., Cameron, Epstein, and O'Halloran 1996, finding that substantive representation of minority voters is maximized outside the South by dividing minority voters equally across districts, while in the South minority voters will achieve the best outcomes legislatively if a maximum number of districts with 47 percent black voting-age population are created; Lublin

1999, refuting their findings on methodological grounds; and Epstein and O'Halloran 1999, confirming their previous results over time. See also Swain 1993 and Guinier 1994.

5. A divided three-judge federal court rejected the state apportionment board's plan on the ground that the board had failed to show any violation of section 2 of the Voting Rights Act; therefore, its creation of new majority-minority districts was unnecessary; since the action was intentional and partisan in purpose, the resulting loss of minority-influence districts violated the Fifteenth Amendment. Furthermore, population disparities in the plan led the court to reject it for a violation of the Fourteenth Amendment equal protection clause (794 F.Supp. 695 [ND Ohio 1992]). The board's revised plan was also rejected by the district court in a 2–1 decision (794 F.Supp. 760 [ND Ohio 1992]). In both instances, the majority judges were Democratic, the dissenter Republican. This was a partisan decision-making pattern that mirrored the apportionment board's partisan division and continued the tradition of judicial partisanship in reapportionment and districting cases in Ohio that is consistent in state and federal courts at least as far back as the post *Baker v. Carr* decisions of the 1960s. See Barber 1969.

6. North Carolina's Twelfth District was, in fact, virtually a mirror image of South Carolina's notorious Seventh Congressional District of 1882, when the population of South Carolina was about 60 percent black and black voters were Republicans. The *New York Times* reported at the time that the Seventh District "contains all the precincts of black voters that could be strung together with the faintest connection of contiguous territory. . . . In canvassing this district the candidates would have to travel about 200 miles within its extreme borders. [The Bourbons] boast that they have so fixed things that but one district, the Seventh, will be given to the Republicans." Referred to at the time as "Dibble's adroit gerrymander," the overpopulated Seventh District was adjacent to the long, narrow First District, constructed by its white Democratic incumbent. The *New York Times* commented: "Mr. [Samuel] Dibble has thus hitched together about all the Democratic precincts he could find in the neighborhood of his home to make his election sure, and to be safe the district is so limited that it contains only 119,000 inhabitants, about 35,000 less than the required population to entitle it to a representation." *New York Times*, 13 July 1882, p. 5. See also Simpkins 1932, 548.

7. The major cases in this ongoing struggle were North Carolina: *Shaw v. Reno* 1993, *Shaw v. Hunt* 1996, *Hunt v. Cromartie* 1999; Georgia: *Miller v. Johnson* 1995, *Abrams v. Johnson* 1997; Louisiana: *U.S. v. Hays* 1995; Texas: *Bush v. Vera* 1996; Florida: *Johnson v. DeGrandy* 1994, *Lawyer v. Dept. of Justice* 1997. Until 1999, in what was an inconclusive procedural decision (*Hunt v. Cromartie*), opinions in these race-based districting cases were sharply split, 5–4, with consistent blocs of justices on opposing sides: in the majority, Justices O'Connor, Kennedy, Scalia, Thomas, and Chief Justice Rehnquist; in dissent: Justices Stevens, Souter, Breyer, and Ginsburg. In one of the few

instances when an allegedly race-based district was upheld, the result was reached because Rehnquist crossed over on technical grounds (the challenged district was the product of a federal court settlement) to support the outcome. *Lawyer v. Dept. of Justice,* 521 U.S. 567 (1997).

8. A second kind of harm identified by the Supreme Court is "stigmatic . . . in the sense that the race-based line-drawing may promote racial hostility." *Shaw v. Hunt,* 517 U.S. 899 at 927. In *United States v. Hays,* 515 U.S. 737 (1995), the Court rejected a Louisiana suit challenging a redrawn majority-minority district because the plaintiffs lived and voted in an adjacent district and therefore were found by the Court to have suffered no "injury in fact" that would give them standing to sue. However, this adjacent district shared a new boundary with the challenged district that the plaintiffs alleged was a race-based line. The Court denied that residents of the adjacent district suffered the "special *representational* harms racial classifications can cause in the voting context" (at 745). For critical analysis of the Court's reasoning with respect to standing to sue, see Justice Souter's dissent in *Shaw v. Hunt, Bush v. Vera* 1996, at 951, and Durschlag 1997.

9. In *Adarand Constructors, Inc. v. Pena,* 515 U.S. 200 (1995), the Court applied the strict scrutiny standard to all racial classifications, whether "benign or otherwise," and to all governmental actors: federal, state, and local. The Court's 5–4 split in this affirmative action case followed the pattern of the race-based districting cases, with Justice Stevens arguing for the dissenters that "there is no moral or constitutional equivalence between a policy that is designed to perpetuate a caste system and one that seeks to eradicate racial subordination. Invidious discrimination is an engine of oppression, subjugating a disfavored group to enhance or maintain the power of the majority. Remedial race-based preferences reflect the opposite impulse: a desire to foster equality in society" (at 243). Justice O'Connor for the majority, however, continued the trend in public contracting and education disputes to restrict the use of affirmative action (*City of Richmond v. Kirwan* 1989). No longer would a historical pattern of racial discrimination justify remedial racial preferences. Even addressing present effects of past discrimination is not a compelling state interest (*Podberesky v. Kirwan* 1995).

10. In 1996, Cleo Fields, by then a two-term Congressman from Louisiana, chose not to run again from "his" district, which had been reduced from 55 to 28 percent black voting-age population (Yeoman 1998, 20).

11. Ironically, in the first post-1990 North Carolina redistricting, a second and more compact majority-minority district could have been drawn in the southeastern region of the state, achieving proportionality without so "bizarre" a shape as the contentious Twelfth turned out to be. This was an option recommended by the state's attorney general. Only Justice White's dissenting opinion in *Shaw v. Reno* revealed the reason that this most "obvious" district was not drawn, namely, incumbency protection. A white Democratic incum-

bent would have been threatened by the creation of a new minority district in that section of the state (at 673n. 10).

12. The Court's action in *Hunt v. Cromartie* had unanimous support. Justice Thomas's opinion, signed by five justices, held that not all consideration of race was impermissible in districting decisions. Evidence of "high correlation between race and party preference" might lead the lower court to decide that the motivation for the Twelfth District lines was (permissibly) partisan instead of impermissibly racial. Justice Stevens wrote a concurring opinion, joined by Justices Breyer, Ginsburg, and Souter, noting the convincing nature of the evidence that the legislature's motivation was partisan. *Hunt v. Cromartie* 1999; *New York Times,* 18 May 1999, A17.

13. *Martin v. Allain,* 658 F.Supp. 1183 (S.D.Miss. 1987); *Martin v. Mabus,* 700 F.Supp. 327 (S.D.Miss. 1988). The election system that was found to be discriminatory required judicial candidates to run in multijudge districts where each judge occupied a particular seat or "slot." A challenger therefore had to run against a single incumbent in a plurality at-large contest. Federal District Judge William H. Barbour Jr. ordered the creation of judicial subdistricts, some with black majorities. See E. Still 1991, 361.

14. In 1998, the National Center for Health Statistics reported that Hispanic children already outnumbered black children. The Census Bureau explains relative growth rates of these groups by both immigration from Latin America and higher birth rates of Hispanic Americans, while birth rates of African Americans have declined. If 925,000 Hispanic blacks (largely from Dominica, Puerto Rico, and Cuba) are subtracted from the black total, the disparity in numbers widens. A countervailing trend is the more frequent practice of intermarriage between Hispanic women and non-Hispanics (as reported by 31.4 percent of Hispanic women in 1990, mostly to non-Hispanic whites) as opposed to 6.3 percent of black women reporting marriage to a husband of another racial group. *New York Times,* 16 August 1998, E3.

15. The Census Bureau reported an uneven distribution of the undercount at 2 percent of the overall population but 4.8 percent of the black population and 5.2 percent of the Hispanic population. *New York Times,* 11 September 1998, A14. The double count occurred because of second-home ownership, adding upper-income people to the total and therefore exacerbating the bias of the undercount. *New York Times,* 26 January 1999, A20.

16. A coalition of large cities sued the Census Bureau to force the statistical adjustment of the 1990 Census. The U.S. Supreme Court ruled unanimously that the adjustment was not required by the Constitution, but it did not address the question of whether such an adjustment was permissible (*Wisconsin v. New York,* 517 U.S. 1 [1996]).

17. Because there are five racial categories protected in the Voting Rights Act and in affirmative action legislation, a multitude of racial combinations becomes possible for non-Hispanics, and just as many for Hispanics, who are

an ethnic group but not a racial group. However, to simplify federal reporting requirements for state and local governments and businesses, the guidelines from the Office of Management and Budget limit the call for data to the five racial groups named in these statutes, plus the four most common combinations of racial groups, as identified in Census Bureau tests (*New York Times*, 11 March 2000, A7).

18. In *Holder v. Hall*, 1994, the Supreme Court declined to find minority vote dilution in the practice of electing a single county commissioner who exercises all executive and legislative power. No black commissioner had ever been elected in Bleckley County. Black voters, who constituted 20 percent of the county's population, argued that the Voting Rights Act should afford a remedy in the form of a five-member commission. In a 5–4 decision, the Court declined to apply section 2 of the act to challenges to the size of a government structure. The decision was of limited significance, since the Court remanded the case for consideration of the same issue by constitutional standards.

19. See, e.g., Zimmerman 1978; Rogowski 1981; J. Still 1981; Note, *Yale Law Journal* 1982a, 1982b; Low-Beer 1984; Levinson 1985; Grofman and Lijphart 1986; Thernstrom 1987; E. Still 1991; Guinier 1991, 1992, 1994.

20. A useful compendium of diverse views is found in Peacock 1997. Thernstrom, Guinier, Engstrom, Bernard Grofman, Mark Rush, Ed Still, and others are represented in chapters, some of which are reprinted from other sources.

21. Asian American Legal Defense and Education Fund 1998, Re: Comment under sec. 5 of the Voting Rights Act, chap. 149, Laws of the State of New York, Re: New York City Community School Board Election Procedures; Center for Voting and Democracy 1998, Submission No. 98–31–93 to the U.S. Dept. of Justice, Re: New York City Board of Education's Submission under sec. 5 of the Voting Rights Act.

22. Illinois Citizens for Proportional Representation is a nonprofit, nonpartisan group organized in 1997 for the purpose of achieving "a more democratic, fairer proportional representation voting system." See www.prairienet. org/icpr. Supporting the efforts of this organization, the *Chicago Tribune* explained its editorial position: "There were liberal Republicans and conservative Democrats. . . . The intermeshing of political and regional interests has all but disappeared in the 15 years since cumulative voting was abolished. In its place, partisan politics has become increasingly shrill and confrontational. . . . For years, many partisans and political independents have looked wistfully at the era of cumulative voting. They acknowledge that it produced some of the best and brightest in Illinois politics." Editorial, "Better Politics from an Old Idea," 30 May 1995.

23. In place of the snakelike district invalidated in *Shaw v. Reno* (1993) as one of twelve existing single-member districts, Lee Mortimer of the Center for Voting and Democracy proposed three multimember congressional districts for the entire state. With boundaries largely following county lines, a

Western District would elect three members, a Piedmont District (incorporating most of the challenged Twelfth District) would elect five, and an Eastern District would elect four. Voters would cast their ballots at-large within the multimember districts, but be able to cumulate their votes as they chose—all for one candidate, or divided among several. The attraction of the plan was its ability to create the opportunity for minorities to win representation without rigidly programming voters into racial districts (*News and Record,* Greensboro, N.C., 9 January 1994, F3; *New York Times,* 3 April 1994, E5; *New Yorker,* 4 April 1994, 7–8).

A CV alternative proposed by Lani Guinier would have North Carolina voters choose their twelve members of Congress by CV with each voter casting twelve statewide votes that could be cumulated in accord with voter preference (*Washington Post Weekly,* 11 April 1994, 24). Both of these CV plans would have enabled the *60 percent* of African American voters in the state who were *not* living in either of the racially designated districts to vote with others of similar interests. However, as noted earlier, since the CV plans would require a change in the federal law that mandates single-member districts for Congress, neither proposal was entered formally in the case.

24. The Cincinnati Charter Committee, an integrated coalition that played a central role in the introduction and continued practice of PR/STV, narrowly lost two initiatives (1988 and 1991) to restore the city's proportional representation (PR/STV) elections. Following the 1991 defeat of PR, fifteen black voters sued the city in federal court, alleging that the plurality at-large electoral system for city council was adopted in 1957 with the intent to discriminate against black voters and that it indeed caused minority vote dilution in violation of the Voting Rights Act. The remedy they sought was not PR but a single-member district system. Judge Herman Weber, to whom the case was assigned, delayed the trial to allow the city council itself to present its preferred remedy to the voters. After public hearings, input from consultants, and lengthy internal debate, the council placed on the May 1993 ballot a council election plan retaining the nine at-large members but providing for their election by cumulative voting. A brief but intense campaign led to defeat of the initiative by a 79 percent majority, and the case went to trial (*Center for Voting and Democracy* 1994, 41–42; *Cincinnati Enquirer,* 7 February 1993, H1–H2; *The Plain Dealer* (Cleveland), 17 May 1993, 3B).

In July 1993, Judge Weber issued his decision upholding the city's 9X voting system. Although conceding that a nasty racial "whisper campaign" had accompanied the 1957 repeal of PR and the adoption of plurality at-large voting, the judge denied that city officials were responsible for it. Furthermore, he attributed PR's repeal to "objective factors such as low voter turnout at a special election; the deficiencies of PR; and partisan political interests" (*Clarke v. City of Cincinnati* 1993). His opinion quoted the U.S. Supreme Court's rejection of race-conscious districting in *Shaw v. Reno* (1993), which was announced between the trial in Cincinnati and Judge Weber's decision.

Since the Cincinnati decision rested on the judge's denial that voting patterns in the city were racially polarized, the relevance of *Shaw* was unclear. The decision, however, was upheld on appeal (*Clarke v. City of Cincinnati*, 6th Cir., 1994; *The Plain Dealer* [Cleveland], 4 November 1994, 5B).

25. In some of these limited voting cases, the total number of candidates was equal to the number of seats, making the victory uncontested. In 1988, however, black candidates won contested LV races in six of seven Alabama towns, and in 1992 they won in four of five. In Lowndesboro in 1988 and in Dora in 1992, the single black candidate finished only one or a few votes behind the winner with the lowest total vote. This outcome suggests that either black turnout was very low or many blacks but virtually no whites crossed racial lines in voting (Engstrom 1992, 758–60).

26. The "States' Choice of Voting Systems Act" would amend 2 U.S.C. §2c by providing that all states entitled in the 108th Congress and in any subsequent Congress to more than one representative may elect members from single-member districts or from multimember districts, or from some combination of these, using a system that maintains equal voting power for each voter and that does not violate the *Voting Rights Act of 1965* (42 U.S.C. §1973 et seq.), H.R. 1173, 106th Cong., 1st sess.

BIBLIOGRAPHY

Legal Cases

Abrams v. Johnson, 521 U.S. 74 (1997).

Adarand Constructors, Inc. v. Pena, 515 U.S. 200 (1995).

Allen v. State Board of Elections, 393 U.S. 544 (1969).

Baker v. Carr, 369 U.S. 186 (1962).

Brown v. Board of Education, 347 U.S. 483 (1954).

Bush v. Vera, 517 U.S. 952 (1996).

Campbell v. Board of Education, 310 F.Supp. 94 (EDNY 1970).

Campos v. City of Baytown, 840 F.2d 1240 (5th Cir. 1988); 849 F.2d 943 (5th Cir. 1989); cert. den. 492 U.S. 905 (1989).

Cane v. Worcester County, Md., 35 F.3d 921 (4th Cir. 1994), overturning 847 F.Supp. 369 (1994); 59 F.3d 921 (4th Cir. 1994), overturning 874 F.Supp. 687 (D.Md. 1995), cert. den. 513 U.S. 1148 (1995).

Chisom v. Roemer, 501 U.S. 380 (1991).

City of Boerne v. Flores, 521 U.S. 507 (1997).

City of Mobile v. Bolden, 446 U.S. 55 (1980).

City of Richmond v. Kirwan, 488 U.S. 469 (1989).

Clarke v. City of Cincinnati, 40 F.3d 807 (6th Cir. 1994).

Cleveland County Ass'n for Gov't by the People v. Cleveland County Bd. of Comm'rs, 965 F.Supp. 72 (D.D.C. 1997), rev'd on other grounds, 1998 WL 210591 (D.D.C. 1998).

Clinton v. The Cedar Rapids R.R. Co., 24 Iowa 455 (1868).

Colegrove v. Green, 328 U.S. 549 (1946).

Connor v. Finch, 431 U.S. 407 (1977).

Cousin v. McWherter, 46 F.3d 568 (6th Cir. 1995).

Cousin v. Sundquist, 145 F.3d 818 (6th Cir. 1998), 119 S.Ct. 1026 (1999), cert.den.

Davis v. Bandemer, 478 U.S. 109 (1986).

DeGrandy v. Wetherell, 794 F.Supp. 1076 (N.D.Fla. 1992).

Department of Commerce v. U.S. House of Representatives, 11 F.Supp.2d 76 (DDC, 1998), 119 S.Ct. 765 (1999).

Dillard v. Chilton County Board of Education and Chilton County Commission, 699 F.Supp. 870 (M.D.Ala. 1988).

Dillard v. Crenshaw County, 640 F.Supp. 1347 (M.D.Ala. 1986).

East Carroll Parish School Board v. Marshall, 424 U.S. 636 (1976).

Fortson v. Dorsey, 379 U.S. 433 (1965).

Gaffney v. Cummings, 412 U.S. 738 (1973).

Gomillion v. Lightfoot, 364 U.S. 339 (1960).

Gray v. Sanders, 372 U.S. 368 (1963).

Gregory v. Ashcroft, 501 U.S. 452 (1991).

Growe v. Emison, 507 U.S. 25 (1993).

Hile v. City of Cleveland, 107 O.S. 144, 141 N.E. 35 (1923), writ of error dismissed, 266 U.S. 582 (1924).

Holder v. Hall, 512 U.S. 874 (1994).

Houston Lawyers' Association v. Attorney General of Texas, 501 U.S. 419 (1991).

Hunt v. Cromartie (Shaw III), 119 S.Ct. 1545 (1999).

Johnson v. DeGrandy, 512 U.S. 997 (1994).

Johnson v. City of New York, 274 N.Y. 411 (1937).

Lawyer v. U.S. Department of Justice, 521 U.S. 567 (1997).

LULAC v. Midland Independent School District, 829 F.2d 546 (5th Cir. en banc, 1987).

LULAC v. Northeastern Independent School District, 903 F.Supp. 1071 (U.S.D.C. 1995).

Martin v. Allain, 658 F.Supp. 1183 (S.D.Miss. 1987).

Martin v. Mabus, 700 F.Supp. 327 (S.D.Miss. 1988).

McSweeney v. City of Cambridge, 665 N.E.2d 11 (Mass. 1996).

Miller v. Johnson, 515 U.S. 900 (1995).

Moore v. Election Comm'rs of Cambridge, 35 NE2d 222 (Mass. 1941).

Nixon et al. v. Kent County, 76 F.3d. 1381 (6th Cir. 1996).

People ex rel. Devine v. Elkus, 59 Cal. App. 396, 211 Pac. 34 (1922), hearing denied by Cal. S. Ct. (1922).

Perkins v. Matthews, 400 U.S. 379 (1971).

Podberesky v. Kirwan, 38 F.3d 147 (4th Cir.), reh'g den. 46 F.3d 5 (5th Cir. 1994) (en banc), cert. den. 514 U.S. 1128 (1995).

Reutener v. City of Cleveland, 107 O.S. 117, 141 N.E. 27 (1923).

Reynolds v. Sims, 377 U.S. 533 (1964).

Reynoso et al. v. Amarillo Independent School District, Civil Action N.2–98–CV-186–J, U.S.D.C., N.D.Texas, 1999.

Rural West Tennessee African-American Affairs Council v. McWherter, 877 F.Supp. 1096 (W.D.Tenn.), summarily aff'd sub.nom. *Rural West Tennessee African-American Affairs Council v. Sundquist*, 516 U.S. 801 (1995).

Shaw v. Hunt (Shaw II), 517 U.S. 899 (1996).

Shaw v. Reno, 509 U.S. 630 (1993).

State ex rel. Howland v. Krause et al., 130 O.S. 455 (1936).

Thornburg v. Gingles, 478 U.S. 30 (1986).

United Jewish Organizations of Williamsburgh, Inc. v. Carey, 430 U.S. 144 (1977).
United States v. Hays, 515 U.S. 737 (1995).
Voinovich v. Quilter, 507 U.S. 146 (1993), 912 F.Supp. 1006 (ND Ohio, 1995), 981 F.Supp. 1032 (1997), aff'd 523 U.S. 1043 (1998).
Wattles ex rel. Johnson v. Upjohn, 211 Mich. 514, 179 N.W. 335 (1920).
White v. Regester, 412 U.S. 769 (1973).
Wisconsin v. New York, 517 U.S. 1 (1996).
Wright v. Rockefeller, 376 U.S. 52 (1964).
Zimmer v. McKeithen, 485 F.2d 1297 (5th Cir. 1973).

Newspapers and Magazines

Ashtabula Star-Beacon. 1916–37. Ashtabula Public Library.
Beacon Record (Ashtabula). 1910–15. Ashtabula Public Library.
Chicago Tribune. 1995.
Cincinnati Enquirer. 1993–94.
Cleveland Citizen. 1921–61. Cleveland Public Library.
Cleveland Plain Dealer. 1917–61. *Plain Dealer,* 1961–2000 (The name changed on September 16, 1961).
Cleveland Press. 1917–37. Cleveland Public Library.
Congressional Globe. 1867–70.
Congressional Record. 1933.
CQ Weekly Report. 1998.
Daily Star (Ashtabula). 1914–16. Ashtabula Public Library.
Equity (formerly *Equity Series*). 1914–1919.
Fraser's Magazine. 1859.
Greater Cleveland (GC). 1923–37. Cleveland: The Citizens League.
Hamilton Evening Journal. 1915–33. Lane Public Library, Hamilton, Ohio.
Hamilton Journal News. 1933–90. Lane Public Library, Hamilton, Ohio.
Jefferson Gazette. 1883 to the present. Ashtabula Public Library.
London and Westminster Review. 1835, 1840.
National Municipal Review (NMR). 1912–58. New York: National Municipal League.
National Civic Review (NCR). 1959 to present. Denver: National Civic League.
News and Record (Greensboro, N.C.). 1993–94.
New Yorker. 1994.
New York Times. 1871–2000.
Proportional Representation Review (PRR). 1893–1932. Chicago and Philadelphia: The Proportional Representation League. Consolidated with *National Municipal Review,* 1932–58; *National Civic Review,* 1993 to present.

Texas Observer. 1994.
Time Magazine. 1994.
Toledo Blade. 1927–57.
Toledo City Journal. 1916–57. Toledo Commission on Publicity and Efficiency.
Toledo News-Bee. 1927–38. Toledo Public Library.
Toledo Times. 1927–57. Toledo Public Library.
Washington Post Weekly. 1994.

Works Cited

Abbott, Virginia C. 1949. *The History of Woman Suffrage and the League of Women Voters in Cuyahoga County, 1911–1945.* Cleveland: Cleveland League of Women Voters.

Addams, Jane. 1960. *Jane Addams: A Centennial Reader.* New York: Macmillan.

Aleinikoff, T. Alexander, and Samuel Issacharoff. 1993. Race and Redistricting: Drawing Constitutional Lines after *Shaw v. Reno. Michigan Law Review* 92:588–651.

Argersinger, Peter H. 1989. The Value of the Vote: Political Representation in the Gilded Age. *Journal of American History* 76:59–90.

Asian American Legal Defense and Education Fund. 1998. Re: Comment under Sec. 5 of the Voting Rights Act, Chap. 149, Laws of the State of New York, New York City Community School Board Election Procedures.

Austen-Smith, David, and Jeffrey Banks. 1991. Monotonicity in Electoral Systems. *American Political Science Review* 85:531–37.

Baker, Keith M. 1975. *Condorcet: From Natural Philosophy to Social Mathematics.* Chicago: Univ. of Chicago Press.

Banner, Lois W. 1980. *Elizabeth Cady Stanton: A Radical for Woman's Rights.* Boston: Little, Brown.

Barber, Kathleen L. 1969. Partisan Values in the Lower Courts: Reapportionment in Ohio and Michigan. *Case Western Reserve Law Review* 20:401–21.

———. 1981. Ohio. In *Reapportionment Politics: The History of Redistricting in the Fifty States,* ed. Leroy Hardy et al., 256–65. Beverly Hills, Calif.: Sage.

———. 1983. Partisan Bias and Incumbent Protection in Legislative Districting. Paper presented at the 1983 meeting of the American Political Science Association, Chicago.

———. 1995. *Proportional Representation and Election Reform in Ohio.* Columbus: Ohio State Univ. Press.

Bartholdi, John J., III, and J. B. Orlin. 1991. Single Transferable Vote Resists Strategic Voting. *Social Choice and Welfare* 8:341–54.

Beard, Mary R. [1915] 1972. *Woman's Work in Municipalities*. Reprint, New York: Arno.

Beard, Charles A., and John D. Lewis. 1932. Representative Government in Evolution. *American Political Science Review* 26:223–40.

Beinart, Peter. 1997. New Bedfellows. *New Republic*, 11 Aug. 1997, pp. 23–26.

Bentley, Arthur F. 1908. *The Process of Government*. Chicago: Univ. of Chicago Press.

Blair, George S. 1960. *Cumulative Voting: An Effective Electoral Device in Illinois Politics*. Urbana: Univ. of Illinois Press.

Blair, Margaret M. 1995. *Ownership and Control: Rethinking Corporate Governance for the Twenty-first Century*. Washington, D.C.: Brookings Institution.

Bogdanor, Vernon. 1984. *What Is Proportional Representation?* Oxford: Martin Robertson.

———. 1993. Israel Debates Reform. *Journal of Democracy* 4:66–78.

———, ed. 1985. *Representatives of the People: Parliamentarians and Constituents in Western Democracies*. Aldershot, England: Gower.

———, ed. 1991. *Blackwell Encyclopedia of Political Science*. Oxford: Blackwell.

Bourke, Paul F. 1975. The Pluralist Reading of James Madison's Tenth *Federalist*. *Perspectives in American History* 9:271–95.

Boyer, Paul. 1978. *Urban Masses and Moral Order in America, 1820–1920*. Cambridge: Harvard Univ. Press.

Buckalew, Charles R. 1872. *Proportional Representation; or, The Representation of Successive Majorities in Federal, State, Municipal, Corporate, and Primary Elections*. Philadelphia: J. Campbell and Son.

Buenker, John D. 1973. *Urban Liberalism and Progressive Reform*. New York: Charles Scribner's Sons.

———. 1988. Sovereign Individuals and Organic Networks: Political Cultures in Conflict during the Progressive Era. *American Quarterly* 40:187–204.

Burnham, Robert A. 1992. The Cincinnati Charter Revolt of 1924: Creating City Government for a Pluralistic Society. In *Ethnic Diversity and Civic Identity: Patterns of Conflict and Cohesion in Cincinnati since 1820*, ed. Henry D. Shapiro and Jonathan Sarna, 202–24. Urbana: Univ. of Illinois Press.

———. 1997. Reform, Politics, and Race in Cincinnati. *Journal of Urban History* 23:131–63.

Burnham, Walter Dean. 1981. The System of 1896: An Analysis. In *The Evolution of American Electoral Systems*, ed. Paul Kleppner et al., 147–202. Westport, Conn.: Greenwood Press.

Calhoun, John C. 1851. *A Disquisition on Government and A Discourse on the*

Constitution and Government of the United States. Charleston, S.C.: Steam Power-Press of Walker and James.

Cameron, Charles, David Epstein, and Sharyn O'Halloran. 1996. Do Majority-Minority Districts Maximize Substantive Black Representation in Congress? *American Political Science Review* 90:794–812.

Cassella, William N. 1975. A Century of Home Rule. *National Civic Review* 64:441–50.

———. 1990. The Model Charters: Continuity and Change. *National Civic Review* 79:318–31.

Center for Voting and Democracy. 1994, 1996. *Voting and Democracy Report, 1993, 1995.* Washington, D.C.: Center for Voting and Democracy.

———. 1998. Submission no. 98–31–93 to the U.S. Dept. of Justice under Sec. 5 of the Voting Rights Act, Re: New York City Community School Board Election Procedures.

Chafe, William H. 1972. *The American Woman: Her Changing Social, Economic, and Political Roles, 1920–1970.* New York: Oxford Univ. Press.

Childs, Richard S. 1952. *Civic Victories.* New York: Harper.

———. 1965. *The First Fifty Years of the City Manager Plan of Municipal Government.* New York: Stratford Press.

City of Cambridge, Mass., Technical Working Committee for Computerization of Cambridge Elections. 1996. Report to the Cambridge Board of Election Commissioners. Cambridge: The City.

Cohodas, Nadine. 1994. Electing Minorities. *CQ Researcher* 4:698–715.

Cole, Alistair, and Peter Campbell. 1989. *French Electoral Systems and Elections since 1789.* 3d ed. Aldershot, England: Gower.

Commons, John R. 1907. *Proportional Representation.* 2d ed. New York: Macmillan.

Conger, J. L. 1920. Justice to Both Minority and Majority through Proportional Representation in City Elections. *American City* 23:58–59.

Congressional Quarterly. 1976. *National Party Conventions, 1831–1972.* Washington, D.C.: CQ Press.

———. 1994. *CQ's Politics in America 1994: The 103d Congress.* Washington, D.C.: CQ Press.

Cooley, Winnifred Harper. 1913. The Younger Suffragists. *Harper's Weekly,* 27 September, 7–8.

Cox, Gary W. 1997. *Making Votes Count: Strategic Coordination in the World's Electoral Systems.* Cambridge: Cambridge Univ. Press.

Davidson, Chandler. 1992. The Voting Rights Act: A Brief History. In *Controversies in Minority Voting: The Voting Rights Act in Perspective,* ed. Bernard Grofman and Chandler Davidson, 7–51. Washington, D.C.: Brookings Institution.

———, ed. 1984. *Minority Vote Dilution.* Washington, D.C.: Howard Univ. Press.

Davidson, Chandler, and George Korbel. 1981. At-Large Elections and

Minority-Group Representation: A Re-examination of Historical and Contemporary Evidence. *Journal of Politics* 43:982–1005.

DeGrazia, Alfred. 1951. *Public and Republic: Political Representation in America.* New York: Alfred A. Knopf.

DeLeon, Richard E., Lisel Blash, and Steven Hill. 1997. The Politics of Electoral Reform in San Francisco: Preference Voting versus Districts versus Plurality At-Large. Paper presented at the 1997 meeting of the Western Political Science Association, Tucson, March 13–15, 1997.

Doron, Gideon, and Richard Kronick. 1977. Single Transferable Vote: An Example of a Perverse Social Choice Function. *American Journal of Political Science* 21:303–11.

Douglas, Paul H. 1923. Occupational versus Proportional Representation. *American Journal of Sociology* 29:129–57.

Draper, Theodore. 1957. *The Roots of American Communism.* New York: Viking Press.

Dreier, Mary E. 1950. *Margaret Dreier Robins: Her Life, Letters, and Work.* New York: Island Press Cooperative.

Droop, H. R. 1881. *On Methods of Electing Representatives.* London: Statistical Society.

DuBois, W. E. B. [1899] 1967. *The Philadelphia Negro: A Social Study.* Univ. of Pennsylvania Studies in Political Economy and Public Law, no. 14. Philadelphia: Univ. of Pennsylvania; New York: Schocken Books.

———. 1935. *Black Reconstruction in America, 1860–80.* New York: Harcourt, Brace.

Durschlag, Melvyn R. 1997. *United States v. Hays:* An Essay on Standing to Challenge Minority Voting Districts. *Univ. of Cincinnati Law Review* 65:341–80.

Dutcher, Salem. 1872. *Minority or Proportional Representation: Its Nature, Aims, History, Processes, and Practical Operation.* New York: United States Pub. Co.

Dye, Nancy Schrom. 1980. *As Equals and Sisters: Feminism, the Labor Movement, and the Women's Trade Union League of New York.* Columbia: Univ. of Missouri Press.

Engstrom, Richard L. 1992. Modified Multi-Seat Election Systems as Remedies for Minority Vote Dilution. *Stetson Law Review* 21:743–70.

Engstrom, Richard L., Delbert A. Taebel, and Richard Cole. 1989. Cumulative Voting as a Remedy for Minority Vote Dilution: The Case of Alamogordo, New Mexico. *Journal of Law and Politics* 5:469–97.

Epstein, David, and Sharyn O'Halloran. 1999. A Social Science Approach to Race, Redistricting, and Representation. *American Political Science Review* 93:187–91.

Everson, David H., and Joan A. Parker. 1983. The Impact of the New Single Member District System in Illinois. Paper presented at the annual meeting of the American Political Science Association, Chicago.

Filene, Peter G. 1970. An Obituary for "The Progressive Movement." *American Quarterly* 22:20–34.

Fishburn, Peter C. 1990. Dimensions of Election Procedures: Analyses and Comparisons. In *Representation and Electoral Systems: Canadian Perspectives*, ed. J. Paul Johnston and Harvey Pasis, chap. 30. Scarborough, Canada: Prentice-Hall.

Fishburn, Peter C., and Steven J. Brams. 1983. Paradoxes of Preferential Voting. *Mathematics Magazine* 56:207–14.

Fisher, J. Francis. 1863. *The Degradation of Our Representative System and Its Reform*. Philadelphia: C. Sherman.

Flexner, Eleanor. 1975. *Century of Struggle: The Woman's Rights Movement in the United States*. Rev. ed. Cambridge: Harvard Univ. Press, Belknap Press.

Ford, Lacy K., Jr. 1994. Inventing the Concurrent Majority: Madison, Calhoun, and the Problem of Majoritarianism in American Political Thought. *Journal of Southern History* 60:19–58.

Foulke, William Dudley. 1915. Address. *Equity* 17:70–76.

Fraga, Luis R. 1991. Policy Consequences and the Change from At-Large Elections to Single-Member Districts. Paper presented at the annual meeting of the Western Political Science Association, Seattle.

Gallagher, Michael. 1992. Comparing Proportional Representation Electoral Systems: Quotas, Thresholds, Paradoxes, and Majorities. *British Journal of Political Science* 22:469–96.

Gilpin, Thomas. 1844. *On the Representation of Minorities of Electors to Act with the Majority, in Elected Assemblies*. Philadelphia: J. C. Clark.

Glendening, Parris N., and Mavis Mann Reeves. 1984. *Pragmatic Federalism*. 2d ed. Pacific Palisades, Calif.: Palisades.

Godkin, Edwin L. 1894. The Problems of Municipal Government. *Annals of the Academy of Political and Social Sciences* 4:857–82.

Gordon, Jeff. 1994. Institutions as Relational Investors: A New Look at Cumulative Voting. *Columbia Law Review* 94:124–92.

Gosnell, Harold F. [1934] 1948. Proportional Representation. In *Encyclopaedia of the Social Sciences*, ed. Edwin R. A. Seligman. vol. 12, pp. 541–45. New York: Macmillan.

Grabowski, John J. 1986. Social Reform and Philanthropic Order, 1896–1920. In *Cleveland: A Tradition of Reform*, ed. David D. Van Tassel and John J. Grabowski, 29–49. Kent, Ohio: Kent State Univ. Press.

Graham, Hugh Davis. 1992. Voting Rights and the American Regulatory State. In *Controversies in Minority Voting: The Voting Rights Act in Perspective*, ed. Bernard Grofman and Chandler Davidson, 177–96. Washington, D.C.: Brookings Institution.

Griffith, Ernest S. 1974. *A History of American City Government: The Conspicuous Failure, 1870–1900*. New York: Praeger.

Grofman, Bernard, and Chandler Davidson, eds. 1992. *Controversies in*

Minority Voting: The Voting Rights Act in Perspective. Washington, D.C.: Brookings Institution.

Grofman, Bernard, and Arend Lijphart. 1986. *Electoral Laws and Their Political Consequences.* New York: Agathon Press.

Grofman, Bernard, Lisa Handley, and Richard G. Niemi. 1992. *Minority Representation and the Quest for Voting Equality.* Cambridge: Cambridge Univ. Press.

Guinier, Lani. 1991. The Triumph of Tokenism: The Voting Rights Act and the Theory of Black Electoral Success. *Michigan Law Review* 89: 1077–1154.

———. 1992. Second Proms and Second Primaries: The Limits of Majority Rule. *Boston Review,* Sept./Oct., 32–34.

———. 1994. *The Tyranny of the Majority.* New York: Free Press.

Haber, Samuel. 1964. *Efficiency and Uplift: Scientific Management in the Progressive Era, 1890–1920.* Chicago: Univ. of Chicago Press.

Hacker, Andrew. 1964. *Congressional Districting: The Issue of Equal Representation.* Washington, D.C.: Brookings Institution.

Hallett, George, Jr. 1940. *Proportional Representation: The Key to Democracy.* New York: National Municipal League.

Hamilton, Alexander, James Madison, and John Jay. [1788] 1945. *The Federalist.* New York: Heritage Press.

Hare, Thomas. [1859, 1860] 1977. *Treatise on the Election of Representatives, Parliamentary and Municipal.* In J. S. Mill, *Thoughts on Parliamentary Reform,* 2d ed., in Mill, *Collected Works,* vol. 19, pp. 491–95.

Hare, Thomas, and John Stuart Mill. 1862. *True and False Democracy: The Representation of All and the Representation of the Majority Only.* Boston: Prentiss and Deland.

Hart, Jenifer. 1992. *Proportional Representation: Critics of the British Electoral System, 1820–1945.* Oxford: Clarendon Press.

Hatton, Augustus R. 1915. Making Minorities Count. *New Republic,* 27 Nov., 96–98.

Hays, Samuel P. 1964. The Politics of Reform in Municipal Government in the Progressive Era. *Pacific Northwest Quarterly* 55:157–69.

Hermens, Ferdinand A. [1941] 1972. *Democracy or Anarchy? A Study of Proportional Representation.* 2d ed. Reprint, New York: Johnson Reprint Corp.

———. 1985. The Record of P.R. in American Local Government: A Critical Review. Paper presented at the annual meeting of the American Political Science Association, New Orleans.

Higham, John. [1955] 1988. *Strangers in the Land: Patterns of American Nativism, 1860–1925.* New Brunswick, N.J.: Rutgers Univ. Press.

Hoag, Clarence G. 1913. The "Representative Council Plan" of City Charter. *Equity* 15:74–83.

———. 1919. P.R. and the League of Nations. *Equity* 21 (2): 74.

Hoag, Clarence G., and George H. Hallett. 1926. *Proportional Representation*. New York: Macmillan.

Hofstadter, Richard. 1955. *The Age of Reform: From Bryan to F.D.R.* New York: Alfred A. Knopf.

Hogan, James. 1945. *Election and Representation*. Cork, Ireland: Cork Univ. Press.

Holt, Thomas. 1977. *Black over White: Negro Political Leadership in South Carolina during Reconstruction*. Urbana: Univ. of Illinois Press.

Hopkins, William R. 1935. Cleveland Still Dissatisfied. *National Municipal Review* 24:27–31, 41.

Howe, Frederic C. [1925] 1988. *Confessions of a Reformer*. Kent, Ohio: Kent State Univ. Press.

Huthmacher, J. Joseph. 1962. Urban Liberalism and the Age of Reform. *Mississippi Valley Historical Review* 49:231–41.

Issacharoff, Samuel, Pamela S. Karlan, and Richard H. Pildes. 1998. *The Law of Democracy: Legal Structure of the Political Process*. Westbury, N.Y.: Foundation Press.

Kendall, M. C., and A. Stuart. 1950. The Law of Cubic Proportions in Electoral Results. *British Journal of Sociology* 1:183–97.

Kent, Sherman. 1937. *Electoral Procedure under Louis Philippe*. New Haven: Yale Univ. Press.

Kingdom, John. 1991. *Government and Politics in Britain*. Cambridge: Polity Press.

Kleppner, Paul. 1982. *Who Voted? The Dynamics of Electoral Turnout, 1870–1980*. New York: Praeger.

———. 1987. *Continuity and Change in Electoral Politics, 1893–1928*. New York: Greenwood Press.

Kneier, Charles M. [1934] 1957. *City Government in the United States*. 3d ed. New York: Harper and Brothers.

Knepper, George W. 1989. *Ohio and Its People*. Kent, Ohio: Kent State Univ. Press.

Kolesar, Robert J. 1996. Communism, Race, and the Defeat of Proportional Representation in Cold War America. Paper presented at the New England Historical Association Conference, Amherst, Mass., 20 April.

Kolko, Gabriel. 1963. *The Triumph of Conservatism: A Reinterpretation of American History, 1900–1916*. Glencoe, Ill.: Free Press.

Kornbluh, Andrea Tuttle. 1986. *Lighting the Way: The Woman's City Club of Cincinnati, 1915–1965*. Cincinnati: Woman's City Club of Cincinnati.

Kousser, J. Morgan. 1984. The Undermining of the First Reconstruction: Lessons for the Second. In *Minority Vote Dilution*, ed. Chandler Davidson, 27–46. Washington, D.C.: Howard Univ. Press.

Lakeman, Enid. 1970. *How Democracies Vote*. London: Faber and Faber.

Lakeman, Enid, and James D. Lambert. 1959. *Voting in Democracies: A Study of Majority and Proportional Electoral Systems*. London: Faber and Faber.

Lamberti, Jean-Claude. 1989. *Tocqueville and the Two Democracies.* Translated by Arthur Goldhammer. Cambridge: Harvard Univ. Press.

Lemons, J. Stanley. 1973. *The Woman Citizen: Social Feminism in the 1920s.* Urbana: Univ. of Illinois Press.

Lerner, Gerda, ed. 1992. *Black Women in White America: A Documentary History.* New York: Vintage.

Levinson, Sanford. 1985. Gerrymandering and the Brooding Omnipresence of Proportional Representation: Why Won't It Go Away? *UCLA Law Review* 33:257–80.

Lijphart, Arend. 1994. *Electoral Systems and Party Systems: A Study of Twenty-seven Democracies, 1945–1990.* New York: Oxford Univ. Press.

Link, Arthur S. 1959. What Happened to the Progressive Movement in the 1920s? *American Historical Review* 64:833–51.

Litwack, Leon F. 1961. *North of Slavery: The Negro in the Free States, 1790–1860.* Chicago: Univ. of Chicago Press.

Lively, Jack. 1965. *The Social and Political Thought of Alexis de Tocqueville.* Oxford: Clarendon Press.

Longley, Lawrence D. 1972. *The Politics of Electoral College Reform.* New Haven: Yale Univ. Press.

Low-Beer, John R. 1984. The Constitutional Imperative of Proportional Representation. *Yale Law Journal* 94:163–88.

Lublin, David I. 1997. The Election of African Americans and Latinos to the U.S. House of Representatives, 1972–1994. *American Political Quarterly* 25:269–86.

———. 1999. Racial Redistricting and African-American Representation: A Critique of "Do Majority-Minority Districts Maximize Substantive Black Representation in Congress?" *American Political Science Review* 93:183–86.

Macaulay, Thomas B. 1877. *Speeches and Poems.* New York: Hurd and Houghton.

McCormick, Richard L. 1986. *The Party Period and Public Policy: American Politics from the Age of Jackson to the Progressive Era.* New York: Oxford Univ. Press.

McCrackan, W. D. 1897. Proportional Representation. In *The Encyclopedia of Social Reform,* ed. W. D. P. Bliss, 1123–27. New York: Funk and Wagnalls.

McFaul, John M. 1975. Expediency vs. Morality: Jacksonian Politics and Slavery. *Journal of American History* 62:24–39.

McGerr, Michael E. 1982. The Meaning of Liberal Republicanism: The Case of Ohio. *Civil War History* 28:307–23.

———. 1986. *The Decline of Popular Politics: The American North, 1865–1928.* New York: Oxford Univ. Press.

MacKenzie, W. J. M. 1958. *Free Elections.* London: Allen and Unwin.

Macklin, Philip A. 1989. Election Systems and Their Consequences. Paper presented to the Butler County Torch Club, Middletown, Ohio, 14 Sept.

McLean, Ian. 1990. The Borda and Condorcet Principles: Three Medieval Applications. *Social Choice and Welfare* 7:99–108.

Maizlish, Stephen E. 1983. *The Triumph of Sectionalism: The Transformation of Ohio Politics, 1844–1856*. Kent, Ohio: Kent State Univ. Press.

Mast, Tory. 1995. History of Single Member Districts for Congress. In *Voting and Democracy Report, 1995*, 37–39. Washington, D.C.: Center for Voting and Democracy.

Maveety, Nancy. 1993. *Representation Rights and the Burger Years*. Ann Arbor: Univ. of Michigan Press.

Maxey, Chester C. 1922a. The Cleveland Election and the New Charter. *American Political Science Review* 16:83–86.

———. 1922b. Cleveland Revolts. *National Municipal Review* 11:13–16.

———. 1924. The City Manager Plan and Proportional Representation. *Western Reserve University Bulletin*, July, p. 5.

Mélonio, Françoise. [1993] 1998. *Tocqueville and the French*. Trans. Beth G. Raps. Charlottesville: Univ. of Virginia Press.

Merrill, Samuel. 1988. *Making Multicandidate Elections More Democratic*. Princeton, N.J.: Princeton Univ. Press.

Mill, John Stuart. [1861] 1962. *Considerations on Representative Government*. Chicago: Henry Regnery.

———. [1865, 1910] 1947. *Utilitarianism, Liberty, and Representative Government* (3d ed. of *Considerations of Representative Government*). London: J. M. Dent and Sons; New York: E. P. Dutton.

———. [1873] 1964. *Autobiography*. New York: Signet Classics, New American Library.

———. 1972–88. *Collected Works*. Vols. 15, 19, 29. Toronto: Univ. of Toronto Press; London: Routledge.

Miller, Carol Poh, and Robert Wheeler. 1990. *Cleveland: A Concise History, 1796–1990*. Bloomington: Indiana Univ. Press.

Miller, Zane. 1968. *Boss Cox's Cincinnati: Urban Politics in the Progressive Era*. New York: Oxford Univ. Press.

Miller, Zane L., and Bruce Tucker. 1998. *Changing Plans for America's Inner Cities*. Columbus: Ohio State Univ. Press.

Mingle, James R. 1974. The Adoption of City Manager Government in Cleveland: A Case Study of Municipal Reform in the Progressive Era. Master's thesis, Univ. of Akron.

Moley, Raymond. 1923. Proportional Representation in Cleveland. *Political Science Quarterly* 38:652–69.

Morgan, Robert J. 1974. Madison's Theory of Representation in the Tenth *Federalist*. *Journal of Politics* 37:852–85.

Mulroy, Steven J. 1998. The Way Out: A Legal Standard for Imposing Alternative Electoral Systems as Voting Rights Remedies. *Harvard Civil Rights and Liberties Law Review* 33:333–80.

Nagel, Jack H. 1994. What Political Scientists Can Learn from the 1993 Electoral Reform in New Zealand. *PS* 27:525–29.

National Municipal League. 1900, 1915, 1925, 1933, 1941, 1964, 1989. *Model City Charter.* New York: National Municipal League.

———. 1921, 1948, 1963. *Model State Constitution.* New York: National Municipal League.

———. 1956. *Model County Charter.* New York: National Municipal League.

National Research Council. 1994. *Counting People in the Information Age.* Duane L. Steffey and Norman M. Bradburn, eds. Washington, D.C.: National Academy Press.

———. 1995. *Modernizing the U.S. Census.* Barry Edmondston and Charles Schultze, eds. Washington, D.C.: National Academy Press.

Newland, Robert A. 1982. *Comparative Electoral Systems.* London: Arthur McDougall Fund.

Newman, Edgar L., ed. 1987. *Historical Dictionary of France from the 1815 Restoration to the Second Empire.* Westport, Conn.: Greenwood Press.

Niemi, Richard G., and John Deegan Jr. 1978. A Theory of Political Districting. *American Political Science Review* 72:1304–23.

Niemi, Richard G., Simon Jackman, and Laura R. Winsky. 1991. Candidacies and Competitiveness in Multi-Member Districts. *Legislative Studies Quarterly* 16:91–109.

Norris, Pippa. 1997. *Electoral Change since 1945 in Britain.* Oxford: Blackwell.

Ohio, State of. 1912. *Proceedings and Debates of the Constitutional Convention of the State of Ohio Convened January 9, 1912.* Columbus: F. J. Heer.

O'Leary, Cornelius. 1979. *Irish Elections, 1918–1977: Parties, Voters, and Proportional Representation.* New York: St. Martin's Press.

Palmer, Robert R. 1959, 1964. *The Age of Democratic Revolution.* 2 vols. Princeton, N.J.: Princeton Univ. Press.

Parker, Frank R. 1984. Racial Gerrymandering and Legislative Reapportionment. In *Minority Vote Dilution,* ed. Chandler Davidson, 85–117. Washington, D.C.: Howard Univ. Press.

Parliament of the Commonwealth of Australia, House of Representatives. 1994. Elections for the House of Representatives. Factsheet no. 8. Canberra: Chamber Research Office.

Parliament of the Commonwealth of Australia, Senate. 1994. Electing Australia's Senators. Senate Brief no. 1. Canberra: Senate Department Research Section.

Patterson, Isaac F. 1912. *The Constitutions of Ohio.* Cleveland: Arthur H. Clark.

Peacock, Anthony A., ed. 1997. *Affirmative Action and Representation: Shaw v. Reno and the Future of Voting Rights.* Durham, N.C.: Carolina Academic Press.

Piccard, Paul J. 1984. Representation and Discrimination: The PR System Alternative. *National Civic Review* 73:516–21.

Pildes, Richard H., and Kristen A. Donoghue. 1995. Cumulative Voting in the United States. *University of Chicago Legal Forum* 1995:241–313.

Porter, Kirk H. [1918] 1969. *A History of Suffrage in the United States*. Westport, Conn.: Greenwood Press.

———. 1924. *National Party Platforms, 1840–1924*. New York: Macmillan.

Rae, Douglas W. 1967. *The Political Consequences of Electoral Laws*. New Haven: Yale Univ. Press.

Reeve, Andrew, and Alan Ware. 1992. *Electoral Systems: A Comparative and Theoretical Introduction*. London: Routledge.

Reynolds, John F. 1988. *Testing Democracy: Electoral Behavior and Progressive Reform in New Jersey, 1880–1920*. Chapel Hill: Univ. of North Carolina Press.

Reynolds, John Schreiner. 1905. *Reconstruction in South Carolina, 1865–1877*. Columbia, S.C.: The State Co., Pub.

Richie, Robert. 1997. Fuller, Fairer Elections? How? *Christian Science Monitor,* July 21, p. 19.

———. 1998. Full Representation: The Future of Proportional Election Systems. *National Civic Review* 87:85–95.

———, ed. 1994. Computerizing a Cambridge Tradition: An Analysis of Cambridge's 1991 City Council Election Using a Computer Program. Washington, D.C.: Center for Voting and Democracy.

Roberts, Sam. 1993. *Who We Are: A Portrait of America*. New York: Times Books.

Rodgers, Daniel T. 1982. In Search of Progressivism. *Reviews in American History,* 113–32.

Rogowski, Ronald. 1981. Representation in Political Theory and Law. *Ethics* 91:395–430.

Rule, Wilma. 1987. Electoral Systems, Contextual Factors, and Women's Opportunity for Election to Parliament in Twenty-three Democracies. *Western Political Quarterly* 40:477–98.

———. 1995. Why Women Should Be Included in the Voting Rights Act. *National Civic Review* 84:355–68.

Scott, Samuel F., and Barry Rothaus, eds. 1985. *Historical Dictionary of the French Revolution, 1789–1799*. Westport, Conn.: Greenwood Press.

Seasongood, Murray. 1933. *Local Government in the United States*. Cambridge: Harvard Univ. Press.

———. 1960. *Selections from Speeches, 1900–1959*. New York: Alfred A. Knopf.

Shannon, David A. 1955. *The Socialist Party of America*. New York: Macmillan.

Shapiro, Henry D. 1983. The Place of Culture and the Problem of Identity. In *Appalachia and America: Autonomy and Regional Dependence*, ed. Allen Batteau, 120–32. Lexington: Univ. Press of Kentucky.

Shortridge, Ray M. 1981. Estimating Voter Participation. In *Analyzing Electoral History: A Guide to the Study of American Voter Behavior*, ed. Jerome

M. Clubb, William H. Flanigan, and Nancy H. Zingale, 137–52. Beverly Hills, Calif.: Sage.

Simkins, Francis B. 1932. *South Carolina during Reconstruction.* Gloucester, Mass.: Peter Smith.

Skowronek, Stephen. 1982. *Building a New American State.* New York: Cambridge Univ. Press.

Spence, Catherine Helen. 1910. *Autobiography.* Adelaide, Australia.

Stanton, Elizabeth Cady, Susan B. Anthony, and Matilda J. Gage, eds. [1881] 1969. *History of Woman Suffrage.* New York: Arno and the *New York Times.*

Steed, Michael. 1985. The Constituency. In *Representatives of the People: Parliamentarians and Constituents in Western Democracies,* ed. Vernon Bogdanor, 267–85. Aldershot, England: Gower.

Steffens, Lincoln. 1905. Ohio: A Tale of Two Cities. *McClure's Magazine* 25:293–311.

———. [1906] 1968. *The Struggle for Self-Government.* Reprint, New York: Johnson Reprint Corp.

Sterne, Simon. [1871] 1970. *On Representative Government and Personal Representation.* Philadelphia: J. B. Lippincott; Chicago: Library Resources, microfiche.

Stetson, Dorothy M. 1991. *Women's Rights in the U.S.A.: Policy Debates and Gender Roles.* Belmont, Calif: Brooks/Cole.

Still, Edward. 1984. Alternatives to Single-Member Districts. In *Minority Vote Dilution,* ed. Chandler Davidson, 249–67. Washington, D.C.: Howard Univ. Press.

———. 1991. Voluntary Constituencies: Modified At-Large Voting as a Remedy for Minority Vote Dilution in Judicial Elections. *Yale Law and Policy Review* 9:354–69.

———. 1992. Cumulative Voting and Limited Voting in Alabama. In *United States Electoral Systems: Their Impact on Women and Minorities,* ed. Wilma Rule and Joseph F. Zimmerman, 183–96. New York: Praeger.

———. 1999. Statement to the U.S. Commission on Civil Rights Regarding the Necessity for Sampling in Census 2000, 12 Feb. 1999. Manuscript.

Still, Jonathan W. 1981. Political Equality and Election Systems. *Ethics* 91:375–94.

Stinchcombe, Jean L. 1968. *Reform and Reaction: City Politics in Toledo.* Belmont, Calif: Wadsworth.

Stone, N. I. 1915. Shall the Majority Rule? *Century* 90:134–43.

Straetz, Ralph A. 1958. *PR Politics in Cincinnati: Thirty-two Years of City Government through Proportional Representation.* New York: New York Univ. Press.

Svara, James H. 1990. Local Government Reform: Its Nature, Impact, and Relevance to Regionalism. *National Civic Review* 79:306–17.

Swain, Carol M. 1993. *Black Faces, Black Interests: The Representation of African Americans in Congress.* Cambridge: Harvard Univ. Press.

Swanstrom, Todd. 1985. *The Crisis of Growth Politics: Cleveland, Kucinich, and the Challenge of Urban Populism.* Philadelphia: Temple Univ. Press.

Thernstrom, Abigail. 1987. *Whose Votes Count? Affirmative Action and Minority Voting Rights.* Cambridge: Harvard Univ. Press.

Thompson, Carl D. 1913. The Vital Points in Charter Making from a Socialist Point of View. *National Municipal Review* 2:416–26.

Thompson, Dennis F. 1976. *John Stuart Mill and Representative Government.* Princeton, N.J.: Princeton Univ. Press.

Tocqueville, Alexis de. [1850] 1959. *Recollections.* Translated by A. T. de Mattos. New York: Meridian Books.

———. [1835/1840] 1966. *Democracy in America.* Translated by George Lawrence. New York: Harper and Row.

Tufte, Edward R. 1973. Relationship between Seats and Votes in Two-Party Systems. *American Political Science Review* 67:540–54.

———. 1975. Determinants of the Outcomes of Midterm Congressional Elections. *American Political Science Review* 69:812–26.

Tuve, Jeanette E. 1984. *First Lady of the Law: Florence Ellinwood Allen.* Lanham, Md.: Univ. Press of America.

Tyson, Robert. 1908a. American Proportional Representation League. In *The New Encyclopedia of Social Reform,* 3d ed., ed. W. D. P. Bliss, 38. New York: Funk and Wagnalls.

———. 1908b. Proportional Representation. In *The New Encyclopedia of Social Reform,* 3d ed., ed. W. D. P. Bliss, 975–78. New York: Funk and Wagnalls.

Unger, Irwin. 1978. *These United States: The Questions of Our Past.* Boston: Little, Brown.

Upton, Harriet Taylor. 1910. *The Western Reserve.* Chicago: Lewis.

U.S. Department of Commerce, Bureau of the Census. 1910–60. *Census of Populations.* Washington, D.C.: Government Printing Office.

U.S. Senate. 1869. Select Committee on Representative Reform. 40th Cong., 3d sess. *Report* no. 271, March 1869.

———. 1877. Committee on Privileges and Elections. 44th Cong., 2d sess. *Report on Inquiry into the Elections of 1874, 1875 and 1876,* no. 704.

———. 1879. Select Committee to Inquire into Alleged Frauds and Violence in the Elections of 1878. 45th Cong., 3d sess. *Report* no. 855.

Warner, Hoyt L. 1964. *Progressivism in Ohio, 1897–1917.* Columbus: Ohio State Univ. Press.

———, ed. 1971. *Reforming American Life in the Progressive Era.* New York: Pitman.

Wayne, Stephen J. 1980. *The Road to the White House.* New York: St. Martin's Press.

Weaver, Leon. 1982. Two Cheers for Proportional Representation in Cambridge, Massachusetts. Paper presented at the annual meeting of the American Political Science Association, Denver.

———. 1984. Semi-Proportional and Proportional Representation Systems in the United States. In *Choosing an Electoral System: Issues and Alternatives,* ed. Arend Lijphart and Bernard Grofman, 191–206. New York: Praeger.

Weaver, Leon, and Judith Baum. 1992. Proportional Representation on New York City Community School Boards. In *United States Electoral Systems: Their Impact on Women and Minorities,* ed. Wilma Rule and Joseph F. Zimmerman, 197–205. New York: Praeger.

Whitlock, Brand. 1914. *Forty Years of It.* New York: D. Appleton.

Wiebe, Robert H. 1967. *The Search for Order, 1877–1920.* New York: Hill and Wang.

Williams, Charles M. 1951. *Cumulative Voting for Directors.* Boston: Harvard University Graduate School of Business Administration.

Williamson, Chilton. 1960. *American Suffrage: From Property to Democracy, 1760–1860.* Princeton, N.J.: Princeton Univ. Press.

Yale Law Journal. 1982a. Note: Alternative Voting Systems as Remedies for Unlawful At-Large Systems. *Yale Law Journal* 92:144–60.

———.1982b. Note: The Constitutional Significance of the Discriminatory Effects of At-Large Elections. *Yale Law Journal* 91:974–99.

Yates, Tyrone. 1992. Letter to Zane Miller.

Yeoman, Barry. 1998. Virtual Disenfranchisement. *Nation,* Sept. 7/14, 18–21.

Zeller, Belle, and Hugh A. Bone. 1948. The Repeal of P.R. in New York City— Ten Years in Retrospect. *American Political Science Review* 42:1127–48.

Zimmerman, Joseph F. 1972. *The Federated City: Community Control in Large Cities.* New York: St. Martin's Press.

———. 1978. The Federal Voting Rights Act and Alternative Election Systems. *William and Mary Law Review* 19:621–60.

———. 1980. Local Representation: Designing a Fair System. *National Civic Review* 69:307–12.

———. 1990. Alternative Electoral Systems. *National Civic Review* 79:23–36.

Zuczek, Richard. 1996. *State of Rebellion: Reconstruction in South Carolina.* Columbia: Univ. of South Carolina Press.

INDEX

Urban Life and Urban Landscape Series
Zane L. Miller, General Editor

The series examines the history of urban life and the development of the urban landscape through works that place social, economic, and political issues in the intellectual and cultural context of their times.